Detector Dogs and Scent Movement

Detector Dogs and Scent Movement

How Weather, Terrain, and Vegetation Influence Search Strategies

Tom Osterkamp

CRC Press
Taylor & Francis Group
Boca Raton London New York

CRC Press is an imprint of the
Taylor & Francis Group, an **informa** business

Cover photo courtesy of Glenda Eichmeyer

First edition published 2020
by CRC Press
6000 Broken Sound Parkway NW, Suite 300
Boca Raton, FL 33487-2742

Library of Congress Cataloging-in-Publication Data

Names: Osterkamp, Tom, author.
Title: Detector dogs and the science of scent : a handler's guide to
environments and procedures / Tom Osterkamp.
Description: Boca Raton, FL : CRC Press, [2020] | Includes bibliographical
references and index. |
Identifiers: LCCN 2019050786 (print) | LCCN 2019050787 (ebook) | ISBN
9780367074296 (hardback) | ISBN 9780429020704 (ebook)
Subjects: LCSH: Detector dogs--Sense organs. | Detector dogs--Training. |
Olfactory sensors.
Classification: LCC SF428.73 .O88 2020 (print) | LCC SF428.73 (ebook) |
DDC 636.73--dc23
LC record available at https://lccn.loc.gov/2019050786
LC ebook record available at https://lccn.loc.gov/2019050787

Typeset in Minion Pro
by Deanta Global Publishing Services, Chennai, India

This book is dedicated to my lovely wife Joan for her assistance, patience, and always being there.

Contents

Preface

This book reviews the scientific literature on scent and scent movement with emphasis on scent movement in outdoor environments. The primary goals are to translate the scientific information into less technical terms and to provide it to search dog handlers. Throughout the book, comments and suggestions are made to show how handlers can use the information in training and deploying search dogs. Several new hypotheses are made about scent and scent movement.

Much of the material presented comes from the literature on dogs trained to find explosives, drugs, people, and cadavers. A large part of it comes from observations and experiences of search dog handlers. All of it can be applied to any type of search dog.

Scent movement is not an easy subject but a better understanding can be achieved by developing an awareness of wind. This can be done by observing wind movement under different weather conditions and how it is influenced by terrain, vegetation and obstacles. Dogs know how to use the wind to detect and find a source and you can learn by observing them. Studying this book will also help to develop that understanding.

Chapter 1 contains a thumbnail history of search dogs, terminology and a few considerations in using them. Chapter 2 discusses different types of scent, scent properties, residual scent, and the effects of surfaces. Multiple ways that dogs use to manipulate sniffing to help them find and recognize a source are described. The use of training aids, scent availability, source placement, and potential problems are also discussed.

Basic information necessary to understand scent movement is addressed in chapter 3. Scent movement is concerned with the interactions among weather and the physical environment (vegetation, terrain) and intervening media (air, soil, ground cover, snow, water) that influence scent movement from the source to the dog's nose. These interactions determine our search strategies and favorable times and places to search; ultimately, they determine the success or failure of our search efforts. Topics include the effects of air stability and turbulence (mechanical and thermal) on scent plumes.

The primary concerns of chapter 4 are searching, detecting and locating sources on the ground surface or above it. Search strategies and special effects associated with slope, valley and prevailing winds are discussed. The effects of scent collectors, ponding, channeling, chimneys, gridding and detection distances are explored. Distant alerts are difficult to resolve. Their causes and strategies for locating the source and examples are provided.

Chapter 5 investigates the complexities of scent movement from a buried source to the soil surface and through ground cover (vegetation, litter, snow) into the air. A simplified approach using air temperature, moisture (humidity), and air pressure is developed that can help handlers understand favorable times to search. The concept of a soil surface scent print is proposed. Tables of soil, weather and vegetative conditions that result in favorable times to search are presented.

Chapter 6 focuses on the use of dogs to detect scent from bodies underwater although the information is also useful when searching for other underwater sources. Information is reviewed on the body in water, scent movement in water and the use of dogs for water searches including problems associated with the selection of sources for training, lateral scent displacement, thermoclines, scent pooling, and natural decomposition gases. The concept of a water surface scent print is proposed. Tactics for shoreline searches and boat searches on lakes and rivers are discussed.

The nature of trail scent is covered in chapter 7 including the effects of environmental conditions (wind, terrain, vegetation, temperature, moisture). It is shown that the presence of a human thermal boundary layer, thermal plume, the wake produced by a moving person, and the bellows action of pant legs and shoes produce trail scent. This means that trail scent comes from every location on the human body and anything attached to the body (drugs, explosives). The use of scent articles is discussed and the effects of wind on turns in a trail and around buildings are reviewed. It is shown that dogs can detect air scent from trails 200 yards distant and at least a day old, determine direction of travel, follow car trails several days old for long distances, and follow trails aged for two weeks or more.

The references are not exhaustive.

While many people have contributed to the information in this book, the errors are mine. I would like to hear from anyone who has found errors which I am sure are present. I would also like to hear from handlers who have been successful on canine searches using the information in this book.

Acknowledgments

My wife Joan and son Jon edited several versions of the manuscript which improved it enormously. Bruce Barton, Susan Bulanda, Mark Holmes, Marcia Koenig, Deborah Pahlman, and Deb Tirmenstein reviewed parts of the book and provided many valuable comments.

Figures, photographs, maps, and information about searches were provided by Kris Brock, Dr. Brent A. Craven, Dr. T. R. Oke, Dr. Gary S. Settles and Deborah Pahlman. Many scientists graciously shared their publications and provided scientific advice on various aspects of the book, especially Dr. Paul A. Moore, Dr. Gary S. Settles, and Dr. Arpad A. Vass.

Numerous law enforcement personnel have been generous in sharing their knowledge and experience in classes and seminars and during evaluations and informal discussions. I am especially indebted to them for providing opportunities for me to serve, especially Major Mike Copeland, Franklin County Sheriff's Office in Missouri.

Search dog handlers from Canada, Alaska and many states helped shape my ideas on using search dogs. My dogs, Ted, Trixie, Rommel, Dolly, Happy, Bitsy, Max, Stormy, and Pepper have taught me much of what I know about scent and scent movement.

I am forever grateful to my Dad, Joe Osterkamp, for starting me down this path of working with dogs and to my wife and family for allowing me to continue it.

Acknowledgments

Introduction

1

1.1 History

Genetic evidence indicates that dogs evolved gradually from wolves beginning about 100,000 years ago. The oldest dog fossils date from about 14,000 years ago. It is likely that ancient hunters used dogs to secure animals for food and as sentry dogs around their camps in a symbiotic relationship. This relationship has evolved and strengthened to the point where dogs and humans enjoy the closest interactions of all species in the animal world.

The evidence of human and canine interactions is well documented (Thurston 1996; Schoon and Haak 2002). Egyptian paintings prior to 3,000 B.C. show dogs being used for hunting, and many mummified dogs have been found in Egyptian tombs, indicating that dogs occupied a special place in their society. Writings and pictures that predate the Roman Empire illustrate the use of dogs for scent detection. Sophocles (496–406 B.C.) wrote a satire about the gods called "The Tracking Dogs," indicating that dogs were used for tracking at that time.

The role of dogs continued to flourish in Roman society. Plinius (A.D. 23–79) described six classifications of dogs: guard dogs, shepherd dogs, hunting dogs, war dogs, sight hounds, and tracker dogs. Roman legions sent packs of armored attack dogs into battle, and Attila the Hun used them as sentries. Worldwide, dogs were used as sentries, guards, messengers, scouts, and fighters by armies and as hunting, herding, tracking, and draft animals by the populace. Except for hunting, a full appreciation of their scenting ability was slow to develop.

During the French and Indian Wars in 1775, Benjamin Franklin recommended the use of dogs by the Army to search for marauders who were attacking and killing colonists near Boston. In 1779, William McClay suggested using dogs to search for scalping parties in Pennsylvania. The first documented air scenting search dog (SD) (Barry, 1800–1812) lived with monks in a hospice in Saint Bernard Pass in the Alps at an altitude of over 8,000 feet. Barry used his scenting abilities to help rescue more than 40 persons during his lifetime. Bloodhounds and their handlers from Cuba were employed by the Army as man trackers in the swamps of western Florida and Louisiana in 1835.

The modern use of dogs for scent detection dates from the late 1800s and early 1900s. In 1888, Scotland Yard used bloodhounds for scent detection work in the infamous "Jack the Ripper" case. Many documented cases exist of the use of dogs in Europe for police work, which involved trailing and scent discrimination in the early 1900s (Schoon and Haak 2002). The British police and military explored the use of dogs in scent work and trained dogs to detect land mines in WWI. In the 1930s, police and military units began extensive training of canine units and the Swiss Army began training SDs to find avalanche victims. Germany had an estimated 30,000 trained dogs at the start of WWII, and Russia had a canine force of over a million animals that included explosive dogs (EDs) trained to detect explosives. The German Army used trailing dogs (TDs) to silently follow British Special Air Service officers who parachuted into Germany to collect intelligence prior to WWII. The dogs were trained to follow a given ground scent (scent discriminating) from a scent article or a footprint and to attack the subject at the end of the trail. The British Army adopted the idea of using silent TDs to find but not attack the enemy hiding on islands in the Pacific theater.

The USA did not have a canine unit in WWI although individual dogs did serve. Scent training in the USA began in earnest in WWII. At the start of the war, the only military dogs to be found within the Army were about 50 sled dogs in Alaska. The Army formed an official K-9 Corps but had to turn to the public to obtain dogs. A civilian organization called Dogs for Defense was established in 1942 to promote a national recruiting drive for canines. In 1944, the Army deployed over 100 dogs with a mine detection unit although the dogs were initially unsuccessful in locating nonmetal mines in Algeria and Italy. Dogs continued to be used in the Korean War, but in 1958 the K-9 Corps was terminated and responsibility for military working dogs was transferred to the Air Force where it remains.

The Vietnam War saw a dramatic increase in the US military canine presence. These four-footed soldiers were used to detect explosives, booby traps, trip wires, underwater enemy swimmers, stockpiles of enemy food, and to trail the enemy. They were credited with finding over a million pounds of stockpiled corn which caused the enemy considerable hardship. The enemy's efforts to distract the dogs with bait and perfumes were not successful, and they offered rewards to anyone who killed a military dog.

Tragically, at the end of the war, the military command left the dogs which had faithfully served them to a culture that considered them food and an enemy who hated them. Some were transferred to the South Vietnamese, some turned loose, many were euthanized, and a few were returned to the USA. This was their fate despite saving an estimated 10,000 American soldiers' lives and preventing many more soldiers from being injured. Military dog handlers are still suffering from the traumatic effects of leaving their dogs behind.

During this same period in the 1960s and early 1970s, the US expanded its detector dog programs with an emphasis on drugs and explosives. A Military Working Dog Program was established in 1968 at Lackland Air Force Base in San Antonio, Texas, that is still in operation. By 1971, they were training drug dogs (DDs) for use on ships and aircraft and had conducted a drug detection program for the Customs Service which showed that dogs could be trained to detect at least four odors. At about the same time, the British began training its military dogs to detect drugs and followed this program with training for explosives detection work to assist in the fighting in Northern Ireland. The US began training and deploying EDs in 1973, and, by the mid-1970s, government agencies in many countries were using SDs for various specialized tasks.

Several reports described the programs and methods used to train the dogs, and these were known to law enforcement and civilian trainers. In 1974, the New York State Police had a trooper handler and a yellow Labrador named Pearl trained for cadaver search by Southwest Research Institute. Law enforcement trainers in the northeast soon developed their own programs. These programs spread rapidly to other parts of the country and to civilian trainers. By the end of the century, it is estimated that there were over 100 volunteer search dog units that performed cadaver searches.

Today, SDs are used for an incredible variety of tasks. The expanding use of SDs in war (Frankel 2014) includes searching for improvised explosive devices (IEDs), body parts after explosions, and clandestine graves of soldiers and civilians, as well as trailing the enemy. Dogs are employed by government agencies to search for all manner of contraband including agricultural products, weapons, ammunition, accelerants, drug money, wildlife and wildlife parts, exotic plants and animals, sewage, bacteria, and people being smuggled into the country in ships, trains, and vehicles. Law enforcement uses SDs at crime scenes to search for evidence, blood, weapons, and clandestine graves. Dogs have been shown to be capable of detecting the scent associated with various diseases including cancer. Other uses include the detection of cows in estrus, poached abalone, termites, indoor air pollution, gas line leaks, rusted pipes, seal and polar bear dens, duck nests, animal scats, noxious weeds, contaminated water, mold, bed bugs, and historical graves—anything that emits scent molecules. The searches are conducted in airplanes, airports, ships, trains, trucks, cars, warehouses, businesses, schools, cities, suburbs, houses, backyards, cemeteries, archaeological sites, fields, forests, deserts, and wilderness.

The ability of SDs to detect and locate faint scent sources continues to amaze. The US Department of Defense has reportedly spent almost $20 billion to develop scent-detecting devices but found that EDs are better than instruments at detecting buried land mines and explosive devices. Dogs are still the gold standard for detection work. They are successful at these searches primarily because of their sensitive noses, but also have other capabilities which support the use of their noses. Dogs are highly mobile and can operate in challenging terrain even at night. They apply efficient search strategies for detecting scent, can actively extract scent from sources, use their wet noses to determine wind direction and the direction to a scent source, and use the wind to follow a discontinuous scent plume to the source. Importantly, because of their long association with humans, they have a special intelligence and bond with humans which exceeds that of other animals.

1.2 Purpose

This book reviews the scientific literature on scent and scent movement which is concerned with the movement or transport of scent from a source to the dog's nose. The emphasis is on scent movement in outdoor environments. The primary goals are to translate the scientific information into less technical terms, to provide it to SD trainers and handlers, and to show how it can be used to improve their skills in training and deploying their dogs on searches.

There are several reasons why SD trainers and handlers need to have information on scent movement.

- First, the primary task of the handler is to place the dog in a position where it can access scent from the search object. The more handlers know about scent movement the more likely they will be successful.
- Second, problems inevitably arise that the dog cannot solve. When this occurs, the handler must understand their behavior and be able to devise a search plan on how to help them. Scent movement will be a critical part of that plan.
- Third, in training and searches it is desirable to maximize the success of the canine team by continually adapting to changing winds and scenting conditions. Careful attention to the wind during training and searching can make the difference between success and failure.
- Fourth, there has been a dramatic increase in the research on scent during the past two decades, and new information on scent and scent movement in training and deploying SDs is available. Trainers and handlers who improve their knowledge of scent and scent movement will improve their success in training and on searches.

1.3 Terminology

While there is no standardized method for naming SDs, a common method that we will use is to name them after the source they are trained to detect. Examples are explosive dogs (EDs) and cadaver dogs (CDs). The terminology for CDs and human remains dogs (HRDs) is confusing and varies with locations and organizations. CDs have been defined as dogs that are specially trained to detect the scent of human decomposition and show their handlers its location. The sources of this scent include complete human cadavers, body parts including bones, tissue, decomposition fluids, blood, and residual scent on anything that comes in physical contact with these sources. Physical contact may not be required for the dogs to alert when objects such as grass, shrubs, trees, leaves, soil, rocks, etc. are in contact with the air flow which contains the decomposition scent. These objects may collect scent on their surfaces and in dead air spaces and may exchange scent molecules with air under favorable conditions.

In the last few decades, there has been a shift in terminology from CDs to HRDs, especially by some certifying agencies. There has also been an attempt to differentiate between CDs, HRDs, and historical human remains dogs (HHRDs). The proposed distinctions are that CDs would be those used to locate recently deceased human remains, whole bodies, and recently disarticulated bodies on the surface of the ground or hanging above the ground. HRDs (also called forensic search dogs) would be those used to locate human remains that range in age from recently deceased through all stages of decomposition, including disarticulated and skeletal remains both above and below ground. They would be trained to locate trace evidence, blood splatters, and residual scent but should not alert on human urine, feces, semen, and items with live human scent on them since this could confuse the investigation. HHRDs would be those used to locate human remains that are very old, most often bones, both above and below ground.

Currently, there is little or no distinction between CDs and HRDs. Agency standards for certification of CDs and HRDs do not include testing to ensure that the dogs do not alert on human urine, feces, semen, and articles with live human scent on them. An example of a potential problem would be when they alert on the back seat of a car or in a bedroom and this is taken as evidence that a body has been there. However, the alert may have been caused by the presence of semen. Another example would be when they alert in a shed, barn, or outdoor setting and this is taken as evidence that a body has been there, or a crime has been committed there. The alert in these cases may have been caused by someone having urinated or defecated there.

It has been shown (Riezzo et al. 2014) that two dogs specially trained only on cadaver blood can detect this blood diluted to 1 ppm (part per million) with urine. This suggests that microscopic quantities of blood potentially present in urine, feces, and semen could cause the dogs to alert. Also, semen contains putrescine and cadaverine, two decomposition compounds that are partly responsible for its smell and flavor, which have been used to train CDs. CDs should not alert on urine, feces, and semen that do not contain blood but may, in fact, alert on these sources if they do contain blood. When a CD alerts on what may be one of these sources, it is desirable to inform law enforcement about whether the dog will alert on urine, feces, and semen that contain blood so that laboratory testing can be used to eliminate these potential sources.

Detector dogs usually refer to dogs trained to find scent from a source while search dogs include detector dogs and dogs trained to follow a scent trail on the ground. The rest of the book will use search dogs to refer to detector dogs and trailing dogs.

1.4 Using Search Dogs

Well-trained SDs should:

- Search independently for an odor using a thorough free search strategy or on lead.
- Be responsive to the handler's directions while searching. Some SDs require control at a distance using voice and/or hand commands.
- Discriminate between sources which have common scents in the presence of distracting odors and environments.
- Detect very faint scents as well as variable and high levels of scent.
- Find the source of the scent once it is detected.
- Communicate the location of the source to the handler.
- Be capable of learning and generalizing from past experiences.

SD searches vary greatly in type, area, and difficulty, which lead to a wide range of requirements for the dog and handler. For example, searches for missing persons who may be alive or deceased in large areas (10s to 1000s of acres) and are likely to be above ground require a dog that will alert to the presence of a live person or cadaver, will range out from the handler, can be controlled at a distance, and a handler who is experienced in large area searches with such a dog. A large area live search dog team that is cross trained in cadaver would be a good choice for this type of search.

Searches for missing teeth or small bones needed for identification of a disarticulated skeleton found in an area of an acre or less require a slow moving, nose-to-the-ground dog and a team that is experienced in gridding and cross gridding a small area. There are similar requirements for teams searching for mines, clandestine graves, and IEDs, while others may be used on or off leash to search vehicles and confined spaces (trains, buildings, aircraft, ships). Most canine teams cannot do large area, large scent source and small area, small scent source searches well. Teams that conduct these searches should have a demonstrated capability for performing the specific type of search that has been requested.

There is a significant difference between searching for live subjects and human remains. Live subjects may not remain in one place for long times, while cadavers stay in position from the time of death until found (discounting disarticulation and movement by animals, people, or water). This means that cadavers continually disperse scent into the atmosphere from one position and create an extensive downwind scent plume. Also, flowing water on the ground surface or underground, in streams, and in rivers may carry scent and/or scent bearing materials downslope or downstream. These airborne and water transport processes can transport scent a mile or more from the source. Under stable weather conditions, scent may be expected to repeatedly (daily) follow the same pathways depending on the local vegetation, terrain, and weather conditions. In these cases, scent may be expected to repeatedly contact and accumulate in or on natural scent collectors or traps (brush, logs, outside bends of streams) that are at some distance from the remains. SDs may show a strong interest and may even alert on these scent collectors but may not be able to find the scent source. Discontinuities in the scent plume or changes in wind direction can make it impossible for dogs to follow a scent plume to the source. These are problems that handlers must solve using their knowledge of scent movement.

There are significant differences between on and off leash use of search dogs. Dogs worked on leash depend on their handlers to guide them through the search area in a way that ensures good coverage of possible source locations and a high probability that they will encounter the scent. Use of the leash allows precise control of the dog's position and helps the handler place the dog in a potential area containing scent. Dogs worked off leash are more independent, only relying on their handlers to place them in the general area of the scent. Some are trained to take visual and/or audible directions at a distance from their handlers. The ability to control the movements of the dog at a distance is highly desirable to minimize time and energy and to ensure the best coverage of the search area. Knowledge of scent movement can increase success when conducting on leash searches and is often critical for the success of off leash searches.

The Dog's Nose and Scent

2

2.1 Sense of Smell

This chapter is concerned with the internal and external aerodynamics of the nose involved in the sense of smell (olfaction) as they relate to training and searching with SDs. The sense of smell involves detection and perception of chemicals (odorants or scent molecules) inhaled by the dog. These scent molecules in the environment enter the dog's nose in the gas phase, in the solid phase as particulates from a source, and attached to particulate matter such as dust or skin flakes. In the warm and humid environment of the nose, scent molecules in the gas phase and those detached from particulates contact sensors (receptors) that generate electrical signals which are sent to the brain. Signal processing and learning by the brain result in the "perception" of an odor or scent.

2.1.1 Physiology and Function

Olfaction links the dog's brain to their external environment. Figure 2.1 is a schematic diagram of the "wiring" system for olfaction in mammals, including dogs.

There is a cavity (olfactory recess) at the rear of the nose behind and below the eyes with a lining of tissue (epithelial layer) that contains the receptor cells (neurons) (Figure 2.1). The ends of the receptor cells have 10 to 30 cilia, tiny hairlike structures immersed in mucous, that are in contact with inhaled air containing odorants (Marples 1969). The binding sites for odorants in the air are located on the cilia. Each receptor binds to a single type of odorant. When this occurs, the reaction produces a tiny electrical signal that is transmitted to a kind of junction box (glomerulus) in the olfactory bulb of the brain. Several thousand receptors for a specific odorant are randomly distributed in the nasal lining and are connected to the same glomerulus. Mitral cells in the glomerulus send the signal to the olfactory cortex of the brain where information from several types of scent receptors is combined into a pattern (an odor object) that characterizes the perception of a scent. The brain can do this because each odorant activates a unique combination of receptors.

An odorant also possesses properties that can contribute to scent discrimination (Schoenfeld and Cleland 2005). These include volatility and

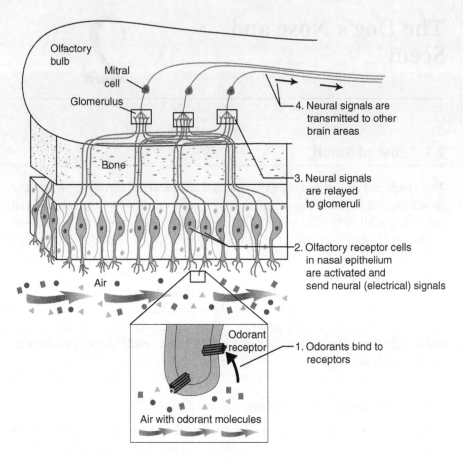

Figure 2.1 A schematic diagram of the olfactory system in mammals which shows how dogs detect scent molecules. (From Conover 2007. Used with permission of the Nobel Committee for Physiology and Medicine.)

water solubility that influence movement of molecules through the nose during inhalation. The random distribution of receptor cells makes it possible for dogs to modify scent patterns by influencing the number of molecules reaching different receptors during a sniff. Dogs can then modify and analyze scent patterns by regulating their sniffing.

There is another olfactory system for detecting scent that uses the vomeronasal organ in the roof of a dog's mouth. It is thought that this system is used primarily for detecting pheromones relating to sexual activity. However, retrievers used in duck hunting, trailing dogs following a trail through water, and water search dogs have been observed tasting the water. The process is different from drinking in that the mouth is partially opened and water flows through it and out the sides of the mouth. This suggests that the dogs may be using the vomeronasal organ to detect scent in or on the water or it may be possible for the dogs to "taste" scent.

The foregoing description of the olfactory system of mammals suggests that the physical and chemical characteristics of odorants that allow them to bind to receptors form the basis for the dog's perception of scent. While binding to receptors is an initial and necessary step in olfaction, it appears that memory and perceptual learning play a fundamental role in scent discrimination and perception (Wilson and Stevenson 2003; Lovitz et al. 2012). The process of perceptual learning involves continued experience (training) with a scent which leads to improved detection, recognition, discrimination, and perception of that scent. It is important to train regularly with all the scent variations that SDs will be tasked to find (Goldblatt et al. 2009).

Most scents are mixtures of many odorants. A mixture of only two odorants can result in a new scent that is weaker or stronger than either odorant or one odorant can mask the other partially or completely. This makes it impossible to predict how a mixture will be perceived by SDs. The results of studies of mixtures of four or more types of scent molecules (Wilson and Stevenson 2003; Lovitz et al. 2012; Goldblatt et al. 2009) indicate that people, dogs, and other animals do not perceive all the individual scent molecules in a source but perceive the mixture as a whole; it is synthesized. The idea that dogs can smell every component in a stew is probably not correct.

Synthetic processing based on experience uses memory and pattern recognition to form an odor object for the mixture. The process is similar to the sense of sight in that the brain does not perceive each pixel of a tree but forms a visual object that it perceives as a tree. Formation of odor objects by the brain is a relatively simple, efficient, and flexible way of perceiving odors in the environment that gives an almost unlimited ability to smell new odors. Thus, the search object that SDs seek is likely an odor object (Gazit et al. 2005a).

The above description of the sense of smell is primarily concerned with the details of sensing and perception that are internal processes. However, considerable practical information can be obtained by considering the fluid dynamics (air and scent movement) interior and exterior to the dog's nose. Dogs smell by sniffing and Figure 2.2 is an accurate, three-dimensional model of the left canine nasal airway, reconstructed from high-resolution MRI scans (Craven 2008; Craven et al. 2010).

When inhaling, air is drawn into the nostril from a distance up to about 4 inches. Dogs tend to reduce this distance to zero (Settles and Kester 2001), which provides them with the highest scent concentration, allows them to sample the source independently with each nostril, and to discern the spatial distribution of the source. Flow paths during exhalation bypass the olfactory recess, leaving scent-laden air there for more time which enhances absorption of scent molecules. Sniffing frequency for free air sniffing is about 4 to 7 times per second in short bouts. Sniffing can be observed in the movement of the thin skin on the side of my Beagle's nose but is difficult to see on the

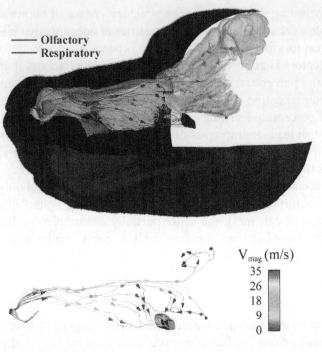

Olfactory
Respiratory

V_{mag} (m/s)
35
26
18
9
0

Figure 2.2 The internal aerodynamics of canine olfaction for the left nostril. Top: The olfactory recess (yellowish-brown) on the right. Flow paths during inhalation are distinct for respiration and olfaction. Bottom: Velocities for the same flow paths show high velocity (red) in the front of the nose and low velocity (blue) in the olfactory recess. (From Craven 2008. Courtesy of Dr. B.A. Craven.)

side of my Lab's nose due to the thicker skin. If the source is inaccessible, the bouts are longer with a frequency as low as of one sniff every 2 or 3 seconds. Notice the long deep sniffs a dog takes when sniffing at the crack of a closed door to an inaccessible room.

Part of the inhaled air is used for respiration and part is directed into the olfactory recess (Figure 2.2) where hundreds of millions of receptor cells are located (I would like to know who counted them). Thus, olfactory and respiratory airflows are separated, each with a distinct flow path and velocity through the nasal cavity.

On exhalation, an interior flap of skin at the front of the nose closes and slits on the side of the nose cause air jets to be directed to the sides of the dog's nose and downward (Settles et al. 2002). This nearly eliminates mixing of the exhaled air with the inhaled air so that fresh uncontaminated scent is introduced into a dog's nose during sniffing. Laboratory experiments have shown that dust particles smaller than about 100 μm can be made airborne and subsequently inhaled (Figure 2.3). This indicates that these jets can also dislodge particulates, skin flakes, and, probably, adsorbed volatile organic compounds (VOCs) from surfaces.

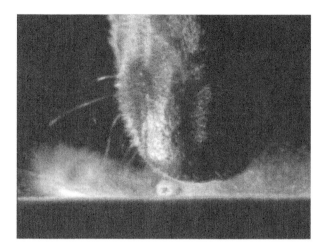

Figure 2.3 Surface dust particles disturbed by exhalation jets from the dog's nose. Flow directions for sources on the surface show that these air jets blow particles in a cloud to both sides of the nose and back in the photo. Some of the airborne particles can then be inhaled. (Courtesy of Dr. G.S. Settles 2002a.)

Observations of CDs show that dogs cast about, typically cross wind, when searching for a buried source or a hidden one on the ground surface. On detecting the source, their movements become more directed as they follow the scent plume. As they approach the source, their noses are close to the ground surface and they typically pass over the source while sniffing and then back up slightly until their noses are directly over the source or downwind of it. The dogs attempt to put their noses as close as possible to the source before giving their alert, a desirable behavior. This method maximizes the ability of the dogs to detect scent since they can detect scent molecules in the air, cause particulates to become airborne and then inhaled, and actively dislodge scent molecules from surfaces which can be inhaled. Not all dogs use this method exactly. There are differences between dogs and between different breeds of dogs (e.g. hounds and some dogs tend to work with their noses always close to the ground).

This abbreviated description of the scenting process of dogs indicates that dogs smell VOCs in the gas phase and from particulates (since these may emit VOCs) that contact the receptors in their nose. They cannot smell particulate materials such as skin flakes and dust particles directly. Skin flakes (Figure 2.4) contain volatile glandular secretions (skin oils) and bacteria which produce VOCs that dogs can smell (Syrotuck 1972). Dust particles may contain VOCs from explosives, drugs, and cadavers since, under dry conditions, dust particles adsorb VOCs on their surfaces. With the dog's head nearly vertical (Figure 2.3), the slits on the sides of the nose direct the exhaled air jets downward and backward along the surface which causes particulates to become airborne and allows the dog to inhale some of them. On

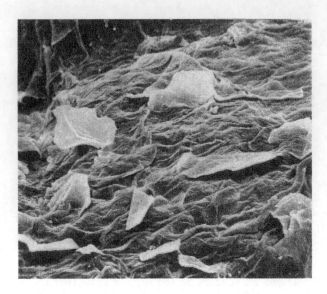

Figure 2.4 Surface of the skin (magnified 2410 times) which shows several partly detached skin flakes and small fragments of detached skin. (From Clark 1974. Used with permission of Cambridge University Press.)

inhalation, the particulates are brought into the warm and humid environment of the nose. For dust particles with adsorbed VOCs on their surfaces, the humid environment provides water molecules that replace the adsorbed VOCs and allows their transfer to the receptors where they can be detected.

McLean and Sargisson (2005) proposed a variation of the effects of the air jets observed by Settles et al. (2002). When sniffing dry soil surfaces, the dog's moist exhaled air jets may cause VOCs adsorbed on the dry dust particles to be replaced by water molecules and be released into the air where the dog can inhale and detect them directly. While this hypothesis is plausible, Phelan and Webb (2002) suggest that it may not be necessary because of the robust scenting ability of dogs.

It appears that the scenting methods used by SDs to detect sources involve direct sniffing of source VOCs and airborne particulates. Dogs can also use exhalation air jets to remove VOCs and particulates from surfaces which can then be inhaled. VOCs adsorbed on the particulates can then be desorbed in the humid and warm air in their noses which frees them for detection. These methods are part of the sniffing process which dogs use to detect scent. In addition, conditions dictate which methods are most efficient and dogs appear to learn to select the appropriate methods for those conditions.

It is of interest to know whether dogs use their eyes in addition to their noses to locate sources. EDs have been tested under both virtually dark (very low light intensity) and full light conditions in controlled (indoor) and uncontrolled (field) environments (Gazit and Terkel 2003b). The main sense used by these dogs for detection was their scenting ability, not only when vision was difficult (in very low light intensity) but also in full light. Neither the presence nor the absence of light influenced the dogs' detection ability. However, in addition to scent, search and rescue (SAR) dogs use their eyes to locate visible sources or subjects. Some hounds that trail with their noses to the ground learn to look for subjects. This difference between EDs and SAR dogs appears to be due to their training. EDs are trained almost entirely with hidden sources that can only be found using their scenting ability. SAR dog training generally includes subjects and sources that are sometimes visible, especially at short distances, so that the dogs learn to look for them.

There is little information on limits to the ability of CDs to detect VOCs from buried decomposing bodies, but experiments with EDs have shown that their sensing thresholds for explosives can be lower than those of laboratory instrumentation (Phelan and Webb 2002 or 2003). There were differences in the sensitivities of the dogs. Not all dogs could reach these low levels and some dogs could not sense even high levels. There were differences in the sensitivity of an individual dog on sequential days and in the reliability of an individual dog at a given level of VOCs. Variations in training history and methods also resulted in different capabilities between dogs. This suggests it would be desirable to test the ability of candidate SDs to detect low scent levels and to select a dog with a suitable nose before investing the time, money, and effort in training and to define and use optimal training methods.

Dogs usually start to pant at temperatures in the 80s°F, but this depends on age, physical conditioning, level of work being performed, and genetic factors. Panting is thought to reduce a dog's scenting ability because, with their mouths open, more air is drawn directly into their lungs through their mouth rather than through their nose. Experience with hardworking airscenting hunting dogs indicates that they appear to work better at air temperatures in the 60s°F or less. However, search dogs and hunting dogs appear to pant while running and are still able to scent the target source, indicating that some of the inhaled scent that enters through the nostrils moves into the olfactory recess.

Studies of racing sled dogs, hunting dogs, and other working dogs (Grandjean and Clero 2011; Reynolds 2017) discuss diet (nutrition) and exercise (physical training) requirements for optimum physical performance. A study by Altom et al. (2003) investigated the effects of diet and exercise on olfactory acuity (scenting ability). A group of dogs was exercised 30 min/day, 3 days per week on a treadmill, while another group was exercised 10 min/day, 1 day per week. After 12 weeks, the two groups were subjected to a stress test (treadmill) for 1 hour, followed by measurements of their olfactory acuity (ability to detect an odorant). The exercise group did not show a reduction in their olfactory acuity from their pretest baseline. However, the non-exercise group showed a 64% reduction in olfactory acuity following the physical stress test. This data shows that a moderate physical conditioning program can help SDs maintain their scenting ability during periods of intense work. Gazit and Terkel (2003a) found that increased panting resulted in a significant decrease in explosives detection, but that the dogs were eventually able to adjust to working in extreme conditions. Grandjean and Clero (2011) point out that nutrition and training are interrelated and provide extensive recommendations for various types of working dogs.

The sense of smell in dogs and other animals has evolved by natural selection for the ability to use chemical cues (scent molecules) in activities associated with finding food, reproduction, and survival. Consequently, they are extremely effective at detecting and discriminating odors associated with these activities. This implies that the threshold for detecting some odorants may depend on their importance for survival to the dog. Some sources (e.g. explosives) that dogs are required to detect do not meet this requirement. However, dogs quickly learn that finding these sources enhances activities that are a normal part of their lives (obtaining food and bonding with pack members, handlers, and others).

The above description of the olfactory system for dogs suggests that the size of the system and the number of receptors would indicate the ability of the system to detect and discriminate scent. Rats, mice, and dogs have about the same number of functional olfactory genes and their olfactory systems are comparable in their ability to detect and discriminate odorants. However, dog olfactory recesses vary widely in size (compare Bloodhounds and Rottweilers to Beagles and Terriers) and all are much larger than those of rats and mice, a seeming contradiction. This suggests that other factors may be involved in the sense of smell in mammals.

2.2 Scent

Training and using SDs efficiently require an understanding of scent characteristics, movement, and interaction of scent with the environment. While information on scent characteristics has been scant in the past, there has been a rapid expansion of information over the last two decades. On the other hand, information on scent movement and the interaction of scent with the environment is sparse. This section reviews some of the information on scent characteristics and scent during training. Chapters 3 through 6 are concerned with scent movement and its interaction with the environment.

2.2.1 Properties

Scent molecules are defined by their physical and chemical characteristics at the molecular level, especially those that allow them to bind to receptors.

Scent is the dog's learned perception in the brain as a result of processing signals from the receptors and their experience.

All solid and liquid phases of matter emit gas molecules that are part of the scent that dogs detect. The process is often referred to as outgassing and can include evaporation (liquid to gas phase changes), sublimation (solid to gas phase changes), and desorption (removal of a substance that has been absorbed or adsorbed by a solid or liquid). We will use the general term, "volatilization", to describe the processes by which scent molecules are transferred from liquids and solids to the gas phase. This transfer of a chemical into the atmosphere involves several steps, including not only phase transformations but also transport processes. The rate of volatilization depends primarily on the material's vapor pressure. Materials with high vapor pressure at normal temperatures are said to be volatile (they outgas readily emitting a lot of molecules, e.g. gasoline). Volatility of a material is measured by its equilibrium vapor pressure. This is done by placing the material in a closed container and monitoring the vapor pressure in the space (headspace) over the material and by more complex methods. The vapor pressure increases as more molecules leave the material than return to it. When the number of molecules leaving the material equals the number returning, the pressure becomes constant at the equilibrium vapor pressure. Volatility increases with temperature so that higher temperatures increase the amount of scent escaping from a source and available for detection. This makes volatility of the scent source an important factor in training, testing, and deploying SDs. Dogs can detect scent emitted from living and dead organisms and matter, both natural and manufactured, provided the scent source is sufficiently volatile or has a component that is volatile. Typical values of equilibrium vapor pressure in mm of mercury (Hg) near room temperature are: water vapor, 8; trinitrotoluene (TNT), 7.0E-6 (0.000007); acetic acid (heroin), 13; and dimethyl disulfide (human decomposition), 28. Normal atmospheric pressure is about 760 mm Hg (29.92 inches or 14.7 pounds per square inch).

Most of the scent from sources that SDs seek are VOCs. VOCs are compounds whose molecules contain carbon although some carbon containing compounds are classified as inorganic. VOCs have high vapor pressures at ordinary ambient temperatures that cause a significant number of molecules to volatilize from the liquid or from the solid form into the air. The scent of ethyl alcohol (C_2H_6O) is an example that even humans can easily detect. Examples of volatile inorganic compounds (VICs) include those containing nitrogen (e.g. ammonia, NH_3) and sulfur (e.g. hydrogen sulfide, H_2S).

Scent density refers to the "weight" of the scent molecules per unit volume and can be an important factor in scent movement. Density is not a significant factor for movement in an open system that is subject to air currents. However, it can be a factor in closed systems (e.g. containers, autos, houses) with no internal air currents and in open systems with restricted pore space (e.g. soils, snow) that inhibit air movement. If the scent density is less than air (e.g. ammonia), the scent can be expected to rise, and if it is greater than air (e.g. dinitrotoluene, DNT), it will sink or flow downward. Almost all VOCs from explosives, drugs, and human remains are heavier than air so they would be expected, in the absence of wind, to drain downward and settle in low areas (depressions over graves, ditches, floor drains, car floors). In outdoor settings, scent can pool in these areas and, under calm and cloudy conditions, can remain there until removed by turbulent air conditions.

2.2.2 Surfaces

Surfaces in contact with airborne VOCs can interact with the VOCs and modify the concentration of VOCs available to SDs. Common surfaces include natural ones (soil and rock, vegetation, wood) and manufactured ones (cloth, plastic, pavement, metal). VOCs in contact with surfaces can produce new chemical compounds that may help or hinder SDs. VOCs may be adsorbed (stick) to surfaces and later serve as sources by desorbing (volatilizing) by natural processes or by air jets from the dog's nose. Some sources, especially drugs and explosives, produce microparticles that are "sticky" and adhere to surfaces where they volatilize or can be removed by the action of dog's exhalation air jets, producing scent for dogs to detect. This sticky nature of VOCs and microparticles can cause contamination of nearby surfaces such as other training aids, clothes, hair, hands, travel bags, and dust particles (Oxley et al. 2008; Goldblatt 2017). Dogs can detect these contaminated surfaces and dust particles (Phelan and Webb 2003).

When scent molecules contact surfaces, their behavior depends on their properties, properties of the surface, and external conditions (wind velocity, temperature, humidity, and other factors). The amount of scent that volatilizes from skin secretions, decomposition fluids, explosives, drugs, and other sources depends on their volatility, surface area of the source, whether it is contained or buried, and environmental factors. A substance that has a larger surface area will evaporate at a faster rate, resulting in more scent (because there are more surface molecules in contact with the air). Wind increases evaporation rates from a source by enhancing the movement of scent molecules away from the surface into the air which increases its volatility. Increased temperatures increase volatility by making scent molecules more energetic which allow them to more easily escape a source.

The amount of scent and the time it remains on a surface also depends on the number of binding sites for the scent molecules. Metals have few binding sites while most natural surfaces such as vegetation, soil, and wood have many. VOCs attach readily to these natural surfaces at cooler temperatures and volatilize at warmer temperatures. This accounts for the daily and seasonal variations of VOCs found in the environment. For example, the air in forests normally emits more VOCs during the day than at night and more during warm seasons than colder seasons (Schade and Goldstein 2001).

Air humidity is also an important factor. VOCs readily attach to dust and very dry soils. With an increase in humidity, water molecules preferentially replace the VOCs on soil surfaces allowing the VOCs to escape into the air, resulting in dramatic increases in VOC emissions from the soil (Petersen et al. 1996).

Once scent has been deposited on surfaces, it has a remarkable ability to survive. Depending on the surface, it can survive washing, radiation, explosions, fire, and even attempts to mask its presence (Stockham et al. 2004; Goldblatt et al. 2009). Some sources (e.g. urine) may contain other chemicals, besides the scent molecules, that stabilize the scent and allow it to remain in the environment longer.

2.2.3 Residual Scent

The above discussion indicates that VOCs can attach to surfaces some distance from the source. In addition, when a source is placed at a site and removed later, VOCs, microparticles, and liquid residuals may be left behind. These materials can be in the form of liquids from the source, liquids that have been in contact with the source, particulates from the source, and VOCs from it. Fingerprints consisting of liquids and particulates (skin flakes) are an example, and VOCs that accumulate on vegetation downwind of a source are another. VOCs from liquids, particulates, and the source, when it was present, can remain in the air and/or may be adsorbed on nearby objects around the former location of the source or downwind from it.

While there are numerous anecdotal examples of residual scent involving SDs, there are few studies of it. Scent from some sources such as explosives and drugs can be transferred to the skin and clothing of persons handling them and to objects they touch (notice airport security wiping baggage surfaces). CDs have alerted on blood in vehicles that were involved in accidents a decade earlier (Osterkamp, unpublished), have alerted in vehicles that were used to transport bodies, and have found clandestine graves where the body had been removed. The FBI has shown that the scent of a person can linger in the neighborhood where their house was located for at least 6 months after they have moved. A trailing dog given a scent article from the person trailed a short distance to the house (Stockham et al. 2004). This could have been a result of VOCs on the nearby vegetation and other surfaces or perhaps the home with its many porous surfaces saturated with the person's scent was acting as a source that attracted the dog.

Volatilized scent molecules from a source that has been removed can cause SDs to alert, but little is known about the conditions that need to be favorable for this to occur. In the short term (days to weeks), scent molecules can probably linger in the air at sites with restricted air circulation (e.g. carpet, grass, leaf layer on the forest floor). In the long term (perhaps weeks to years), it appears that the scent molecules would have to be adsorbed on or absorbed in objects around the site. Changes in temperature, wind, humidity, the mechanical action of sniffing (air jets), or the dog's movement may cause the scent molecules to dislodge or volatilize from the objects which makes them available for detection.

A study of the residual scent left by marijuana, hashish, amphetamine, cocaine, and heroin in unsealed plastic bags used the number of alerts of trained DDs to evaluate the persistence of scent at 24/48 hours after the drug was removed from the site of the hide (Jezeirsky et al. 2014). The residual scents of hashish and marijuana were the most persistent and that of heroin the least, although it has a high vapor pressure. The percent of dogs alerting on the former location of hashish sources in open plastic bags after 24/48 hours was 100/80% and on heroin 33/8%. The VOCs causing the alerts may have diffused through the plastic bags to the surface on which they were resting or may have passed directly to the air from the unsealed bags and then adsorbed on nearby surfaces. It is known that airtight containers used to transport sources to training sites may eventually develop contaminated exterior surfaces that leave residual scent wherever they are placed. These results suggest that care must be taken to allow time (several days or more) for residual scent to dissipate when using areas (buildings, vehicles, field sites) repeatedly during training and testing. They also suggest that an alert during a search where nothing is found may mean that a source was previously present at the site or nearby. For most applications, it is desirable to train the dogs to offer their alert only when the source is present.

2.3 Training Aids

Training SDs requires that we have an example (training aid) of the target source to use to communicate to the dogs the scent we wish them to find. Training aids are commonly packaged and/or put in containers to prevent the dogs from coming in contact with the source. The packaging should not look like toys that are used to reward them since this may lead the dogs to pick them up, an undesirable behavior (Goldblatt et al. 2009). Aids should have the same scent expected to be found in searches. If the aids do not have the same scent, their scent should be sufficiently similar to the target source to allow the dogs to generalize and detect the source. It appears that the ability to generalize depends on the similarity of the scent of the trained and untrained target source, breadth of training with different variations of the source, and, possibly, the dog's intelligence. If the target source is a single chemical compound the task is easier, but most sources contain many chemical compounds and it may not be known which chemical(s) triggers the dog's alert.

The training aid could be some of the source material, something to which the source scent has been transferred, or a mimic (simulant) of the source. While the source material used with direct scenting is an ideal training aid, it can be difficult to obtain, inconvenient, sometimes requiring numerous source variations, and even dangerous or illegal to use (e.g. explosives, drugs, cadavers). Transferring the source scent to a sorbent material (e.g. gauze pad) alleviates these problems (this method is also used by trailing dog handlers to create human scent articles). The transfer can be accomplished by direct contact with the source (e.g. wiping a solid or transferring part of a liquid source onto the material), passively adsorbing scent from the source onto the material, and by actively drawing scent through sorbent material to which the scent molecules adhere. Wiping a source with sorbent material transfers some of the scent to the material. However, in some cases, wiping may destroy evidence such as fingerprints.

Passive adsorption involves placing the sorbent material in contact with the source or placing the source and the material, without contact, in a closed container. A significant time may be needed to transfer the scent and, if the material contacts the source, it may modify or destroy a fragile source. Actively drawing scent from the source through and onto sorbent material to create the training aid is a relatively fast process that still preserves the source for forensic analysis. The Scent Transfer Unit 100 (STU-100) is a portable, low power vacuum cleaner which uses this method of scent collection (Tolhurst 1991; Eckenrode et al. 2006).

Training aids may attempt to simulate the scent source by using the pure chemical, chemical mixtures, a chemical component(s) of the source that is a major portion of its vapor headspace, or by using a small amount of the active chemical in a nonhazardous matrix (e.g. silica, fiber, inert chemical). Another method separates the components of an explosive mixture but allows their gases to combine and form a merged scent (Lazarowski and Dorman 2014).

It has been shown that some simulants may not elicit an alert by SDs which indicates that not all the dominant components are the actual odorants used by the dogs to detect explosives and drugs (Macias et al. 2008; Macias 2009). Regardless of the method used to develop an aid, it should be confirmed that SDs trained using the aid recognize and alert on the target source during field operations and that trained canines recognize and alert on the aid. Training procedures may also need to be modified to proof the dogs off scents introduced by the method. Also, the dogs still need to be trained on variations of the actual sources encountered while working.

Dogs are the gold standard for detecting sources under field conditions because of their scenting ability that allows them to distinguish the source from a diverse scent background, their mobility in difficult terrain, their use of highly efficient methods for detecting and precisely locating a source, their intelligence, and their rapport with humans. While electronic "noses" may be able to detect the presence of a source, they must be transported or directed around the search area by a human that understands the effects of weather (especially wind), terrain, and vegetation on scent movement; have a reliable way of precisely locating the source once it has been detected; be able to work through turbulence and discontinuous scent plumes, and be able to distinguish the source from similar background scents. Also, an instrument cannot provide emotional support and rapport that may be desirable under the stressful conditions associated with finding some sources (e.g. explosives).

2.3.1 Explosives

The importance, difficulties, inconveniences, and dangers of using the actual explosives as training aids have resulted in extensive efforts to develop aids that are safe and convenient to use. These efforts have been hampered by the possible explosive nature of the aids, the large number of different explosives, possible improvised explosives, lack of knowledge about what chemicals trigger the dog's alert, debate over training methods, and other factors. Table 2.1 shows some common explosives and their vapor pressures; many more exist.

Table 2.1   Mean Vapor Pressures of Select Explosives at 25°C (77°F)

Name, Abbreviation	Mol Weight (g/mol)	Formula	Vapor Pressure (mm of Hg)[a]
Nitromethane, NM	61	CH_3NO_2	36
Hydrogen peroxide, HP	34	H_2O_2	2.2
Diacetone diperoxide, DADP	148	$C_6H_{12}O_4$	1.9E-1
Triacetone triperoxide, TATP	222	$C_9H_{18}O_6$	4.8E-2
Nitroglycerin, NG	227	$C_3H_5N_3O_9$	4.9E-4
2,4-Dinitrotoluene, 2,4-DNT	182	$C_7H_6N_2O_4$	3.1E-4
Ammonium nitrate, AN	80	NH_4NO_3	1.1E-5
2,4,6-Trinitrotoluene, TNT	227	$C_7H_5N_3O_6$	7.0E-6
Urea nitrate, UN	123	$CH_5N_2ONO_3$	2.9E-7
Cyclotrimethylene trinitramine, RDX (C4)	222	$C_3H_6N_6O_6$	3.7E-9
Ammonium perchlorate, AP	118	NH_4ClO_4	3.0E-11
Cyclotetramethylene tetranitramine, HMX	296	$C_4H_8N_8O_8$	1.8E-14
1,3,5-Triamino-2,4,6-trinitrobenzene, TATB	258	$C_6H_6N_6O_6$	1.8E-15
Hexanitrostilbene, HNS	450	$C_{14}H_6N_6O_{12}$	4.6E-18
Guanidine nitrate, GN	122	$CH_6N_3NO_3$	2.0E-20

Source: Data from Ewing, R.G. et al. 2013. *Trends Anal Chem* 42:35–48.

[a] 1.9E−1 means the number with the decimal point moved one place left (0.19).

Generally, explosives in the top half of Table 2.1 are readily detected by dogs. Some explosives such as RDX and HMX have extremely low vapor pressures that indicate so few scent molecules are emitted from them that dogs are not likely to be able to detect the explosive component directly from the VOC emissions resulting from vapor pressure. Goldblatt (2017) suggests that stickiness of explosive microparticles may be as important as vapor pressure. The ability of dogs to use nasal air jets to dislodge and inhale particles of explosives and dust containing explosive VOCs may account for the ability of dogs to detect some explosives.

Vapor pressures of some explosives vary strongly with temperature. While there is considerable variability in the data, it appears that the vapor pressure of TNT increases about 10 times when the temperature increases from 25°C (77°F) to 40°C (104°F) (Oxley et al. 2005) indicating that much more scent would be available at higher temperatures.

The mol weight of dry air is 29 g/mol and that of humid air is less because the water vapor in it is just 18 g/mol. In the absence of wind or air currents, all the scent molecules from the explosives shown in Table 2.1 would eventually drain to the lowest point in the area because their mol weight is greater than that of air. This suggests, *when there is no wind or there is a downslope flow*, it would be desirable to search for hazardous sources (e.g. buried explosives) on a slope by gridding across the slope and advancing the grid upslope.

Commercial explosives are often mixtures of other explosives and contain chemicals in addition to the parent explosive. These additional chemicals may be a result of the manufacturing process, weathering, chemical reactions between components, and other factors. They are commonly more volatile than the parent explosive and may account for most of the vapor in the headspace of the parent explosive (Goldblatt et al. 2009). For example, military TNT consists of about 99.8% of 2,4,6-TNT and less than 0.1% of 2,4-DNT but the vapor in the headspace consists of 58% 2,4,6-TNT and 35% 2,4-DNT, a result of DNT's higher vapor pressure (Table 2.1). The primary component of US military C4 (cyclonite, RDX) is about 91% by weight, but it is not present in the headspace because of its low vapor pressure.

It seems logical to conclude that EDs would detect the more common chemicals in the vapor headspace. The problem for training is that while it may be thought that the dogs are detecting the parent explosive, they may be learning to detect a volatile component(s) rather than the parent explosive. Since TNT is found in about 80% of all land mines, this can have serious consequences. For example, a dog trained on TNT that contains DNT may learn to detect DNT. Russian and some other manufactured TNT does not contain DNT and neither does some weathered TNT which may result in a failure of the dog to alert on them (Goldblatt et al. 2009).

In a study to evaluate the ability of EDs to generalize from a pure potassium chlorate (PC) source to PC-based mixtures (Lazarowski and Dorman

2014), it was found that 87% of dogs trained with pure PC alone did not correctly alert to the presence of one or more of four PC-based explosive mixtures (PC plus a fuel). However, after training with a device that kept the components separated but allowed the vapors to combine, a significant improvement was seen in the number of dogs alerting to PC-based mixtures compared to training with PC alone. A similar inability of the dogs to generalize from pure ammonium nitrate to ammonium nitrate-based explosives was also noted. If it is desired to have dogs reliably alert to a mixture of components X and Y, then it is not sufficient to train them on only one of the components. This is not surprising since for a mixture of two scents (X and Y), one may partially or completely mask the other or a totally new scent may be produced as noted previously.

Jezierski et al. (2012) conducted a study of 80 ED teams used by Polish police to determine the effectiveness of the teams in finding explosives in training and testing environments. The study was conducted using rooms known and unknown to the dogs and the exterior of cars outdoors (Table 2.2). Each search was limited to 10 minutes.

Dynamite (NG based) was the easiest explosive to find based on the shortest search time, most correct alerts (82%), least misses (2%), and less false alerts (17%). TNT was the most difficult explosive to find based on longer than average search time, least correct alerts (49%), most misses (17%),

Table 2.2 Selected Results from a Study of 80 ED Teams Used by Polish Police to Determine the Effectiveness of the Teams in Finding Explosives in Training and Testing Environments

	Search Time (sec)	Correct Alerts (%)	Missed Sources (%)	False Alerts (%)
Explosive				
Dynamite	68	82	2	17
Semtex	107	74	13	13
PMW-8	113	79	7	14
TNT	99	49	17	33
Search Type				
Known rooms	113	66	11	23
Unknown rooms	79	73	23	4
Car exteriors	64	83	1	16
Training Stage				
Final	91	66	19	15
During examination	99	67	12	21
During annual reexamination	93	76	5	20

Source: Data from Jezierski, T. et al. 2012. Poster presented at the Canine Science Forum, Barcelona, Spain.

and most false alerts (33%). These results may be primarily due to the higher vapor pressure of dynamite compared to TNT.

Teams were less successful searching known rooms compared to unknown rooms based on much longer search times, fewer correct alerts, and many more false alerts (although misses were fewer). The exteriors of cars outdoors were less difficult to search than the rooms although the rooms appear to have been much larger. Experienced teams that reexamined produced more correct alerts and fewer misses but did not produce fewer false alerts.

2.3.2 Drugs

As with explosives, it is not necessary to use parent compounds for training DDs. Research that includes studies of the compounds present in the vapor headspace coupled with studies of the response of dogs to these compounds indicates the dogs use the most abundant chemical component(s) in the vapor headspace to detect and find drugs (Furton and Myers 2001). Most of the VOCs in drugs have a high vapor pressure (Table 2.3).

Marijuana is a commonly used drug in the USA and is now legal in several states. Studies of the headspace volatiles have shown that there are many; however, α-pinene, β-pinene, myrcene, limonene, and β-caryophyllene occupy a major portion of the headspace (Hood et al. 1973). Additional studies with canines indicate that α-pinene, β-pinene, and limonene are important for developing training aids for marijuana (Lai et al. 2008).

Cocaine was an early example of dogs alerting on the primary headspace component of the target source, methyl benzoate. Methyl benzoate is a decomposition product of cocaine with a high vapor pressure (Table 2.3). Field tests of 28 DDs showed that a threshold level of 1 μg (microgram) of methyl benzoate spiked with cocaine on US currency was required to initiate an alert by 50% of the dogs (Furton et al. 2002). However, the majority

Table 2.3 **Summary of the Vapor Pressures for Select Drugs near Room Temperature**

Drug	Scent Volatiles	Formula	Mol Weight (g/mol)	Vapor Pressure (mm Hg)
Marijuana[a]	α-Pinene	$C_{10}H_{16}$	136	3
	β-Pinene	$C_{10}H_{16}$	136	3
	Limonene	$C_{10}H_{16}$	136	1.3
Cocaine[a]	Methyl benzoate	$C_8H_8O_2$	136	0.4
Heroin[b]	Acetic acid	$C_2H_4O_2$	60	13
Methamphetamine[b]	Benzaldehyde	C_7H_6O	106	1.3
Ecstacy (MDMA)[a]	Piperonal	$C_8H_6O_3$	150	0.01

[a] *Source:* Data from Lai, L.H. et al. 2008. *J Sep Sci* 31:402–412.
[b] *Source:* Data from https://pubchem.ncbi.nlm.nih.gov/compound/.

of dogs did not alert to pharmaceutical grade cocaine at levels as high as 1 g. Methyl benzoate is not found on circulated currency in sufficient quantities to cause an alert from a DD. Consequently, an alert on currency by a DD dog indicates that the currency was recently exposed to cocaine since no other drugs are commonly found on currency.

Acetic acid is the primary volatile in the headspace of heroin and vinegar (Macias et al. 2008). Since vinegar may be commonly found in the search environment, acetic acid is not a good choice for a training aid for heroin and it will be necessary to find some other compound or to use the drug itself as a training aid.

Benzaldehyde is a primary scent volatile of methamphetamine (Vu 2001). Results from tests with a small number of DDs (6) showed that they alerted on street methamphetamine but did not alert on pharmaceutical grade methamphetamine.

Impurities in drugs because of the manufacturing process may produce volatiles and some manufacturing processes may result in the presence or absence of certain volatiles. Dogs trained on training aids developed from drugs manufactured by one process may not alert on similar drugs produced by another process. For example, the volatile piperonal is a recommended training aid for MDMA (Macias 2009). It has been shown that dogs trained to alert on piperonal will alert on MDMA and dogs trained on MDMA will alert on piperonal. However, piperonal occurs in widely varying amounts in MDMA depending on the manufacturing process, a condition that may create difficulties for dogs using piperonal as a training aid to detect MDMA.

A study of 164 DD teams in 1219 searches for marijuana, hashish, amphetamine, cocaine, and heroin evaluated the abilities of the dogs to detect and locate these drugs as shown in Table 2.4 (Jezierski et al. 2014). Street drugs were used for searches in rooms familiar to the dogs, rooms unknown to them, outside rooms (stables, storerooms), exteriors and interiors of cars, and lines of luggage. Each search was limited to 10 minutes.

Marijuana was the easiest drug to detect based on the shortest search time, 92% correct alerts, only 4% misses, and 4% false alerts. Heroin was the most difficult drug to detect with the longest search time, 70% correct alerts, 12% misses, and 18% false alerts. This difficulty occurs even though the primary scent volatile in heroin is acetic acid (Table 2.3) which has a high vapor pressure that should make it relatively easy to detect. The ranking from the easiest to the most difficult was marijuana, hashish, amphetamine, cocaine, and heroin. The areas searched had more than 83% correct alerts except for the interiors (58%) and exteriors (64%) of cars. False alerts were generally less than 15% except for the interiors (36%) and exteriors (22%) of cars. The large fraction of false alerts inside cars was thought to be caused by the odor plume that was distributed throughout the interior space. In the US, some DD handlers close car doors with their dogs inside and other handlers open

Table 2.4   Selected Results from a Study of 164 DD Teams Used by Polish Police to Determine the Effectiveness of the Teams in Finding Drugs in Training and Testing Environments

	Search Time (sec)	Correct Alerts (%)	Missed Sources (%)	False Alerts (%)
		Drug		
Marijuana	50	92	4	4
Hashish	54	82	6	12
Amphetamine	74	78	5	17
Cocaine	79	74	13	13
Heroin	81	70	12	18
		Search Type		
Known rooms	70	83	7	10
Unknown rooms	64	83	4	12
Outside rooms	61	86	8	6
Cars outside	64	64	15	22
Cars inside	78	58	6	36
Luggage lineup	23	84	2	15
		Training Stage		
Final	53	87	4	10
During examination	71	75	3	22
During annual reexamination	69	85	9	6

Source: Data from Jezeirsky, T. et al. 2014. *Forensic Sci Int* 237:112–118.

all car doors to help localize the scent plume but there does not appear to be any research to verify either method. Misses were less than 8% except for the exteriors of cars (15%) where the large fraction of misses was thought to be caused by air turbulence around them.

Comparison of the results for explosives and drugs indicates that explosives are much more difficult to detect and locate compared to drugs based on 72% vs 88% correct alerts and 20% vs 5% false alerts for explosives and drugs, respectively. This may be caused by the much lower vapor pressures of explosives and subsequent reduced scent availability compared to drugs. However, the question remains open as does the reason for the large percentage of false alerts by the ED teams.

2.3.3 Human Scent

Human scent from live persons consists of VOCs produced by bacteria acting on the skin and skin flakes (including skin flakes from breath), volatilization of secretions (oils) on skin and skin flakes, and VOCs from breath. Except for breath, this scent is carried upward by body air currents (Figure 2.5) and

Figure 2.5 Drawing of the rising boundary layer and human scent plume from a person in calm air.

exits the body at the top of the head and on horizontal surfaces. The scent is carried away from the body by the wind which produces a human scent plume. It is this airborne scent plume that SDs detect. See Chapter 7 for a detailed description of scent movement on and away from the body.

CDs search for decomposing bodies, body parts (large ones like a head or limbs to small ones like teeth or a piece of bone), bones, tissue, blood, body fluids, and trace (residual) evidence of these in all stages of decay. It is not feasible for handlers to obtain and store such a wide variety of aids; they usually resort to using a dozen or so types of aids in varying stages of decay.

Scent from human remains is emitted from the remains as gases or is readily volatilized from liquids and solids. There are nearly 500 VOCs from decomposing bodies that comprise the total VOC profile for them (Vass et al. 2004, 2008), but the specific compounds that elicit an alert by CDs are unknown. Some of the VOCs are present throughout the decomposition process and others are limited to certain stages of decomposition.

2.3.3.1 Decomposition

Decomposition processes include autolysis, putrefaction, liquefaction and disintegration, skeletonization, and diagenesis. These processes are represented by stages of decomposition (e.g. fresh, early decomposition, advanced decomposition, skeletonization, and decomposition of skeletal material) that are largely based on the visual appearance of the remains (Rebmann et al. 2000; Vass 2001; Dent et al. 2004).

The effects of decomposition processes are to reduce the body to elemental solids, liquids, and gases. These materials and gases evolving from them eventually pass into the soil and/or to the atmosphere where the gases can be detected. Bodies exposed to air decompose roughly eight times faster than buried bodies and about twice as fast as submerged bodies although many factors can modify these estimates. The slow decomposition rates of buried cadavers compared to those on the ground surface are generally a result of cool soil temperatures, soil moisture, lack of insects and scavengers, and other factors. For buried bodies, except for shallow graves and/or coarse-grained soils, decay is mostly anaerobic because of oxygen depletion in graves.

2.3.3.1.1 Autolysis   Autolysis is defined as self-digestion. Without oxygen, cells begin to decay a few minutes after death (Vass 2001). Decay proceeds from within the cells with enzymes that dissolve the cells, eventually causing them to rupture and release fluids that are rich in nutrients. Bacteria in the respiratory and digestive systems multiply rapidly. Autolysis becomes apparent in a few days when fluid-filled blisters appear on the skin and sheets of skin slough off the body. When enough cells have ruptured, the nutrient-rich fluids become available and putrefaction occurs.

2.3.3.1.2 Putrefaction   Putrefaction is the consumption of the soft tissues of the body by microorganisms such as bacteria, fungi, and protozoa (Vass 2001). The microorganisms feed on the nutrient-rich fluids produced during autolysis. Body tissues are converted into gases, liquids, and simple molecules. There is a greenish discoloration of the skin and it is easily detached. The gases cause tissues in all areas of the body to swell or bloat (including organs and the circulatory system), which increases body volume. Gas and fluid accumulations in the intestines eventually purge from the body, usually from the rectum. Further, protein and fat decomposition produce putrescine, cadaverine, and other volatile fatty acids.

Saponification, freezing, and mummification are the processes that retard decomposition. Saponification produces a kind of soap under favorable conditions (warm and moist environments in the presence of bacteria) called adipocere, which is formed from the adipose fat layer lying just beneath the skin. It is a rancid, greasy, soapy, wax-like, and malodorous substance and its formation inhibits further decomposition. A saponified body recovered from a deep, water-filled South African cave 10 years after the person drowned looked like it was in good condition but smelled badly (Zimmermann 2006). Mummification is the process of desiccating tissue into a leathery form under conditions of dry heat or very cold temperatures and low humidity which tend to preserve the tissue. This process occurs naturally in deserts and Arctic regions. Freezing a body at the time of death preserves it by stopping the decomposition process. Permafrost (perennially frozen ground with temperatures less than 0°C (32°F)) underlies about 20 to25% of the exposed land surface of the earth (Osterkamp and Burn 2002). Bodies buried in permafrost for more than a century have been found almost intact, and animals buried in permafrost for tens of thousands of years have been found remarkably preserved. Likewise, bodies encased in glacier ice for several thousand years have been found well preserved.

2.3.3.1.3 Liquefaction and Disintegration   The body's tissues and organs soften during decomposition and degenerate into a mass of unrecognizable tissue that becomes liquefied with continued decomposition. Liquefaction products may exude from the natural orifices. In the case of a body buried directly in the soil, a mucus sheath may form around the body consisting of liquid body decomposition products and fine soil (Dent et al. 2004). Ultimately, liquefaction and disintegration of the soft tissues leave behind skeletonized remains. At this stage, the skeletonized body will be held together by ligaments and surrounded by a putrid, liquefying mass. Eventually the liquefaction products may be incorporated within percolating water and enter surrounding soil and groundwater.

2.3.3.1.4 Skeletonization and Diagenesis   Skeletonization refers to the removal of soft tissue from bone. Skin, muscle, and internal organs are generally lost to the environment well before a skeleton becomes disarticulated. In dry or freezing environments and in water where saponification has occurred, skeletonization may be incomplete. Bone may be broken down over time by diagenesis and physical breaking. Diagenesis of bone exposed to the environment refers to the alteration of bone composition by several complex processes (Dent et al. 2004).

2.3.3.2 Scent Sources

2.3.3.2.1 Chemical Compounds   Decomposition odor increases with time and then decreases through the skeletonization phase until it may no longer be detectable by humans. During putrefaction, microorganisms destroy soft tissues in the intestines and elsewhere, producing gases such as hydrogen sulfide, carbon dioxide, methane, ammonia, sulfur dioxide, hydrogen, and fatty acids (Vass 2001). Putrescene and cadaverine are significant decomposition products that have been used to train cadaver dogs but are toxic and should not be used since other training aids are available.

VOCs emanating from buried cadavers in shallow graves that are not in coffins are under investigation in long-term experiments (Vass et al. 2004, 2008). These field experiments are valuable because the environmental conditions (soil, flora, fauna, moisture, thermal, and atmospheric) can add to, reduce, or eliminate VOCs from decomposition scent. Decomposition compounds occur in the following classes: acids, alcohols, halogens, ketones, aldehydes, cyclic hydrocarbons, sulfides, and nitrogen-containing compounds. The best represented class is cyclic hydrocarbons, with toluene and p-xylene being reported regularly. Putrescene and cadaverine have not been detected and extremely light VOCs (ammonia, hydrogen, carbon dioxide, methane) could not be detected with the methodology used.

It required 17 days for the first compounds to be detected at the surface from a 1.5 ft burial depth with most compounds apparent after the first month. These findings have implications for training, evaluating, and searching with CDs (Vass et al. 2004, 2008). Depth of burial, class of compound, and season of burial influenced this timing.

Soil temperatures are also important and BADDs (burial accumulated degree days) are used to calculate the cumulative effects of variable soil temperatures over time. These factors are not all independent since BADDs depend on the depth of burial and the season of burial. A cadaver buried at a depth where the average soil temperature was 5°C for 1 day, 7°C for 1 day, and 10°C for 2 days would have BADDs = 32 degree-days for these 3 days. An estimate of average annual BADDs for shallow burials near Phoenix is about 8,000 degree-days. Estimates for areas where soils at the depth of burial freeze, must have thawed soil temperature data available to estimate BADDs since cadavers do not decompose at temperatures below freezing. Where bodies are buried in permafrost (e.g. near Fairbanks), BADDs would be near zero. These estimates can vary significantly from year to year, from site to site, and from region to region even when at the same latitude because of the influence of soil properties, elevation, and distance to the ocean or large water bodies on soil temperatures.

Thirty cyclic compounds that were detectable at the soil surface over buried cadavers have been identified as key markers of decomposition and therefore of importance for CDs. They were grouped according to those found throughout the time of burial, only early in the burial (<7,300 BADDs), and those persisting until all soft tissue was gone (<18,000 BADDs). Compounds present throughout the decomposition process would be desirable choice for training aids. However, there is still too little known about the decomposition compounds that dogs use to detect human remains to state this as more than a hypothesis.

The bad news is that this group of compounds (including toluene, ethane, sulfides, methane, aldehydes) is not unique and can be found in many outdoor samples taken virtually anywhere. Their ubiquitous presence may account for some of the false alerts by cadaver dogs.

2.3.3.2.2 Compounds in Near-Surface Soils A global study of the near-surface chemical compounds of soils associated with graves (60+ years old) and the downslope surface and subsurface plumes in different environments identified more than 50 human decomposition compounds detectable in the near-surface soils as shown in Table 2.5 (Vass 2012). Their presence depends on environmental conditions and their properties (solubility, density, molecular weight, etc.) determine whether a compound is detected in close association with the remains (corpse) and/or in the downslope chemical plume.

The vapor pressures of the VOCs in Table 2.5 are high, which indicates that their volatility is high and that dogs could easily detect them if the grave soils are sufficiently porous to allow the scent to reach the surface and they are not removed by chemical or biological processes in the soil.

Decomposition in the grave environment was found to be aerobic (involves oxygen) if it was a surface or near-surface event, the remains were loosely wrapped in clothing, in a non-airtight container above ground, or covered by <0.3 m (1 ft) of loose material. The environment was anaerobic (doesn't involve oxygen) if the remains were buried a minimum of 0.61 m (2 ft) deep in clay textured soils, 0.76 m (2.5 ft) in peat or silty textured soils, 1.07 m (3.5 ft) deep in sand or loam soils, or the remains were wrapped or placed in an airtight container or matrix. These results indicate that training aids for CDs used to detect graves should include materials that have decomposed both aerobically and anaerobically.

Some compounds tend to concentrate near the remains rather than in the plume as the gravesite ages. Thus, when searching for clandestine graves, the compounds that appear predominantly near or at the corpse as opposed to those present in the plume may be more valuable as

Table 2.5 Properties of Selected VOCs Associated with Decomposition of Human Remains

Volatile Organic Compound	Formula	Mol Weight (g/mol)	Vapor Pressure (mm of Hg)	Occurrence (Corpse/Plume or Human/Animal)	
Nonanal	$C_9H_{18}O$	142	0.3	Corpse/plume	Human/animal
Toluene	C_7H_8	92	28	Corpse/plume	Human/animal
Dimethyl disulfide	$C_2H_6S_2$	94	29	Corpse	—
Acetone	C_3H_6O	58	226	Corpse/plume	Human/animal
Hexane	C_6H_{14}	86	150	Corpse/plume	Human/animal
Chloroform	$CHCl_3$	119	200	Corpse/plume	Animal
Carbon disulfide	CS_2	76	350	Corpse/plume	—
Styrene	C_8H_8	104	4.5	Corpse/plume	—
Pentane	C_5H_{12}	72	500	Corpse	Human only
Carbon tetrachloride	CCl_4	72	110	Plume	Human only
Decane	$C_{10}H_{22}$	142	1.3	Corpse	Human only
Undecane	$C_{11}H_{24}$	156	0.4	Corpse/plume	Human only

Source: Data from Vass, A.A. 2012. *Forensic Sci Int* 222:234–241.

training aids. These include benzene, some fluorinated halogens, sulfur compounds (dimethyl disulfide, dimethyl trisulfide), and a few aldehydes (heptanal, hexanal, nonanal, octanal). Using this information requires that we know which VOCs are present in training aids used for CDs. None of the VOCs associated only with human decomposition (Table 2.5) were present in a study of training aids (Hoffman et al. 2009). Unfortunately, not enough is known about the effects of age, storage conditions (temperature, humidity, aerobic or anaerobic decomposition), and other factors on training aids to predict the specific VOCs that would be present in the aids.

2.3.3.3 Live vs Dead

Decomposition scent differs from live scent since it is thought to be generic. The scent specific to an individual is eventually replaced by decomposition scent consisting of elemental compounds thought to be common to all cadavers since it involves the decomposition of proteins, fats, and carbohydrates. It has been shown there is less variation in VOCs among recent cadavers than among the living, and decomposition may reduce the differences among cadavers (DeGreeff and Furton 2011). However, each living person's scent is unique, specific to the individual, which indicates that some of the chemicals that make up scent may be controlled by the individual's genetics. It is also known that dogs can detect bones, teeth, and hair in older burials and that these materials retain their DNA. This raises the possibility that dogs may be capable of distinguishing between individual cadavers (skeletons) by the unique scent of their bones, teeth, and hair.

The time frame for decomposition to occur is highly variable and depends on temperature, availability of oxygen, moisture, types of available fauna (bacteria), soils, diet, medicines, obesity, and other factors. Typical times required would be a few weeks to a few months. Under hot and moist conditions, the time can be significantly shorter. At the time of death, breath and metabolism cease but scent from glandular secretions and bacteria remain for an undetermined period. Dogs appear to be able to recognize when a person is dead, but it is not known how they do this. They may be detecting a lack of visual cues of life, lack of breath in the scent bouquet, a scent associated with the death of cells, and/or some other effects. Some nurses report that people who are about to die have a certain smell, but this does not appear to have been verified.

Carrion flies, when present and under favorable environmental conditions, have been observed to appear on a corpse in a matter of minutes after death (Haskel et al. 1997). The flies are attracted to the nose and mouth most likely because of the odors emanating from these two sites that attract them. These observations suggest that there may be a scent associated with death, an "odor mortis," that appears within minutes of dying or possibly before.

In response to a suspected murder investigation, an attempt was made to answer two questions raised by law enforcement (Oesterhelweg et al. 2008). How long would a deceased body have to be in contact with a material for the scent to be detectable by a CD, and how long would detectable scent remain on the material? Carpet squares were placed under two cadavers wrapped in a thin cotton blanket at postmortem intervals < 3 hours and removed after 2 min for one and 10 min for the other. Three CDs alerted on the carpet squares up to 35 days (2-min exposure) and 65 days (10-min exposure). The authors also concluded that a person dead for 2 hours could be detected by CDs.

2.3.3.4 Cadaver Scent and Discrimination
CD handlers have long believed that dogs can discriminate between human and animal remains, and VOC profiles from human and animal remains have been shown to be different (DeGreeff and Furton 2011). CDs can detect blood from cadavers at concentrations of 1 ppm and can distinguish it from distractions including blood in urine, swine blood, and dog menstrual blood (Riezzo et al. 2014). CD handlers also believe that dogs can discriminate between fresh human and animal blood stains and this has been confirmed in two instances by laboratory analysis (Osterkamp unpublished). Human blood stains on automobile upholstery can be detected for a decade under favorable conditions (Osterkamp unpublished).

2.3.3.5 Specific Training Aids
Desirable training aids for CDs would be bodies, body parts, bones, blood, and other body fluids in various stages of decay including saponification, mummification, and under different decomposition conditions (e.g. wet, dry, aerobic, anaerobic). Collection and storage of these aids would be a daunting task, so handlers must resort to using human remains that may be lawfully obtained. Handlers obtain human remains for training aids from other handlers, coroners, medical examiners, morgues, hospitals, and elsewhere. Several universities in the US, Canada, and Australia, offer classes for CDs that include detection of full body cadavers (i.e. the full VOC scent profile for deceased humans).

An assumption in the use of aids is that the dog will generalize from the limited number of compounds that it is trained to alert on. Also, it will perform its alert when encountering larger cadaver parts or the whole cadaver with the full VOC profile (as modified by local conditions). The basis for making this assumption is not well established. Handlers compensate by using as many different training aids as possible. Since these training aids are limited, it is unknown if they contain sufficient components of the VOC profile to enable the dog to generalize to the odors that they encounter when finding human remains. However, while we do know that CDs trained on a few small amounts of human remains do find bodies, it would be desirable to have a better understanding of what the dogs smell and what is needed to train them.

Historically, CDs trained with putrescene or cadaverine have been successful in finding cadavers in the field (Rebmann et al. 2000). These compounds were not found at the ground surface in the grave study. Studies of EDs suggest that dogs trained on limited varieties of smokeless powders were only able to reliably detect the specific types on which they were trained. Buried bodies may present more difficult conditions because the soil environment (which includes chemicals and bacteria in the soil) can add to, remove, and/or modify the VOCs emanating from a decomposing buried body.

In a study of training aids contributed by CD handlers (Hoffman et al. 2009), 33 VOCs occurred in the headspace of 14 decomposing training aids that included blood, tissue, skin, fat, adipocere, bone, and teeth. No information was given about the storage conditions (e.g. aerobic, anaerobic, temperature, humidity) during decomposition of these aids. Comparing these results to 30 key VOCs present at the ground surface over graves (Vass et al. 2008), only four of the compounds (dimethyl disulfide, toluene, nonanal, and tetrachloroethylene) were found in the training aids. It is of interest to cadaver dog trainers and handlers that the first three compounds occurred in only one of the training aids, body fat attached to skin. However, the effects of decomposition and environment on the compounds emanating from body fat and skin are not known. Tetrachloroethylene was found in blood, muscle, skin, adipocere, bone, and teeth.

None of the 14 training aids contained VOCs known to be specific to human decomposition only (pentane, carbon tetrachloride, decane, undecane) (Table 2.5). The training aids did contain seven of the compounds found in the global grave study. Six were found in bone; five in muscle; four each in blood, body fat attached to skin, adipocere, and fat; and three each in skin and teeth.

Disarticulated bodies can be widely scattered by animals, dispersed downhill under the influence of gravity, and transported by water. Since searches may be conducted specifically for cadaver parts that can yield DNA (bones, teeth, and hair), it is desirable to store training aids for them separately. Bones can be obtained from companies that sell bones and even complete skeletons although little is known about how these were processed and handled. Some appear to have been chemically cleaned. Teeth are especially important since they are commonly used for identification of the body. In some states, dentists may be able to provide teeth that have not been cleaned or autoclaved. Hair can be obtained from barbers, hair dressers, and friends.

The large numbers of VOCs produced during decomposition and the lack of information on what compounds the dogs use to detect decomposition scent pose significant problems for developing training aids for CDs.

A viable alternative to using human remains for training aids would be to transfer scent from the remains to a material that would become the training aid. DeGreeff and Furton (2011) used the STU-100 (with Dukal cotton gauze (Dukal Corporation, Syosset, NY) for the scent collection pads) to obtain VOCs from cadavers in a morgue and a crematorium, and from gauze containing decomposition fluid, adipocere, bone residue, or blood. These scent pads were stored in glass jars and used later in tests of trained CDs. The majority of dogs alerted on the aids with different concentrations and from different odor sources in every scenario tested.

Another way to collect cadaver scent would be to place sterile gauze pads in contact with a cadaver for a length of time similar to the method used by Oesterhelweg et al. (2008). The experience of trailing dog handlers indicates this would be about 10 to 30 minutes. Store the pads in clean, sealed glass vials or jars for later use. The method requires access to cadaver sources in different stages of decay but does not require an expensive STU-100 unit. This method is not intrusive so that morgues and crime scene investigators may be willing to allow this type of scent collection. The advantages are that handling the pads would not be as hazardous as cadaver materials and it does not appear that there are legal restrictions to possessing them.

Artificial scents such as Sigma Pseudo Corpse I and II (Sigma Aldrich Chemical Corporation) have been used to train cadaver dogs. While the scents appear to have a limited scent profile, CDs trained with them have found bodies (Rebmann et al. 2000), but it is not known if the handlers observed a full alert or a CB (change of behavior). Training aids have been made from chemical solutions of the most commonly occurring VOCs found in human remains. These aids were used in trials with cadaver dogs, but the dogs showed inconsistent interest in them.

2.3.4 Other Sources

It appears that training aids for most other types of SDs rely on some of the source material to communicate to the dog the scent that results in being rewarded. A novel training aid for SDs used to search for bed bugs was developed by immersing the bugs in solvents (pentane, acetone, methanol, and water) (Pfiester et al. 2008). It was determined beforehand that the dogs did not alert on these solvents. The solvents were then sealed in containers. For training, 1 ml of the extract (equivalent to five bed bugs) was placed on filter paper inside a vial. All dogs trained on bed bugs alerted on the pentane extract but not on the other extracts indicating that the scent of the bed bugs was transferred to that solvent.

Training aids for dogs used to detect human diseases, especially types of cancer, have used breath from affected individuals, even though the cancer may not directly affect their respiratory system (Lippi and Cervellin 2011).

2.3.5 General Recommendations

Research is currently being conducted to develop training aids for EDs, DDs, and CDs so that any recommendations may soon be out of date. ED and DD handlers usually have access to scent kits and source materials from their organizations. Given the success of the STU-100 for making training aids for CDs, it would seem obvious to use it for making aids for EDs and DDs. CD handlers generally use whatever scent sources they can obtain. The STU-100 is too expensive for many teams, and until new information and/or products are available, handlers will need to continue using a wide variety of cadaver materials in different stages of decay or scent pads that have been in contact with them. Commonly used aids include placentas with blood and body fluids, skin, tissue, blood, adipocere, body fat, bone, and teeth. Soil from under a decomposing body (hanging, on the surface, or in a grave) and clothes or articles that have been in contact with a decomposing body can be also used. Body fat attached to skin, blood and body fluids, muscle, skin, bones, and teeth may be especially important in searches for clandestine graves. It is important to expose CDs to aids of varying sizes and types.

2.3.5.1 Storage

Glass containers with glass stoppers that are not exposed to ultraviolet light have been shown to offer greater stability for stored human scent samples and probably for other scent samples as well (Hudson et al. 2009). Glass jars with plastic, perforated lids have also been used. If canning jars are used, decomposition chemicals and chemicals from other sources may cause the metal lids to rust. Rust can be detected by dogs (Schoon et al. 2014) and its presence contaminates the stored scent source. Freezing training aids for long times can cause them to desiccate, possibly changing their properties, because the duty cycle of a freezer causes moisture to migrate from the source to the inside walls of the storage container.

Training aids for all SDs should be carefully handled, stored, and transported to prevent contamination. Contamination can occur by transfer of trace fluids, microparticles, and VOCs from the aids to other aids and surfaces nearby. It can also be a result of background scents in the location where they were prepared, contact with humans (primarily from skin secretions, perfumes, lotions, smoke, skin flakes), type of clothing and gloves used by the preparer, the environment (vehicle fuel and fumes, oils, grease, buildings, sewage) and animals present such as pets and other SDs. Cross contamination can result when aids are in close proximity while in semipermeable containers (e.g. paper or canvas bags) during handling, shipping, storage, and placement. Cross contamination can also occur if two different drugs or explosives are handled with the same pair of gloves. The problem is that it may be thought that the dog is being trained for one source, but the dog is alerting to the presence of another.

Handling aids with clean tongs or forceps while wearing clean medical examination gloves helps to keep human and other scent off them. SD handlers often use these gloves to handle their aids. However, if the outside of the fingers of the gloves are touched by their skin when putting them on or if any object is touched that has previously been touched by bare hands (e.g. door knob, scent container) then human scent will be transferred to the gloves and aids. Do not hide training aids where dogs can touch the aids with their wet noses or mouth them. Training aids hidden for a long time or repeatedly in the same place may cause the location to be contaminated with residual scent.

It can be argued that ED and DD training aids (explosives and drugs) will commonly contain the scent of the people that packaged them (from skin flakes, secretions, breath, lotions, perfumes, etc.), so that human contamination should not create problems. However, limited information indicates EDs may prefer the scent of one person over that of others to the point that it influences their success during training (Goldblatt 2017). The question may be more important for training than for searches, but it remains open.

2.4 Scent in Training

2.4.1 Scent Availability

Scent availability refers to the quantity of scent (concentration of scent molecules) available for a dog to detect. It has usually been assumed that scent availability depends on the amount (volume or mass) of the source, but there are other factors. Lotspeich et al. (2012) have shown that scent availability in containers also depends on the container volume, explosive vapor pressure, and temperature. The primary consideration for reliable detection of a source by SDs is for the headspace of the container to be saturated with scent molecules volatilized from the source. Once the headspace is saturated any increase in the amount of sample will not result in an increase in scent availability.

Calculations and studies with EDs have shown that the amount of sample that is needed to saturate different size containers normally used for training is relatively small. For nitromethane, nitroethane, and nitropropane, the amounts recommended to saturate a container and allow for stable concentrations over time are 10 µl (microliters) for 20 ml (milliliters) headspace vials, 100 µl for quart cans and 1000 µl for gallon cans (1000 µl = 1 ml = 3.38E-2 oz).

Generally, factors influencing scent availability include the characteristics of the container (scent containment, volume, materials) and the source (phase, type, amount, surface area, diffusivity and vapor pressure (includes the effects of temperature)). Adhesion of some VOCs and microparticles to the container surface may also be an important factor (Schade and Goldstein 2001; Goldblatt 2017). Scent availability depends critically on the degree of scent containment provided by the container (packaging). Source containers can be completely closed, diffusion limited, partially open, or open.

Completely closed containers do not allow scent molecules to pass through their walls. Common examples include those made of metal (antipersonnel mines), glass, tires, and some plastics. While plastics generally allow gas transport through them, from an operational viewpoint the flux rate of VOCs through the container material does not have to be zero; it just needs to be below the limit of detection by dogs. A potential problem is that the VOCs of some sources may degrade the container material (e.g. corrode some metals, chemically break down plastics).

Diffusive containers are those that allow scent molecules to pass through the container material by diffusion or have such small openings that scent escapes through them by mass flow, but very slowly. Diffusion is such a slow process that it becomes important only over long time periods or with very thin container walls. Slow mass flow (such as through small holes) can appear to behave like diffusion but the scent flux would be much larger than for diffusion. Examples of diffusive containers include thin plastic and rubber packaging (food storage bags, balloons) that allow scent molecules to diffuse through their thin walls. Windproof clothing consists of materials that allow a small amount of air and scent to flow through them but restrict the passage of wind (they are not truly diffusive).

Diffusive training aids have been developed for explosives, drugs, cadavers, and other scent sources called COMPS (Controlled Odor Mimic Permeation System) (Furton and Harper 2017). In use, some of the source or a mimic is placed in the solid form or, for a liquid, on a sterile gauze pad in a plastic bag that is then sealed. The thickness of the bag is chosen to allow scent to diffuse through it at a relatively constant and reproducible rate that produces a fixed amount of scent available to the dogs. Scent availability can be controlled by the diffusion rate of the scent molecules through the bag which is determined by the type of material, thickness of the bag, and the properties of the scent molecules. The bags can be stored and used as training aids later. Additional details and variations of the method for making training aids for EDs, DDs, and CDs can be found in Macias (2009) and DeGreef (2010).

Partially open sources are those that have restricted access to the external air. These include unpackaged sources in containers that are open at the top (cans and jars) and containers that have significant holes in them (luggage, boxes, back packs, canvas bags). The National Odor Recognition Test (NORT) for explosives is such an example. It has the source in a small can with holes in the lid that is placed in an open quart can that is placed in an open gallon can.

If more scent is available than needed to completely saturate a partially open container, the excess scent may overflow the container and flow to low levels in the surrounding area because the VOCs are typically heavier than the air. This means that in training, testing, and searching, SDs should be encouraged to search the lowest areas around a known or suspected position of the source. For sources in closed rooms, scent would be expected to exit at the bottom of the doors, and for luggage to be present at the bottom edge. In outdoor areas, scent pools in depressions near the source until turbulence mixes it with the air and it is transported away by the wind.

Completely open sources are those that are exposed with unrestricted access to the external air. Examples are sources attached to surfaces (explosives) and those lying on the ground surface (spilled gunpowder, shell casings, drugs, bodies, and teeth). Scent availability depends on their size, surface area, and volatility (vapor pressure which depends on temperature). On volatilization from the source, scent molecules enter the air where any wind moves them away from the source in a scent plume detectable by dogs.

It is possible that the scent from a training aid may remain constant with increasing size of the source, but this may not be true for all sources. For some sources, the perceived nature of the scent is thought to change with size. CD handlers have observed that cadaver dogs trained on small sources may fail to indicate a body or may not perform their trained alert on one. A similar situation seems to occur with EDs and DDs that encounter very large sources.

The performance of CDs seems to improve once they have found a body or two. So, it is desirable to use large sources to train the dog although these may be difficult to find. One solution may be to put all the sources used by a group of handlers into an open or ventilated box and work the dogs on it at a group training or seminar. This may not be the best procedure due to the differing ages of the sources, cross contamination of the sources, and other factors.

A curious fact is that agency certifications generally use relatively small sources. The certified teams are then deemed qualified to search for large explosive and drug sources and for bodies without ever having demonstrated in either training or testing that they will alert on them. The assumption that, if the team can find and alert on small sources, then they can find and alert on large ones, does not appear to have been evaluated.

2.4.2 Use of Aids

2.4.2.1 Preexposure and Prescenting

Preexposure is exposing an untrained dog to a source prior to initial training. A kind of preexposure occurs with some training methods that use a scented toy as the first step in training. Hall et al. (2013) have shown that preexposure increases the success rate during initial training. Prescenting is exposing a trained dog to a source prior to performing a search for that source (Papet and Minhinnick 2016). Prescenting in the present context is used by scent discriminating trailing dog handlers prior to starting a trail to communicate to the dog the person the dog is to follow. It has also been used by a few CD handlers prior to land and water searches, especially when the search is for specific items (hair, bone, teeth) or for specific stages of decomposition.

2.4.2.2 Type of Reward

Play/retrieve as a reward (reinforcement) has been widely used. It is thought that dogs trained with this method are highly motivated to find scent. However, some agencies use food and select dogs for their food drive (Department of Agriculture). Food rewards require less skill to deliver, allow more trials per day, and it is easier to find food-motivated dogs. Some dogs are trained every day with their food reward for finds being their only source of food. A potential disadvantage is that in some situations (disaster, crime scenes) food at the site may become a distraction and even ingested by the dogs. Food rewards used in training are often dropped by the handler or the dog so that any dogs working the same hide afterward may be distracted by the food and ingest it.

Using multiple rewards during training can be helpful when working the dog in hazardous (along a highway) or difficult (steep terrain) conditions. Rewards can include food, praise, touch (petting, scratching), games (keep away), tugging, retrieving, combinations, and others. The handler then has the option to select the reward best suited to conditions.

2.4.2.3 Number of Aids

During the initial training, the number of aids hidden from the dog (hides) should be large to establish initial discrimination and variable to keep the dog from getting used to finding a fixed number of aids (Goldblatt et al. 2009). As the dog becomes reasonably proficient at detecting and locating the scent and the handler proficient in working the dog, the number can be systematically reduced. For example, a line of ten blocks could contain 3 to 4 sources initially and eventually be reduced to 0 to 2.

It is necessary to use a null line (no source present) regularly. It appears that dogs that always make a find each time they are trained are more prone to false alerts. For an operational dog, the number of aids needs to be large enough to keep the dog motivated to search. It is usually recommended (e.g. J. Joyce in seminars) for dogs used to search large areas to occasionally search a large null area.

2.4.2.4 *Reward Schedule*

During initial training, SD trainers generally recommend rewarding the dog for every correct response. However, most SD handlers continue to reward their dog in training every time it detects, finds, and alerts on a source. They do not reward them for a positive response on a search since it is not known if a source is present. For SDs, it is desirable to use a variable schedule of reinforcement in training to condition them to not having a reward every time for a find (Goldblatt et al. 2009). A typical reinforcement schedule in training might be 80% (4 of 5) of the correct responses, although there are considerable variations between trainers. SDs training on multiple sources (e.g. graves in a cemetery) may be worked on 5 or more sources before they get their reward. However, their handlers must be acutely aware of any reduction in focus and motivation to avoid developing problems with their alert.

2.4.2.5 *Multiple Component Sources*

SDs may be required to find many different sources with each source consisting of multiple chemical components. For example, EDs may be required to find different types of explosives, DDs, different types of drugs, and CDs, different body parts. Each one of these sources consists of multiple chemical components. Two distinct methods have been developed for introducing these sources to EDs and DDs (Goldblatt et al. 2009). One combines sources to produce a scent mixture that is introduced to the dogs. Once the dogs recognize and alert on the mixture, the sources are separated for the rest of the training and never recombined. However, Goldblatt et al. (2009) recommend introducing each source separately either sequentially or during the same time frame.

2.4.2.6 *Distractions*

Distractions include sights, sounds, and scents that distract a SD while working. A SD is not fully trained until it works reliably in different places in the presence of distractions. Other dogs or animals that SDs see or hear while working are common distractions. Distraction scents are any non-source scents that cause interest or an alert by the dog which confuses the issue of whether a source is present. Blood, bones, and other remains of animals, fish, and birds can be distractions for CDs. Food, fish bait, trash, animal scents, and human and animal urine and feces are other common distractions encountered on searches (there are many others). SDs should be discouraged from showing an interest in or alerting on distraction odors although some are problematical (feces, urine, and semen for CDs) as noted previously. This can be done for any SD by routinely including distractions in yard work and in field problems and discouraging any interest in them. Distractions may also have an impact on the handler and anything that distracts the handler may be expected to influence handler-dog interactions and thereby affect the performance of the team. Thus, the handler should also become accustomed to training in the presence of distractions that may be encountered during searches. A potential distractor is the state of stress of the handler which increases their anxiety and may result in a change in the dog's performance during testing or searching (Zubedat et al. 2014).

This idea was evaluated with handlers of military EDs. Superior offi-cers of the handlers told the handlers prior to a test that they were to be reassigned and/or were present at the tests where they pointed at the han-dlers and appeared to write notes about them. The results showed that the handlers' stress decreased their attention and elevated their anxiety level but increased the activity level of the dogs. Surprisingly, this improved the dog's performance as shown by the reduced time to detect the explosives. It was thought that the external stress disturbed the handler's focus which resulted in reduced control of the dog and allowed the dogs to work in a less handler-dependent manner. These results emphasize the importance of SD-handler interactions in all searches and suggest that reduced control of the dog (e.g. off leash vs on leash) may be desirable. Trainers have long recognized this and often recommend that handlers "let the dog work" (i.e. reduce their control).

2.4.3 Source Placement

If a certain type or part of a regularly used search area never has a source, a dog's motivation to search it and the dog's POD (probability of detec-tion) when a source is present may be reduced. In a study of EDs (Gazit et al. 2005b), experienced handlers and dogs trained on two different roads on alternate days for 20 days. Road A had sources every time and road B never had a source present. Sources were then placed on road B at a frequency of one every third day, but the dogs detected only about 50% of them whereas their success on road A was much higher (about 90%). The dogs were then retrained on road B with sources placed there every day but the dog's moti-vation to search road B never recovered. Additional research confirmed this result (i.e. reduced motivation and reduced ability to detect a source in an area despite continued reinforcement).

These results appear likely to apply to other SDs. It is suggested that SDs be trained in as many different environments as possible and that source placement be varied so that the dogs find sources in all types and parts of the areas being searched, especially regularly used training areas. This includes buildings with different types of rooms (e.g. bathrooms, bedrooms, kitchens, living rooms, etc.) and outdoor settings with different terrain and vegetation. A way to avoid problems here would be to keep a record of where aids are placed in each area, to regularly review this information, and to make sure that all subsets of an area are used.

2.4.4 Potential Problems

Papet (2016) has reviewed the use of training aids for DDs and EDs, including aspects of selection, packaging, handling, storage, and transporting aids. Contamination can occur between aids stored in proximity and by human scent in all aspects of use. CD handlers have observed that their dogs may not come to a full alert on aids used by other handlers which probably indicates contamination. Aids can be contaminated by materials in the area where they are placed as hides and can also contaminate these areas with residual scent as noted (Jezeirski et al. 2014). Cross contamination of sources during use, especially storage, by VOCs and microparticles can be a potential problem for SDs. This indicates that it is desirable to store training aids separately to avoid cross contamination.

Contaminating aids with human scent can occur during packaging and handling. Using medical examination gloves that are put on by handling the wrist section only and clean metal tongs can be helpful. Skin flakes falling on an aid or its container and particulates from sources are problems that are difficult to eliminate. Complete separation of all types of sources during all phases of use is desirable. The primary handler problem appears to be contamination with skin secretions since we leave scented skin oils (fingerprints) on everything we touch. An example in training occurs when a container contaminated with live human scent is used to package the training aid.

In addition to scent from the surroundings, there are seven possible scents: source, container, human, and their four combinations. We would like the dogs to alert on the source scent and any combination that includes it but not on the container or human scent or both. However, experience with EDs, DDs, and CDs shows that dogs will often alert on the container with live human scent on it and no source. This makes it important to include containers with human scent on them, but no source, in yard and field work and to ignore interest or alerts on them. Since contamination and deterioration of training aids due to ageing and weathering can create training problems, Papet (2016) recommends that training aids for EDs and DDs be put on a regular replacement schedule where they are cycled sequentially through usage conditions such as initial training, testing, routine training, training in contaminated environments, and then replaced.

As noted above, not enough is known about the scents from specific sources that cause a dog to alert, and the initial training of many SDs is done with training aids with an unknown scent profile. Special care should be taken at this stage to make sure that the aids are not contaminated (Goldblatt et al. 2009; Papet 2016). It is also necessary to use many variations (types, sizes) of the aids to help the dogs generalize and to eventually train them on the sources found in the field of operations.

Once scent recognition training has been done and the dog has an identifiable and reliable alert that the handler is proficient at recognizing, it is important for the handler to start running blind problems regularly, including null problems. The reason is that, if the handler usually knows the location of the aid, they are likely to give involuntary cues to the dog. Cueing is a major problem when training SDs (Ensminger and Papet 2011a and b). When training on a line of scent containers, handlers may alter their pace, body posture, or eye position at a container with scent which cues the dogs to the location of the scent. In working field problems, handlers are likely to become lax in the control of the dog while searching until in the vicinity of the aid and this too is a cue to the dog. Furthermore, if the handler places the aid and happens to be in a hurry, there is a tendency to hurry the search, not covering the area thoroughly, and effectively lead the dog to the source to get finished, a sure recipe for failure since these actions are the opposite of what must be done during a real search. One of the most important factors when training SDs is to cover the area thoroughly just as in searching.

During training, it is important to make sure that the dog responds to the scent of the aid and is not responding to human, container scent, their combination, or to any other possible contaminant odor. Varying the type, size, and placement of the aids; running blind problems; and having distractions present (scent, sight, and sound) are important.

SDs often learn to trail their handlers or others who place the source, not only in field and forest settings, but also in buildings. Some strategies to prevent trailing to the source are to throw the source (no scent trail), to crisscross the area with a bewildering array of human scent trails, and to enter all the rooms in a building. For buried sources, it is desirable to place the sources several weeks before the dog is used to find them; sources buried for weeks to months are much more realistic for training. This requires a large area dedicated to training and several buried sources. Experience shows that dogs can remember the location of sources if they are worked more than every four months on them. Care in burying the sources is necessary because of possible ground surface contamination from source liquids or particles that the dogs can easily detect. Cadaver sources may need to be placed in a wire mesh cage for shallow burials (<0.30 m or 1 ft) since roaming dogs and wild animals may dig them up. Excessive digging by CDs during training usually requires a long time for the site to return to its natural condition. With care, sites can be useful for years. A site with a placenta and a large handful of hair buried <0.30 m deep in 2005 can still be detected about 50% of the time 13 years later.

Assuming they are properly trained, the most common reasons for SDs not finding a source during searches are (i) the handler missed the change in behavior in the dog and (ii) the dog was never in scent, both handler errors. On searches, SDs that have never found the type and size of source and the amount of scent available from a source may not give their alert but rather some other change in behavior (CB). Consequently, handlers must be aware of changes in the dog's behavior and be able to interpret them. If the dog was never in scent, it is likely a result of poor search methods during training. It is very important during all training to cover the search area thoroughly. Blind trials help to make sure of this. Variable winds may require changes in search plans to cover an area thoroughly. The idea of training like you would search is especially important in SD training. The dog should not be able to tell if they are training or searching. This is difficult to do because the dogs are so expert at reading the handler's emotional, mental, and physical states.

When a dog or handler works harder and longer during a search than during training, the dog is more likely to give a false alert and the handler is more likely to make mistakes. A dog or handler that has only worked 30 min problems cannot search effectively for several hours. Trainers (e.g. J. Joyce in seminars) recommend that "nose time" (the amount of time that the dog and handler can work continuously and reliably) be determined during training. It is also important during training to condition the dog and handler for the longest searches they will be asked to do in the terrain or physical settings where they will do them. Occasionally doing long unknown null problems and problems where the dog will not make a find until after several hours of searching is helpful. For known problems, bringing a dog back to the area of a source repeatedly or hanging out there encouraging the dog to search and make the find may result in a tendency (it is a cue to the dog) to false alert.

A common question of SD handlers is how often the dogs should be trained. Research shows that daily training and encounters with scent sources by SDs improves their ability to recognize and discriminate between sources and background scents and lowers their threshold of detection (increases their sensitivity) for detecting weak sources.

Some agencies recommend 16 hours of training per month in their general guidelines but do not say if this is actual training time or includes travel or other time. If this is training time only, small-area searches for buried sources and some structure searches typically require about 30 min which would be more than 30 such searches per month, an improbable number. Some arson dogs are trained daily, and some EDs not worked for 3 days must be reevaluated before going back into service. Clearly, training almost daily is desirable, but few teams can do this using field problems entirely.

Experience suggests that a mix of yard work (blocks, boxes, carousel, wall) and field training totaling four or five times a week seems to keep CDs and handlers sharp in detecting faint scents.

Do not cross -train SDs to detect articles with live human scent on them unless that is the application you desire. You may have law enforcement or other agencies dig up or recover some buried clothes or shoes instead of the desired source. Do not train CDs in cemeteries unless it can be verified that the bodies were not embalmed with formaldehyde. Plywood manufactured before the mid-1990s was made with glue containing formaldehyde. A dog trained in a cemetery on graves with embalmed bodies may alert on disintegrating plywood made with formaldehyde glue. It appears that the emissions from the glue are similar enough to embalming fluid for the dog to generalize and alert.

2.5 Summary

Scent molecules are volatile organic compounds, VOCs. Scent is the dog's perception of these molecules as a result of processing by the brain. During sniffing, exhalation causes air jets to be directed to the sides of the dog's nose and downward. These air jets can dislodge particles of dust, skin flakes, and adsorbed VOCs from surfaces which can then be inhaled. Scent molecules on dust and skin flakes can be liberated in the dog's warm and humid nose and then be detected by the dog. It may also be possible for the humid air jets impinging on dry soil surfaces to free VOCs adsorbed on dry soil particles to be inhaled for detection of buried sources such as land mines. The warmth of the air jets may also help free VOCs adsorbed on surfaces allowing them to be inhaled and detected.

Sources emit scent by evaporation, sublimation, and desorption. These processes are collectively referred to as volatilization which depends on the vapor pressure of the source which depends strongly on the temperature. For example, the amount of scent volatilizing from TNT increases about ten times when the temperature increases from 77°F to 104°F.

Drugs and explosives produce "sticky" microparticles that adhere to surfaces and humans produce skin flakes that come to rest on surfaces where they can be dislodged by air jets from the dog's nose to produce a detectable scent. This sticky nature of microparticles can contaminate nearby surfaces such as other training aids, dust particles, rooms, and people. For detection of explosives with very low vapor pressures, stickiness may be as important as vapor pressure. The ability of dogs to dislodge these particles by sniffing and inhaling them may account for the ability of EDs to detect explosives with very low vapor pressures such as RDX.

VOCs from explosives, drugs, human remains, and live persons are heavier than air and are expected, in the absence of wind, to drain downward and settle in low areas (depressions over graves, ditches, floor drains, car floors). In outdoor settings, scent can pool in these areas and, under calm and cloudy conditions, can remain there until removed by turbulent air conditions. This suggests, *when there is no wind or there is a downslope flow*, it would be desirable to search for buried explosives and other sources on a slope by gridding across the slope and advancing the grid up the slope.

It is not always necessary to use parent compounds for training EDs and DDs because the dogs use the most abundant chemical component(s) in the vapor headspace. Dogs trained on aids developed from explosives and drugs manufactured by one process may not alert on similar explosives and drugs produced by another process. For example, EDs trained on TNT that contains DNT may learn to detect the more volatile DNT. Russian, other manufactured TNT, and some weathered TNT does not contain DNT, which may *result in a failure* of the dogs to detect the TNT.

Residual scent from sources can remain in hides for days or much longer and possibly result in alerts where nothing is found. Care must be taken to allow time (several days or more) for residual scent to dissipate when using areas (buildings, vehicles, field sites) repeatedly during training and testing. It is also desirable to train dogs to offer their alert only when the source is present.

Favorable times to search for sources buried in dry soil are when humidity is high, or when the ground has been recently wetted by dew, very light rain, or mechanically misted.

Variability in scenting thresholds by different dogs indicates it would be desirable to test the ability of candidate SDs to detect low scent levels in order to select a dog with a suitable nose.

SDs that were not physically conditioned showed a 64% reduction in olfactory acuity following a physical stress test. A moderate physical conditioning program can help SDs maintain their scenting ability during periods of intense work.

CDs can detect blood from cadavers at concentrations of 1 ppm and can distinguish between living and dead humans, human and animal remains, cadaver blood and swine blood, and between cadaver blood and dog menstrual blood. Human blood stains on automobile upholstery can be detected for a decade under favorable conditions.

Body fat attached to skin, bones, blood and body fluids in various stages of decomposition and aerobic and anaerobic decay, adipocere, and mummified tissue are especially important training aids for CDs.

Glass containers with glass stoppers not exposed to ultraviolet light, glass jars with plastic, perforated lids, and canning jars are desirable (in this order) for storing aids. Scent availability from aids depends on the amount; presence of source particulates; vapor pressure; temperature; size of the containers; and whether the containers are closed, partially open, or open. Humidity can also be a factor.

During initial training, SDs should be rewarded for every correct response. A variable reward schedule is phased in for later training. SDs are not fully trained until they work reliably in different places in the presence of distractions (scents, sights, sounds). If a certain type or part of a regularly used search area never has a source, a dog's motivation to search it decreases significantly and may never recover.

SDs and handlers should be conditioning for the longest searches they will do in the weather, terrain, and environments where they will search including occasional long unknown null problems. Do not cross train SDs to detect articles with live human scent unless they will be tasked to search for it. Daily training improves SDs' ability to recognize sources, discriminate between background scents, and lowers their threshold of detection for detecting weak sources. Do not train CDs in cemeteries unless it can be verified that the bodies were not embalmed with formaldehyde.

Scent and Wind

3

3.1 Scent Movement

3.1.1 Introduction

Chapter 3 addresses basic information necessary to understand scent movement. While a technical treatment of the subject is beyond the scope of this book, it is desirable to have a basic understanding of scent and air movement and how weather, terrain, vegetation, and any intervening medium influence that movement. This information can be used to deploy a SD in an efficient manner that is most likely to result in detection and location of the source. These involve both art and science developed through personal observation, experience, and study of scent movement. Do not be discouraged by failures because scent movement and transport of scent by moving air is complex. It is impossible to understand all the situations faced by SD teams due to continuously changing weather and environmental settings (vegetation, terrain) that control scent movement.

Scent movement begins when scent molecules leave the source and diffuse through a thin surface boundary layer and then into the atmosphere from above ground sources or through an intervening medium (soil, ground cover, snow, water). People and probably some warm-blooded animals have a warm thermal boundary layer that carries all the scent from their bodies upward (see Figure 2.5) and in a plume into the atmosphere. Scent movement is concerned with the interactions between the physical environment, weather processes and conditions, and any intervening medium that influences scent movement to the dog's nose. These interactions can determine our search strategies and favorable times and places to search and, ultimately, the success or failure of our search efforts.

The movement of scent molecules occurs by chemical diffusion, gravity, buoyancy, and transport by wind, water, and other fluids. Water transport refers to scent carried by water movement in above ground streams and water bodies, in underground streams, on the ground surface, and in thin water films on soil particle surfaces. Chemical diffusion is the movement of scent molecules from regions of higher to lower chemical concentration in any medium. Concentrations are highest at a source and decrease with distance from the source so that the movement is radially away from the source in all directions unless prevented by obstacles. This movement is so slow that it would require about 2 hours to move scent 1 ft by diffusion while a wind speed of 1 ft/sec or 0.7 mph would require 1 sec to move scent the same distance. This means that chemical diffusion is not a factor in scent transport in moving air or water. It can be a factor in scent transport in fine-grained soils and snow where long times or very short distances exist.

Gravity flow of scent is the downward settling of scent molecules that are heavier than air in settings (soils, enclosed spaces, buildings, vehicles) where there is little or no wind. Scent can also be transported (carried) by wind in the downslope and down valley gravity flow of colder air at night. Buoyant flow refers to upward movement of scent molecules that are lighter than air (ammonia, methane) where there is little or no wind. Scent can also be carried by the convective transport of warmed buoyant air that transports scent molecules and scent plumes upward (Figure 3.1). Thus, scent transport

Figure 3.1 A dark cedar tree in calm air, warmed by the sun, caused air in contact with it to warm. The warmer air is lighter and buoyant which caused it to rise carrying smoke or scent upward. A small gust was observed to bend this plume toward the ground.

by the gravity flow of air, convection, and wind are the primary methods of scent transport in the atmosphere. These processes create scent plumes that are thought to behave like smoke plumes from a chimney or a camp fire. The analogy is not precisely correct since smoke consists of particles and scent consists of molecules, but it appears to be a good approximation.

3.1.2 Scent Plumes

Scent plumes carried by the wind are subject to all the conditions that influence wind behavior including the type of flow, atmospheric stability and instability (thermal turbulence), and mechanical turbulence. The flow of air can be laminar (layered without vertical mixing) but is generally turbulent with eddies in the plume swirling and moving with the wind (Schroeder and Buck 1970) as shown in Figure 3.2. Eddies vary in size from tiny ones that are barely visible to huge ones produced by large terrain elements such as mountains and can rotate in any direction independent of the prevailing wind direction.

Much of the information on scent plumes comes from studies of insects (Carde and Willis 2008). Some of it may not apply to the typically much larger sources that search dogs are tasked to find using their relatively large noses. Since our interests are in the behavior of wind at the height of the dog, interactions of wind with features that influence wind behavior at this height are of primary importance. The plumes appear to be continuous close to the source and about the same size as the source. The effective size of a source can be much larger when it is in a turbulent location (e.g. interior to shrubs and trees, behind obstacles in the wind). Plumes increase in size with distance downwind, primarily because of lateral turbulence that causes them to spread or disperse when the eddies are smaller than the plume. If the size of the eddies is larger than the plume, they can transport the plume long distances.

As the plumes move downwind, turbulence eventually deforms (stretches, twists, bends, breaks) them which creates gaps of clean air within the plume as it expands and disperses downwind (Figure 3.2). At this stage, plumes may be described as patchy distributions of scent clouds that move with the wind. The regions between the scent clouds consist of relatively clean air. The distance between scent clouds increases downwind, which indicates that dogs encounter an increasingly intermittent scent signal in the plume. At large distances, the separation between scent clouds becomes much larger than the size of the dog. The plume may also meander at very low wind speeds and, at high wind speeds, is influenced by turbulence elements and random wind gusts in the flow. If the dogs detect scent at this stage, they cast about trying to acquire the plume and may or may not be successful.

(a)

(b)

Figure 3.2 Smoke plumes showing (a) laminar flow with some turbulence at the top edge and (b) turbulent flow features including size at the source, continuity near the source, dispersal, and intermittent smoke clouds as the plume moves downwind.

This scent plume structure has several implications for search dogs. Most scent is a mixture of multiple VOCs, and when turbulence is present, different compounds will be influenced similarly. The ratios of compounds in the scent clouds should be the same as the ratios emitted by the source. This has the effect of preserving the scent picture for the dogs and helps them to recognize it. Intermittent scent plumes with scent concentrations which are relatively undiluted can move significant distances downwind before they disperse to the point where dogs can no longer detect them. This picture of scent plumes is one where the scent is distributed in scent clouds separated by relatively clean air. It indicates that the use of changes in scent concentration (scent gradient) by a dog as a directional guide to the source may not be reliable unless they are close to the source.

Discounting visual means, successful location of a scent source requires at least two sensory inputs: detection of the presence of scent and the wind direction bearing that scent. Dogs detect the presence of scent with their noses and may determine the direction of scent concentration gradients at small scales due to scent discrimination between the nostrils or by moving along the plume. Wind direction may be determined by differential cooling. A dog's wet nose and your finger wetted and held in the air are sensitive indicators of wind direction. However, in many cases, proceeding into the wind after detecting a source may not enable the team to find it.

The rest of the book explores the influence of weather, terrain, vegetation, and intervening media on scent and scent plumes.

3.1.3 Wind

Wind occurs in response to changes in buoyancy caused by heating or cooling air in contact with the earth's surface materials such as soil, vegetation, and water (Schroeder and Buck 1970). Irregular heating or cooling of the earth's surface produces temperature differences in the adjacent air. Convection occurs when warmer, lighter, buoyant air rises. Horizontal winds occur as colder and heavier air moves to replace the warm air that moved upward.

Wind is usually thought of as the horizontal motion of air with respect to the earth's surface. The wind reported on the evening news is the prevailing horizontal wind high above surface obstacles. We are primarily interested in winds that carry scent to the dog's nose. These winds are the prevailing horizontal winds modified by obstacles such as terrain, trees, vegetation, buildings and by processes such as uneven surface heating (convection).

SD handlers obtain information about wind speed and direction from the feel of the wind on their body, visual observations (waves, vegetation, dust, smoke, clouds, soaring birds), and handheld devices (powder puffers, surveyor tape). Handheld anemometers are useful for determining wind speed and direction at the height of the dog. The Beaufort wind scale (Table 3.1) is an approximate method that allows rough estimates of wind speed based on visual observations. Observed items are near the ground surface (dust, leaves, paper), exposed skin, and much higher (leaves on trees, wind vanes, flags, smoke). These estimated wind speeds are not usually those at the height of the dog because wind speed typically increases with elevation and is modified by surface obstacles.

Table 3.1 Modified Beaufort Wind Scale

Beaufort Number	Description	Wind Speed (mph)	Visible Effects on Land
0	Calm	<1	Calm, smoke rises vertically.
1	Light air	1–3	Direction of wind shown by smoke drift but not by the wind vanes.
2	Light breeze	4–7	Wind felt on face; leaves rustle; wind vanes moved by wind.
3	Gentle breeze	8–12	Leaves and small twigs in constant motion; light flags extended.
4	Moderate breeze	13–18	Raises dust and loose paper; small branches move.
5	Fresh breeze	19–24	Small trees in leaf begin to sway; crested wavelets form on inland waters.
6	Strong breeze	25–31	Large branches in motion; whistling heard in telegraph wires; umbrellas used with difficulty.

Source: Modified from https://en.wikipedia.org/wiki/Beaufort_scale#Modern_scale. The scale is approximate because of the differences between observers and motion of leaves and branches depend on the type of tree. Personal observations indicate that a wind speed of 1 to 2 mph can be felt on damp skin.

True laminar flow is relatively rare in the air near the surface but does occur (Figure 3.2). Low wind speed over flat, smooth, and gently sloping terrain favors laminar flow. Rough surfaces with obstacles and frequent changes in vegetation and topography favor turbulent flow. Atmospheric turbulence is often large at the leading edge of a cold front.

Laminar flow produces continuous layered scent flow not broken by scent clouds. A dog that detects scent from a source in laminar flow should move directly upwind toward the source, although there are few observations to confirm this conclusion (they may also do this in light wind conditions when turbulence is low). Turbulent flow consists of eddies in a swirling, gusting, chaotic flow with rapid changes that redirect, fragment, and dilute the scent which increases the difficulty of detecting and locating a source. A dog that detects scent from a source in a small scale turbulent flow will usually quarter upwind to find the source.

The distance that scent can be transported in a relatively short time by even light winds is large. For a wind speed of 3 mph or 4.4 ft/sec, scent would move 264 ft in 1 min, almost the length of a football field.

The wind can transport particulates such as airborne skin flakes, soil particles with attached scent, and small scent particles. Gravity causes these tiny particulates to settle, but at very slow rates. These particulates suspended in the air by the exhalation jets from a dog's nose could remain in the air for up to several minutes and create a plume many tens of yards long.

3.1.4 Air Stability

3.1.4.1 Stability Conditions

Air is a mixture of gases, primarily nitrogen and oxygen. A one square-inch column of dry air weighs 14.7 lb at sea level and its density is about 0.08 pounds per cubic foot at 32°F. Warm air is lighter than cooler air (e.g. air density at 90°F is about 0.072 pounds per cubic foot) and water vapor molecules are lighter than air molecules so that air containing water vapor (humid air) is lighter than dry air.

Solar radiation passing through the air typically warms it <1°F in a day. Air is heated or cooled primarily by contact with surfaces such as soil, water, vegetation (leaves, grass, tree trunks), rocks, and others. Darker surfaces absorb more heat from the sun than lighter ones and become warmer than lighter ones. (Put your hand on the same horizontal surface of light and dark colored cars in sunlight and feel the temperature differences.) Since this warm air is lighter than the air above, it rises in a process called convection (Figures 3.1 and 3.3). Convection cells have been observed to rise from ground surface areas that were about a square yard at speeds of about a 1 ft/sec at intervals of about 4/min. At night and when a surface is shaded from the sun, it cools by radiating to the sky and cools the air in contact with the surface. Since colder air is heavier than warmer air, colder air remains on the surface and cannot rise through the warmer air above, a highly stable configuration called an inversion.

Air stability is an important factor in searches with search dogs because it influences our success in detecting and locating a scent source in the natural environment. Scent from a source in unstable air is subject to convective turbulence that causes it to rise with the air above the height of the dog and disperse, which makes it difficult or impossible for a dog to detect. Scent

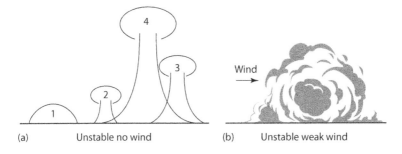

Figure 3.3 Microscale development of convective structures associated with instability. Surface heating (a) causes tiny bubbles of heated air to form (1) which lift off the surface in a mushroom shape (2) and grow vertically (3 and 4). Wind (b) mixes these structures into a thin layer at the surface that can grow into large convection cells.

from a source in stable air remains closer to the surface where it is possible for a dog to detect it.

The change in temperature with elevation above a surface determines air stability or instability. This information is not normally accessible to a handler. Stability must be determined by alternate methods. For calm conditions, stability is sensitive to the amount of solar radiation incident on a surface, which depends on the angle of the sun above the horizon, latitude, time of day, time of year, slope of the surface and the direction that the surface faces. While these factors can vary substantially on the earth's surface, it is convenient to describe their effects by three categories of radiation: strong, moderate, and slight. Fortunately, the factors influencing radiation incident on a surface and the corresponding radiation categories can all be determined in the field by measuring the length of your shadow (Lavdas 1976). For a person who is 6 ft tall, a shadow <3½ ft long indicates strong radiation, a shadow between 3½ ft and 8½ ft long indicates moderate radiation and a shadow >8½ ft long indicates slight radiation. While shadow lengths can be prorated for persons of any height, the above results can be used by persons between 5½ and 6½ ft tall without significant error.

However, air stability also depends strongly on wind, cloud cover, and whether it is day or night. Meteorologists have combined these factors into a set of six stability classifications: Class A—very unstable, B—moderately unstable, C—slightly unstable, D—neutral, E—slightly stable, and F—stable. The factors influencing atmospheric stability, except for the color of the surface, are combined in Table 3.2. Shadow lengths are for a person 6 ft tall and wind speed is estimated with the Beaufort scale. The stability classes in the three columns for day use hold for up to 4/8 cloud cover or any high clouds. For 5/8 to 7/8 cloud cover, use class C. Class D should be used for overcast conditions, day or night, independent of wind speed. Cloud cover is

Table 3.2 Approximate Air Stability Classes Illustrating the Strong Influence of Day, Night, Wind Speed, Solar Radiation, and Cloud Cover

Wind Speed (mph)	Day			Night	
	Solar Radiation			Cloud Cover (cc)	
	Strong <3½ ft	Moderate 3½–8½ ft	Slight >8½ ft	Cloudy > or = 4/8	Clear < or = 3/8
<4	A	A–B	B	E	F
4 to 7	A–B	B	C	E	F
7 to 11	B	B–C	C	D	E
11 to 13	C	C–D	D	D	D
>14	C	D	D	D	D

Source: Modified from Lavdas, L.G. 1976. *J. Air Pollution Control Assn* 26(8):794, and https://en.wikipedia.org/wiki/Outline_of_air_pollution_dispersion

Table 3.3   Cumulative POD by Air Stability Class and Distance from the Source for a Dog/Handler Team Searching for a Live Subject

Air Stability Class	100 m (109 yards) (%)	50 m (55 yards) (%)	25 m (27 yards) (%)
A	13	56	82
B	22	60	84
C	40	71	91
D	82	91	97
E	91	96	98
F	95	97	99

Source: Data from Graham, H. 1994. *NASAR Response Mag* Winter.

the fraction of sky covered by clouds. Night is defined as the period from 1 hr before sunset to 1 hr after sunrise.

3.1.4.2 Effects of Stability on Searching

Graham (1994) developed an empirical method based on air stability for choosing grid/lane widths for a desired probability of detection (POD) and for estimating the POD of canine teams when searching during the day for live subjects. This method is based on stability estimates (Tables 3.2 and 3.3) and his experience with canine training and searches and includes the effects of wind for all stability classes. There is little published information for other above ground sources in the outdoor environment.

While there are limitations to this empirically obtained stability method for estimating POD, it is more valuable than guesses by handlers or incident command (IC). Unfortunately it is not generally taught or required of handlers, their support, and/or search personnel.

The stability method of Graham (1994) can be used by teams to select grid/lane widths for a desired POD by consistently using the method during training. The results would be site specific for the conditions that exist in the training areas and specific to the individual dog and handler. This information on detection distances (hits and misses) can provide a starting point for selecting grid/lane widths. For example, when searching for a source under similar conditions, if the handler has information that their dog rarely detects a source beyond a certain distance, then the grid/lane width should be less than that distance. Also, if the handler has information on POD for a certain detection distance, then this distance would be a starting point for selecting grid/lane widths that would result in that POD. The method has the added benefit of making the handler acutely aware of the effects that wind and air stability have on the success of searches in their local environmental settings.

In addition to air stability, POD for canine teams also depends on the handler, dog, and other factors. Estimates of wind speed using the Beaufort scale are only approximate for field conditions. Stability classes for different

observers using Table 3.2 can easily vary by a class or more. Efforts to cat-
egorize atmospheric conditions by stability classes as in Table 3.2 take the
effects of thermal turbulence into account but do not address the effects of
mechanical turbulence produced by wind and local site conditions. Since the
scent plumes associated with typical scent sources are normally close to the
ground, their plumes are likely to encounter various obstacles in the airflow
and result in mechanical turbulence. This can have a major impact on the
scent plume, which makes searches and success of the search team dependent
on the site conditions.

The primary utility of Tables 3.2 and 3.3 is not so much for making precise estimates of POD but rather for determining favorable and less favorable
times to search. Favorable times exist for stability classes D, E, and F that
occur at night (as defined in Table 3.2), on completely overcast days all year,
and during early morning and late afternoon hours all year, especially when
wind is present. Difficult times exist for stability classes A, B, and C that
occur during the middle of the day during late spring and summer, especially
when there is little or no wind. For these difficult conditions, it is necessary
to reduce normal grid spacing or lane widths to achieve PODs comparable to
those for favorable conditions. While searching in the natural environment
is not an exact science, handlers can develop a sense of what works for them
and their dogs by paying attention to the factors noted in Tables 3.2 and 3.3
during training.

3.1.4.3 Effects of Stability on Plumes
Information on air stability can also be obtained from observations of dust
movement and smoke plumes. The presence of dust devils indicates a high
degree of convective instability. Table 3.4 shows the effects of three stability

Table 3.4 Stability and Some Typical Conditions for Smoke (scent) Plume Patterns

Plume Pattern	Stability	Some Typical Conditions
Looping	Strong convective instability	Sunny, daytime, gusty winds, dust devils, hot, dry, usually summer
Coning	Close to neutral	Cloudy, day or night, windy, all seasons
Fanning	Strongly stable, inversion commonly present	Clear, night, very light winds, low turbulence
Lofting	Inversion layer below, unstable above	Clear, after sunset or night, ground cooling with light winds above developing inversion layer, transitory
Fumigating	Inversion layer above, unstable below	Clear, after sunrise, ground warming destroying inversion layer from below, light winds, transitory

Sources: Bierly, E.W. and Hewson, E.W. 1962. *J Appl Meteorol* 1:383–390. Graham, H. 1979. *NASAR Search and Rescue Dogs Tech. Note* 2:1–4.

Figure 3.4 Looping and coning scent plume patterns (see Table 3.4 and text) and their effects on dog teams. Looping plumes are carried upward with rising air over a warm surface and downward with falling air over a cooler one. Wind causes the rising and cooling air and plume to angle downwind. Coning plumes expand horizontally and vertically and, if the source is elevated, will contact the ground downwind. (Modified from Graham 1979.)

classes with five possible smoke (scent) plume patterns and common conditions when these occur. Other more complex patterns have been observed. Strong instability produces a looping plume pattern typical of daytime and windy conditions during late spring and summer (Figure 3.4). This type of plume is a result of wind that moves the plume horizontally and thermal convection cells that move it up and down over alternating warm and cooler surface temperatures. Looping can repeatedly bring the relatively undiluted plume in contact with the ground downwind from the source. When a dog encounters the scent plume near the ground, it will often look up, whine in frustration, alert or self reward. If possible, the team should move upwind and try to detect multiple places where the scent plume loops to the ground. The source should be upwind along a line connecting these places. Hilly, mountainous, and forested terrain can redirect the wind and confound such efforts.

For stability close to neutral, a cone type of plume develops that expands about equally in both the horizontal and vertical directions as it moves downwind, unless the source is on the ground where it can only expand horizontally and upward. If the scent source is elevated, it will contact the ground at some distance downwind (Figure 3.4). Coning is characteristic of windy and cloudy conditions that can occur during the day or night in all seasons.

When a dog encounters this type of scent plume, it can usually follow it to the source.

Inversions are highly stable air conditions that occur when warmer air exists over colder air. The radiation type tends to occur in valleys, gullies, and depressions on clear nights with little wind when radiational cooling of the ground cools the air in contact with it and produces a layer of colder air with warmer air above. They are shallow initially, tend to increase in thickness through the night, and are very stable. These inversions are destroyed when the morning sun heats the ground or surface vegetation and causes convective turbulence that results in fumigation, and by prevailing winds that produce mechanical turbulence. They may persist during the day under cloudy and relatively calm conditions in depressions, shade and valleys, especially during the winter at high latitudes and low sun angles.

Radiation inversions are important for SD teams because upward movement of scent is effectively eliminated, trapping it below the inversion. Dogs working above an inversion cannot detect scent from a source below it and dogs working below the top of the inversion cannot detect scent from a source above it (Figure 3.5). Inversions can be detected when the handler passes through them, by a distinct change in temperature over a short distance from colder to warmer (moving uphill) and from warmer to colder (moving downhill). The behavior of a smoke plume can indicate the presence of an inversion. When a smoke or a scent plume above an inversion encounters it, the bottom of the plume becomes flat. When a rising plume from below encounters the top of an inversion layer, it flattens and spreads horizontally. Rising smoke from a campfire or house is an example.

Strongly stable air at night (common with an inversion present) with light winds and little turbulence, produces a vertically thin plume that spreads horizontally downwind in a fan shape (fanning, Figure 3.5) or a straight or meandering ribbon when it encounters the top of the inversion. If the source is above the inversion, scent would flow downslope and fan out on top of the inversion and a dog worked just above the top of the inversion could detect it. The dog may also be able to detect a source on the far side of the valley if it is not too wide but note that the source may be above the level of the inversion. Lack of vertical mixing above the inversion allows scent plumes of this type to be transported long distances without much change in concentration so that fanning conditions can be favorable for distant alerts.

Late in the day when an inversion is building up from the surface, the atmosphere above it may still be unstable. This allows vertical mixing of the plume upward while the stable inversion layer below prevents downward mixing. For a source above the inversion layer, this process (lofting, Figure 3.5) creates a plume with increasing thickness downwind and a flat bottom on the developing inversion layer. A dog working within the inversion layer cannot

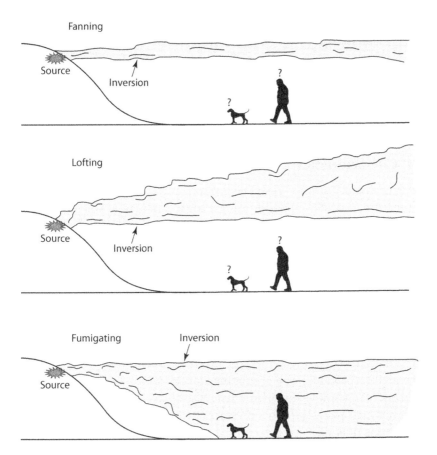

Figure 3.5 Fanning, lofting, and fumigating scent plumes in the presence of valley inversions (see Table 3.4 and text) and their effects on dog teams. Wind is to the right. For sources above the inversion, fanning plumes spread downwind on top of the inversion in a fan shape and lofting plumes occur when conditions are favorable for vertical mixing. Fumigation is the reverse of lofting. (Modified from Graham 1979.)

detect the source above the layer. If there are terrain changes downwind so that the scent plume intersects the ground, a dog working above the inversion layer may be able to detect it.

Fumigation (Figure 3.5) is the reverse of lofting and occurs with the reverse transition in stability in early morning. When the sun strikes and warms the ground surface, it warms the air in contact with the ground and causes buoyant mixing upward while the inversion layer still exists. If the source is elevated but below the top of the inversion, the air above the source is stable and prevents transport upward while the unstable layer below mixes the plume vertically downwind, likely bringing it in contact with the ground where a dog can detect it. Fumigation is transitory and ceases when the buoyant convecting air layer exceeds the inversion depth.

Valley inversions behave differently when the rising sun contacts one or both side slopes. The air in contact with the slope, including that below the inversion level, is warmed, becomes bouyant, and flows upward along the slope. This means a dog would have to be above the source to detect it.

3.2 Turbulence

3.2.1 Characteristics

Turbulent flow is common near the ground, and as the turbulence increases the difficulty in detecting and finding a source increases. Since the primary task of a SD handler is to get the dog into the scent plume from the source, recognizing and evaluating the presence, characteristics, and effects of turbulent flow are necessary skills for them. A high degree of skill at this task will increase the team's probability of success.

Turbulent flows may be viewed as a spectrum of eddies with a wide range of sizes. Mechanical turbulence depends on surface roughness, obstacles in the flow, and wind speed and direction (Schroeder and Buck 1970). The general roughness of an area's surface contributes to the formation of larger eddies that move over the landscape. Like a boulder in a stream, an obstacle in the airflow produces a recirculating mix of eddies behind it with eddies that break off and move downwind from the obstacle. Every obstacle, including porous ones like vegetation, produces turbulent eddies. The sizes, shapes, and motions of eddies are determined by the characteristics of the obstacle and the speed and direction of the wind.

An important feature of these turbulent eddies is their size relative to the size of the scent plume. If the eddies are smaller than the scent plume, they dilute the plume; if they are larger than the scent plume, they can transport the plume or parts of it with little change for relatively long distances. Thus, the size of the eddies determines detection distances for a scent plume and is important for distant alerts.

Thermal turbulence associated with air instability consists of convection cells with warm buoyant upward air movement and adjacent cooled downward air movement (Figure 3.4). Since it is the result of surface heating, thermal turbulence increases with the intensity of surface heating. Mechanical and thermal turbulence frequently occur together and create a mixed convection. Turbulent flow can also bring higher wind speeds from aloft down to the surface, usually in spurts and gusts (large scale looping). There is also small-scale turbulence produced by the dog's movement and by exhalation during sniffing which appears to help the dog find sources.

Eddies may form with their axes of rotation in any plane. Dust devils and thunderstorms are vertical eddies. Rotation speeds in eddies are often much greater than the average horizontal wind speed. Eddies associated with an obstacle tend to hold a stationary position in the lee of the obstacle, although secondary eddies may break off and move downwind. A rule of thumb is that an obstacle influences the airflow for a downwind distance 5 to 10 times the height of the obstacle. An appreciation of eddy characteristics can be gained by observing the flow of water over and past obstacles in a river and the flow of smoke plumes and clouds moving over the terrain (especially with time lapse photographs).

Variable heating and cooling across the terrain causes typical daily cycles in wind behavior. Daytime surface winds in flat terrain increase to their highest speeds and turbulence (primarily thermal turbulence) about the time of maximum heating. With the onset of nighttime cooling, surface winds normally decrease in speed and turbulence.

3.2.2 Thermal (Convective) Turbulence

Prevailing winds often dominate near the surface but when these winds weaken in the presence of clear skies that produce strong daytime heating, local convective winds become important. Convective winds can enhance or oppose prevailing winds, and interactions between the two can result in local variations in speed and direction over distances of a few yards in complex terrain.

3.2.2.1 Surface Temperatures

Microclimatic conditions that influence scent movement vary tremendously over the arctic, temperate, and tropical zones. These variations are made more complex by seasonal effects and changes in vegetation, topography, moisture, and other factors that produce different ecosystems. This global complexity in physical settings and conditions produces tremendous variability in the behavior of the wind that carries scent to the dogs. Most of the following material focuses on temperate zone conditions unless noted otherwise.

The sun warms the exposed earth surfaces and these surfaces warm the air in contact with them. The resulting convection can transfer scent well out of reach of SDs (like looping inFigure 3.4). Thus, surface temperatures can influence the ability of a dog to detect a source and may suggest where and when a dog should be deployed for the highest probability of success.

Daily temperature variations of the earth's land surface are typically 10 to 30°F but can be much smaller or larger. Small variations are associated with light colored and wet earth surfaces, low sun angles, coastal regions, and cloudy days. Large variations are associated with dry, dark colored surfaces, high sun angles, high altitudes, desert regions, and sunny days (Figure 3.6).

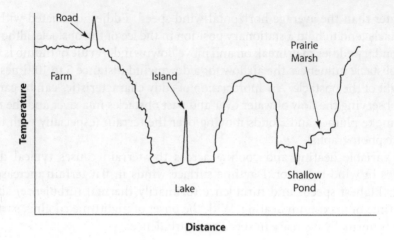

Figure 3.6 Schematic of earth surface temperatures across a varied landscape on a summer day. The difference between the road surface and the lake surface can exceed 50°F. Hot air over the road and island would likely cause convection cells.

3.2.2.2 Non-Vegetated Surfaces

Common non-vegetated surfaces include water, snow, ice, soil, sand, rock, and manufactured ones (concrete, asphalt). It requires much more radiative heat from the sun to increase the temperature of water, snow, and ice surfaces compared to other surfaces. Water, snow, and ice allow some of the radiation to penetrate which reduces their impact on surface temperatures. Moving water can carry some of the radiant energy away from the surface. Snow and ice surfaces cannot exceed 32°F (the equilibrium temperature of water and ice in contact). At night and when in shade, snow surfaces cool quickly and, under favorable conditions, develop strong inversions at the surface. Daily surface temperature variations for water are small and limited for snow and ice compared to the relatively large variations for other non-vegetated surfaces.

Bare soil, sand, rocks, and asphalt tend to dry and warm quickly when exposed to solar radiation. Some soils, vegetation, and asphalt are relatively dark and good absorbers of solar radiation. These properties lead to large daily variations in their surface temperatures that favor formation of small-scale surface convection (Figure 3.3) and large-scale convection cells (thermals) (Figure 3.4, looping) when the overlying air is unstable. The impact of solar radiation on air over surfaces depends on whether the surfaces are level or sloped and on the characteristics of the surfaces. From sunset to sunrise and when a surface is in shade, the surface radiates to a cold sky causing it to cool which cools the air in contact with it and creates a layer of colder air near the surface with warmer air above it. This is a stable configuration for level surfaces since the colder air is heavier than the warmer air above (lighter, warmer air "floats" on the heavier, colder air below it). Under calm

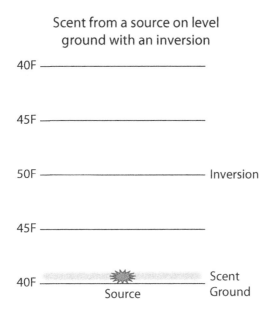

Figure 3.7 Scent from a source on or emitted from the surface of level ground with an inversion. The coldest air is at the surface and scent concentrates there. Temperatures increase up to the inversion and decrease above it.

conditions, an inversion begins to form and scent from a source on or emitted from such a surface will concentrate in a layer near the surface without mixing with the warmer air above (Figure 3.7). Dogs may need to get their noses down to detect scent close to the surface, especially from buried sources. Wind may reduce or prevent the formation of these night inversions.

When the sun is shining on a level, horizontal surface (roughly sunrise to sunset), it absorbs solar radiation and causes the surface to warm and to warm air in contact with it. Since the warmer air at the surface is lighter than the colder air above it, the warmer, buoyant air can rise. This initially creates vertical air currents in the form of tiny convection cells (Figure 3.3) that form a thin turbulent surface layer. If the atmosphere is stable, the thickness of this layer of convection cells will be limited or disappear. If it is unstable, the convection cells can grow into thermals (looping, Figure 3.4) and eventually become large cells (thermals). Thermals can grow thousands of feet high and can transport air from near the ground surface to these high elevations. Glider pilots and soaring birds use thermals to gain or maintain altitude and vultures use them to sample air from near the ground to detect the scent of food. Thermals carry scent out of reach of dogs and make it difficult or impossible to find the source.

The effects of radiation on sloping surfaces differ substantially from those on horizontal surfaces (Mahrt et al. 2001). When in the shade and at night, sloping surfaces also cool by radiating to a clear sky, which makes the

Figure 3.8 Thin downslope flow about 15 min after the slope went into shade.

adjacent air cooler and heavier than the air above and gravity causes it to flow downslope. Under these conditions, scent is transported downslope with the cold air in a thin layer adjacent to the surface (Figure 3.8) and possibly pools in depressions. Under these conditions, SD teams should search at the bottom of the slopes or below the expected position of the source.

East facing ridges go into shade some time before sunset (Figure 3.9), allowing canine teams to take advantage of them during daylight hours. This setting is reversed in early morning when the west facing ridges remain in shade for some time after sunrise, again allowing canine teams to take advantage of them during daylight hours. In summary, "Sun up, scent up and sun down, scent down," but remember shade.

In the sun, sloping surfaces are also heated and warm the adjacent air which makes it lighter than the air above. Buoyancy causes it to flow upslope and into the atmosphere at the top of the slope where it may continue to move upward into the unstable air or be carried away by prevailing winds. This upslope flow is typically thicker and more turbulent than the nighttime downslope flow. Under these conditions, SD teams should search on ridges or hill tops or at elevations higher than where the source may be.

These upslope and downslope winds may not be continuous but may start and stop during the day and night. Downslope gravity flow can occur in areas with hardly noticeable slopes. They may occur with prevailing wind and flow from side slopes that can enhance, eliminate, or redirect them sporadically or continuously creating complex scenting conditions. Figure 3.10 shows downslope gravity flow that consists of a primary down valley flow and flow from both side slopes.

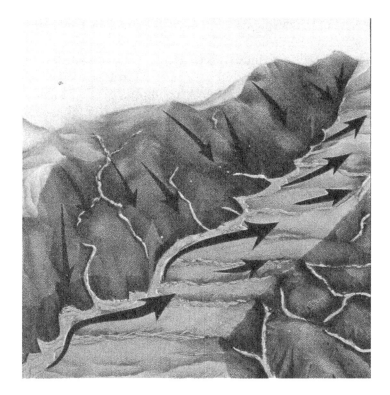

Figure 3.9 Downslope gravity flow of wind begins when the slope goes into shade. Canine teams searching the left slope need to be at the valley bottom or below the source while teams searching the right slope need to be on top the ridge or above the source. (Modified from Schroeder and Buck 1970.)

Figure 3.10 Downslope night time gravity flow consisting of a primary down valley flow and flow from both side slopes. Prevailing winds can enhance, redirect, or eliminate gravity flows resulting in complex scenting conditions. (From Schroeder and Buck 1970.)

Canine searches during the day can be frustrated by the depth and turbulence associated with upslope flow and prevailing winds. At night and
in the shade, prevailing winds tend to decrease and become less turbulent.
Downslope gravity flow is in a thin layer and the scent is closer to the ground,
which results in more favorable scenting conditions than during the day.

3.2.2.3 Thermal Reversals

Air movement caused by radiant cooling and heating of sloping surfaces
produces downslope flow of cold air at night and upslope flow of warmer
air during the day. This results in thermal reversals (reversals in wind
direction) every morning and evening under stable weather conditions.
Thermal reversals can occur in any terrain with sloping surfaces even if the
slopes are very small. Under stable weather conditions, the usual wind is
downslope or down valley at night, as noted. When the sun rises, it warms
surfaces and the adjacent air at higher elevations, with the warming pro-
gressing downhill as the sun gets higher. This warm air moves upslope and
reverses the nighttime flow progressively down valley until it has the usual
upslope daytime flow. If an inversion is present, it may take some time for
it to dissipate.

As sunset approaches, the lower elevations go into shadow first and start
to cool by radiating to the sky. This cools the adjacent air and the colder
air moves downslope and down valley which reverses the daytime flow progressively up the valley until it has the usual downslope nighttime flow. This
downslope flow (katabatic wind) can travel at very high speeds, especially
over long slopes and on glaciers.

When and where the thermal reversal occurs, there is a cessation of the
airflow followed by a variable calm period of minutes to an hour or more and
then the reversal. The timing of these reversals depends on the incoming and
outgoing radiation on the valley slopes and bottom, which depends strongly
on local conditions, especially slope orientation. It is expected to vary seasonally, earlier each morning and later each evening from winter through spring
and later each morning and earlier each evening from summer through fall.
The morning reversal may occur well after sunrise because of the buildup of a
cold air pool or inversion in the valley. The strong dependence of these reversals on local conditions indicates that handlers must become familiar with
thermal reversals in their search areas in order to be at the right place at the
right time to take advantage of them. Thermal reversals are also associated
with sea and land breezes.

3.2.2.4 Sea and Land Breezes

A sea breeze is a wind that flows from the sea to the land while a land breeze
flows from the land to the sea (Figure 3.11). The amount of heat energy
required to change the temperature of water is much larger than the heat

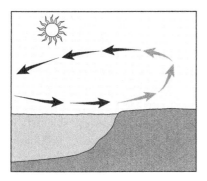 

Figure 3.11 Sea breezes are from the sea and land breezes are from the land. (From Schroeder and Buck 1970.)

required to change the temperature of earth materials like soil, rock, and vegetation. As the day begins, the sun heats both the land and water but the land surface temperatures increase faster and their increase is greater than the water. Air in contact with the land is warmed and becomes lighter, less buoyant and rises. The colder air over the water flows toward and over the land, called a sea breeze, replacing the rising air. The strength of the sea breeze depends on the temperature difference between the land and the water. If there is no prevailing wind, a convective cell may form with air falling over the water and rising over the land. A prevailing wind can enhance, redirect, or prevent the sea breeze from forming. At night, the land cools faster, more than the water, and the process reverses, creating a land breeze (Figure 3.11).

When a sea breeze is present, a dog searching along the shore can detect sources somewhat offshore and when a land breeze is present it can detect sources somewhat inland. It may be possible to search a difficult shoreline with a dog in a boat close to shore when a land breeze is present. Similar breezes may be produced by lakes and ponds but modified by their smaller size compared to the sea and influenced by nearby terrain and vegetation.

If conditions are favorable, convection cells can be observed when the colder air from a land breeze or from gravity flow contacts warmer water and causes fog to form over water bodies such as swamps, ponds, lakes, and sea. These fog layers are common during the transition to colder night temperatures in fall. On ponds they are typically a few feet thick but can be much thicker (hundreds of feet) on large water bodies or when temperature differences between the air and water are large and can persist well into the day. Initially, the upward movement of warm moist air in convection cells from the surface is marked by patches of fog and the downward movement of cold air by the absence of fog. At the onset, the upwelling fog cells are usually less than a yard square and a light wind can destroy them.

3.2.2.5 *Vegetated Surfaces*

Vegetation (grasses, bushes, trees) that is darker than its surroundings and the dark bark of some deciduous trees without leaves can produce convective flow during sunny days (Schroeder and Buck 1970), which can carry scent upward and out of reach of search dogs. This type of convective flow can occur with any dark horizontal or vertical surface (clump of grass, single bush or tree (Figure 3.1), grasslands, forests, and buildings). It exists when these darker surfaces are in the sun and disappears when they go into shade and at night. It can also exist in forest clearings where sunlight can reach dark ground and warm it which causes the air in contact with the ground to warm and rise (Figure 3.12). This draws cooler air from the adjacent forest so that SDs worked in the shade around the clearing can detect sources deeper in the forest. For clear and relatively quiet conditions at night, the ground cools by radiation and causes the flow to be from the clearing into the forest. SDs can then detect sources in the clearing. Fields that are darker than the surrounding fields and islands of darker soil or vegetation in fields can also create isolated convection cells.

The presence of a vegetative canopy (grass, weeds, crops, shrubs, trees) on or over the ground surface causes significant changes in the microclimate. These changes vary seasonally because of seasonal changes in vegetation, foliage, and other factors (e.g. snow). Canopies range in depth from grass prairies and short shrubs to tall forests and differ substantially in characteristics (structure, type of foliage, density, etc.). Grasslands and crops typically have a single layer structure. Managed forests and some mature forests may

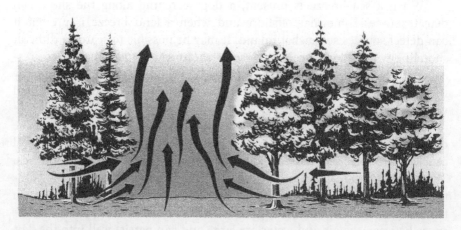

Figure 3.12 Openings in forests where sunlight can reach the ground and where the adjacent forest shades the ground can act as chimneys under conditions of daytime heating and light winds. Cooler air from the forest is drawn to the opening and replaces the heated air that rises. (Modified from Schroeder and Buck 1970.)

have two layers (foliage and tree trunks). Forests with mixed tree types of differing ages are more complex.

Canopies influence the microclimate by their impacts on moisture, temperature, wind, and radiation. Moisture is intercepted and used by canopies. Canopy foliage shades the ground day and night which alters the ground and air temperatures and soil moisture. During the day, it shades the ground and stem or trunk layer from the sun and makes the ground cooler. This can create an inversion beneath the canopy in the trunk layer of a forest. At night, the upper canopy cools by radiating to the cold sky and cools the air in contact with it. If the canopy blocks radiation from the trunk layer it will be warmer than the air in the upper canopy. Heat from the soil and woody mass in the trunk layer also helps to keep this layer warmer. This is an unstable configuration that makes it possible for cooler (heavier) air in the canopy to drain downward and the warmer air carrying scent to move upward, which possibly results in difficult scent conditions for the dogs. Wind blowing over the forest and variations in terrain can dramatically change these conditions.

Thus, forest canopies may produce lower maximum temperatures during the day and higher minimum temperatures at night in the air near the ground than adjacent grasslands or forest clearings. Lower maximum temperatures may induce flow of colder air from the forest into the grasslands by day. However, this process may compete with upper canopy heating that would draw air from adjacent fields toward the forest, possibly with restricted exit flow (from the field) caused by the dense vegetation commonly found at forest edges. Handlers need to observe air flow at the forest edge close to the ground to determine if conditions are favorable for dog teams to search along the edge of the forest and detect sources within the forest close to the edge. Higher minimum temperatures at night may induce flow from colder grasslands and clearings into the forest although this may be modified by cold air draining down through some canopies. Handlers must assess local conditions to determine an effective search strategy.

3.2.3 Mechanical Turbulence

3.2.3.1 Surface Roughness

Mechanical turbulence results from the interaction of wind with surface roughness elements in the flow. These roughness elements can be any obstacle that projects into the flow including both porous and solid ones such as pebbles, rocks, grass, crops, trees, buildings, and terrain features such as hills and valleys. Important characteristics are their size, especially height, number, and spacing. Their impact on the flow can extend upward several times their height and many times their height downwind. Turbulence and reverse flow (recirculation) can develop immediately upwind and downwind of an obstacle in steep terrain and at sharp changes in vegetation.

3.2.3.2 Terrain Effects

Modification of wind by roughness elements makes the behavior of the wind unique in every landscape and impossible to predict in detail. Generally, terrain elements redirect the airflow, accelerate it over their tops (even when the maximum slopes are small), and create turbulence and recirculation in the flow. These changes strongly influence scent movement for short distances upwind and to the sides and long distances downwind in the wake of the elements. These areas require special care and consideration when conducting canine searches.

The following discussion of terrain effects assumes that there is level homogeneous terrain upwind of the elements, neutral atmospheric stability, and wind direction perpendicular to the terrain elements. The results differ if these assumptions are not true. Nevertheless, these simple examples can help in developing an improved understanding of terrain effects on airflow and turbulence. There are two broad classes to consider: moderate terrain with slopes typically <17° (rise/run < 3/10) and steep terrain with slopes >17° (rise/run > 3/10).

3.2.3.2.1 Moderate terrain   For the gentle topography of large terrain elements (hills, valleys, ridges) and low wind speed, the wind can be expected to flow over the terrain with relatively little turbulence except for that produced by much smaller surface elements (boulders, gullies, ditches). However, high wind speeds may lead to turbulence similar to that found in steep terrain at lower wind speeds. Wind speeds can be expected to be higher at the top of terrain elements and in terrain constrictions and lower at the toe of slopes and in valley bottoms.

3.2.3.2.2 Steep terrain   Significant turbulence near the ground surface can be generated by steep terrain elements that influence search strategies and the ability of dogs to detect and locate sources. An understanding of this turbulence can help the team find sources in steep terrain. The location and the characteristics of the turbulence for some simple terrain elements are shown in Figure 3.13; however, changes in air stability, wind velocity, variable terrain, angle of wind to the element, and vegetation can make flow over these elements more complex.

Wind accelerates along a vertical cross section through the centerline of a hill or island or perpendicular to a ridge when it encounters the slope and is maximum as it passes over the crest. A recirculation zone (bolster eddy) may form near the toe of the slope with surface winds that are weak, variable, intermittent, turbulent, and downslope. A much larger near-surface recirculation zone (lee eddy) may form downwind of the crest. The winds are light, variable, intermittent, turbulent, and upslope. The effects of this lee eddy may extend downwind many times the height of the ridge or hill. Consequently, it

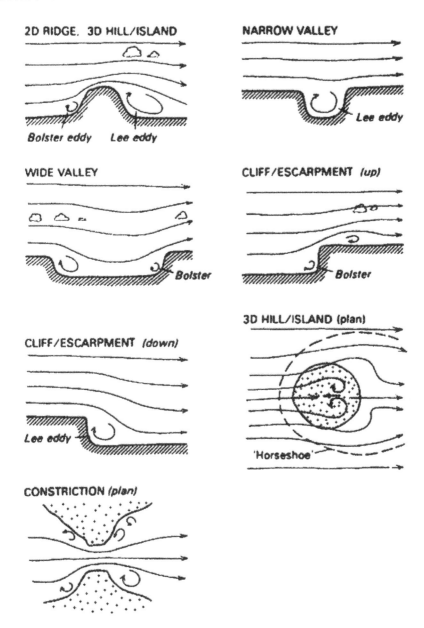

Figure 3.13 Effects of steep terrain elements on wind flowing over them. These effects will be the same for any features with the same density and geometry independent of their size. (From Oke, T.R. 1987. Courtesy of Dr. Timothy R. Oke.)

may be possible for dogs to detect a source downwind of the toe of the slope by working them in the lee eddy along the slope or even near the top of the slope. On the upwind slope, it may be possible for dogs to detect a source somewhat upslope by working them in the upwind eddy along the toe of the slope. For a cliff with a sharp break at the top, an eddy may also form at the top slightly back from the edge.

The above discussion holds for other changes in steep topography associated with airflow into and out of a wide valley, river channel, lake, and on the approach to or leaving a steep change in topography.

An eddy may be created in a depression, gully, valley, road cut, or narrow canyon with light, variable, intermittent, and turbulent winds near the ground with flow opposite to the direction of the flow aloft.

The plan view of a symmetrical hill or island shows the lee eddies in more detail. Airflow increases in speed on the front and sides of the hill and the lee eddies extend farther past the hill than shown.

A plan view of a sharp constriction in river channels, valleys, mountain passes, and road cuts shows the turbulent recirculation zones that form at the upstream and downstream sides of the constriction. The eddies in the recirculation zones shown in vertical sections rotate in a vertical plane but those in the plan views rotate in a horizontal plane.

The results for airflow and turbulence over the above terrain features are general in the sense that they can be applied to a wide range of scales provided the cross-sectional form is similar. For example, the results for ridges can be applied to levies and those for valleys to ravines and road cuts. If the airflow is less than perpendicular to the long axes of two-dimensional features, the strength and persistence of the flow features will be reduced and modified. If the air is unstable, formation of eddies is enhanced relative to neutral stability. If the lee slope is in sunshine, the upslope flow will strengthen the lee eddy.

3.2.3.3 Effects of Vegetation

Isolated trees and bushes produce mechanical turbulence on their upwind sides, and for 5 to 10 times their height in the downwind wake. This turbulence depends on the type of vegetation, its size and density, and wind direction and speed. At low wind speeds, scent can be channeled around dense isolated trees and bushes, and at higher speeds turbulent eddies form on their windward and lee sides. An isolated tree trunk, or one in an open forest, can trap scent in turbulent recirculating eddies on the downwind side (Figure 3.14). Scent from a scent plume upwind accumulates in the eddies and on the bark; dogs typically alert there.

The behavior of scent in islands of trees and bushes may be expected to be like that of individual vegetation if the islands are small (width a few times the vegetation height) or like forests for large islands (width many times the vegetation height).

3.2.3.3.1 Shelterbelts Shelterbelts are long, narrow barriers that provide shelter from the wind. They are commonly porous features (fences, bushes, hedges, trees) but can also be nonporous (berms, stone walls).

Figure 3.14 Smoke from a source placed on the upwind (right hand) side of the tree was caught in recirculating eddies on the downwind side of the tree. Scent accumulates in the eddies and on the bark on the downwind side and dogs typically alert there. The sticks leaning against the nearside of the tree created a smaller eddy.

A high-density shelterbelt is like a ridge (Figure 3.13), where similar eddies can be produced on the upwind and downwind sides. The magnitude of these eddies is determined by the height of the canopy and its porosity to airflow. An upward flow of air on the sunny side of the canopy may occur when it is in the sun and winds are calm or light. The upwind eddies influence scenting conditions immediately in front of the shelterbelt while the influence of the downwind eddies extends from the shelterbelt to many times its height downwind. Wind incident at an angle (up to about 25°) tends to flow perpendicularly through a shelterbelt and to mix downwind with the air flowing over it which produces lateral turbulence. The areas upwind and in the turbulent eddies downwind of shelterbelts require special attention when searching.

A shelterbelt that is open at its base (Figure 3.15) may allow a substantial flow of air through it. This air can act as a "cushion" that may persist many times the height of the vegetation downwind and inhibits downward mixing. This makes it difficult to detect elevated sources in the vegetation of the shelterbelt when downwind from it. An elevated structure or vehicle (tractor trailer) that is open underneath may have a similar effect. It may be desirable to start the search from a distance downwind rather than close to it.

3.2.3.3.2 Forests Wind approaching, leaving, and blowing through forests (and clearings in them) produces turbulence in the form of updrafts,

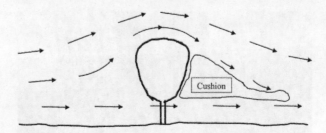

Figure 3.15 Vertical profile of a shelterbelt showing a possible cushion on the downwind side which inhibits downward mixing of scent from above for many times the tree height downwind. (Modified from Oke 1987.)

downdrafts, frequent changes in direction, recirculation, sweeps, ejections, and low speed zones that make it difficult to find sources in and adjacent to the forest. The effects of a forest on wind depend on the air stability, wind velocity, forest density, presence or absence of leaves, and other characteristics of the forest.

Wind incident on a forest edge produces turbulence and updrafts in front of the edge and some distance downwind of it in the forest. If the forest is sufficiently dense, a recirculation zone may develop immediately in front of the edge like that upwind of a steep change in terrain or dense shelterbelt (Figure 3.12). If the forest is sparse in the trunk space, a jet of air into the forest may develop near the ground (Figure 3.16). Deep in the forest, wind directions are highly variable, wind speeds are greatly reduced, and turbulent eddies are much smaller compared to those in an open field.

A comparison of wind in a field and adjacent forest (Table 3.4) showed that in the field above the vegetation, a relatively steady wind direction and speed of 5 to 10 mph existed for more than an hour. In the forest (below the canopy), the wind direction was highly variable with long periods of very light wind (<½ mph) and then several minutes of 2 to 5 mph wind gusts.

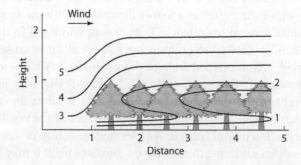

Figure 3.16 Schematic drawing of a jet of air penetrating into a sparse forest near ground level. Distance is scaled according to forest height and wind speeds; 1 to 5 are relative speeds. A low speed wind jet, 1, penetrates almost five times the forest height. (Modified from Belcher et al. 2012.)

Table 3.5   Comparison of Field and Forest

Wind	Field	Forest
Duration	>1 hour	Long periods of calm (<1/2 mph) then
Speed	4.5 to 9 mph	several minutes 2 to 4.5 mph
Direction	Steady	Variable 360°

These intermittent wind gusts are energetic sweeps of air that move downward through the canopy from above. Weaker ejections of air upward and out of the top of the canopy occur in association with the sweeps. Sweeps and ejections can also exist in other types of vegetative canopies such as grasses, weeds, crops, and bushes. These sweeps and ejections would be expected to cause significant vertical mixing of scent and make scenting conditions difficult while they occur (Table 3.5).

Immediately downwind of a forest edge, wind speed increases and moves downward in response to the presence of grassland. If the forest is sufficiently dense, a recirculation zone may develop in the lee of the edge like that downwind of a steep change in terrain or dense shelterbelt (Figure 3.12). These effects may not occur or would be substantially modified for deciduous forests without leaves.

The above differences between wind in fields and forests indicate that scent plumes will behave differently. The relatively constant wind direction in a field indicates that a dog that detects a scent plume there and moves upwind should be able to follow the plume to the source. However, the variability of wind direction in a forest indicates that a dog that detects a scent plume there and moves upwind at that instant will not likely be moving in the direction of the source. This makes it increasingly difficult to find sources beyond 100 yards distance in forests and indicates that closer grid spacing may be required in forests compared to fields. However, as the wind speed increases, the variability in wind direction decreases (i.e. the path of the scent plume becomes straighter), which should reduce this difficulty somewhat.

Managed forests are usually uniform in the sense of having trees of the same type, height, and density while natural forests, especially old growth, have canopies with irregular upper surfaces that contain openings and clearings as a result of the death of old trees, windstorms, and selective cutting. These gaps in a forest may have downdrafts carrying scent which increase the likelihood of sweeps and ejections. Gaps in the forest canopy may be barely noticeable from the ground.

Wind over forest openings and clearings is sensitive to their size and orientation. Gaps about the width of the tree heights in a dense forest may develop a recirculation zone within them that can cause air flowing over the forest to sweep down into the openings along with any scent in the air

(Figure 3.12). This recirculation zone may exist until the gap widths are many times the tree heights. Flow over very wide gaps (10 times the height of the trees or more) may behave like the flow on the lee side and upwind side of a wide valley (Figure 3.13).

Patterns of snow accumulation in clearings are a result of the airflow in the clearings and the adjacent forests (Gary 1974). Snow accumulations are greater in clearings and less in the forest downwind of clearings. Where the width of the clearing is about the same as the height of the trees, snow may accumulate on the upwind side of the clearing with reduced accumulations on the downwind side and some distance into the forest. This pattern of snow accumulation reflects the average direction and duration of airflow rather than the values at any instant of time.

The above patterns of wind behavior at forest edges, within forests and in clearings vary with the physical settings (e.g. air stability, type of trees, old growth, new growth, tree density, etc.) so that somewhat different results may occur depending on the setting. Handlers need to be familiar with the effects of wind behavior in forests in their local training and search areas and this is best done during training.

3.2.3.3.3 Combined terrain and forest effects   Airflow and turbulence are influenced by even gently undulating topography and forest canopies. When a forest canopy covers large variations in topography, the effects on flow and turbulence are even greater (Belcher et al. 2012). Typically, wind velocity in the canopy increases on an upwind slope, is largest near the crest, and decreases in the lee of a hill or ridge. If the slope is sufficiently large or the canopy sufficiently high, a recirculation zone may exist in the canopy in the lee of the hill and a smaller one on the upwind slope of the hill. With increasing slope, the depth of the lee recirculation zone can increase to where it spans the depth of the canopy. The presence of a recirculation zone on the lee side indicates that, under some conditions, it may be possible for a dog to detect a source that is in the forest far down the slope in the prevailing wind direction by working the dog in the recirculation zone across the slope or near the top of the zone.

3.3 Summary

Scent movement is concerned with the interactions among weather and the physical environment (vegetation, terrain) and any intervening medium (air, soil, ground cover, snow, water) that influences scent movement from the source to the dog's nose. These interactions determine our search strategies and favorable times and places to search; ultimately, the success or failure of our search efforts.

Processes that cause scent molecules to move are chemical diffusion, gravity, buoyancy, and transport by wind, water, and other fluids. Chemical diffusion is the movement of scent molecules from regions of higher to lower chemical concentrations in any medium. The movement is radially away from the source in all directions, very slow and not significant for scent transport in calm air. It can be a factor in fine-grained soils and snow for long times or very short distances. Gravity flow is the downward settling of scent molecules that are heavier than air when there is no significant wind. Buoyant flow refers to the upward movement of scent molecules that are lighter than air (ammonia, methane) and to convective transport of warmed air that carries scent molecules and scent plumes upward (Figure 3.1). Scent in air, water, and other fluids can be transported by the movement of these fluids.

Wind is the primary method of transporting a scent in the atmosphere where scent plumes behave like smoke plumes from a chimney or campfire. The initial size of a scent plume is about the same as the source. Close to the source, scent plumes appear continuous, but turbulence creates scent clouds with gaps of clean air as the plume expands and disperses downwind (Figure 3.2). This means the use of scent gradients by a dog as a directional guide to the source is unreliable except close to the source; wind direction is the primary method used to find the source.

Successful location of a scent source requires detection of scent and wind direction. A dog's wet nose is a sensitive indicator of wind direction but *proceeding into the wind after detecting a source may not enable the team to find it.*

Wind occurs in response to changes in buoyancy caused by heating or cooling air in contact with the earth's surface materials. Vertical convection occurs when this warmer buoyant air rises. Horizontal winds occur as colder and denser air moves to replace warm air.

Wind flow can be laminar or turbulent (Figure 3.2). It is usually turbulent, consisting of eddies of all sizes that cause rapid changes which redirect, fragment, and dilute scent. This increases the difficulty of detecting and locating a source. Observations of smoke plumes suggest scent plume patterns of looping, coning, fanning, lofting, and fumigating (Figures 3.4 and 3.5).

The impact of radiation on or from surfaces depends on whether the surfaces are level or sloped. At night, outgoing radiation cools level surfaces that cool the adjacent air which causes scent to remain on the surface where it may be detected by dogs (Figure 3.7). This is a highly stable configuration called an inversion (Figure 3.5). During the day, dark surfaces absorb more incoming solar radiation than lighter ones and become warmer, sometimes several tens of degrees above the air temperature (Figure 3.6). Warm surfaces warm the adjacent air which causes it to rise (convection) and transport scent above the height of the dog where it is impossible for the dog to detect.

The effects of instability caused by radiation on search strategies can be determined in the field by measuring the length of your shadow. The difficulty in locating a source increases as your shadow length decreases. Taking air stability into consideration, favorable times to search occur at night, on completely overcast days all year, and during early morning and evening hours all year, especially when wind is present. Difficult times occur during the middle of the day and afternoon during late spring and summer, especially when there is little or no wind (Tables 3.2 and 3.3).

At night and when in shade, a sloping surface cools by radiation and cools the adjacent air, which makes it heavier and less buoyant than the air above. This causes it to flow downslope in a thin layer carrying scent with it (Figures 3.8 and 3.9). Dogs must be lower than the source to detect it. In sunlight, a sloping surface warms and warms the adjacent air, which makes it lighter and more buoyant than the air above. This causes it to flow upslope carrying scent with it. Dogs must be above the source to detect it (Figure 3.9). The upward flowing layer is thicker than the downward flowing layer which makes the downward flowing layer (at night and in shade) easier for dogs to detect.

Sea and land breezes occur as a result of heating and cooling of land surfaces adjacent to the water. A sea breeze allows a dog searching along the shore to detect sources offshore and a land breeze allows it to detect sources inland (Figure 3.11). Similar breezes are associated with other bodies of water (ponds, lakes, rivers, swamps) but modified by their size.

Air flow at forest and field edges is strongly dependent on site conditions. Handlers must assess local conditions to determine an effective search strategy. Openings in forests where sunlight can reach the ground and where the adjacent forest shades the ground tend to act as chimneys under conditions of daytime heating and light winds (Figure 3.12). Cooler air from the forest is drawn to the opening replacing the heated air that rises.

For terrain with slopes <17° and low wind speed, wind can be expected to flow over the terrain with relatively little turbulence. In steeper terrain, an eddy forms near the toe of the upwind slope and a much larger lee eddy forms downwind of the crest (Figure 3.13). Surface winds in these eddies are weak, variable, intermittent, turbulent, and opposite to the direction of the prevailing wind. The effects of this lee eddy may extend downwind many times the height of the ridge or hill. Canine teams can use these eddies to search parts of the slopes.

On the upwind slope, dogs can detect a source somewhat upslope by working in the upwind eddy along the toe of the slope. On the downwind slope, dogs can detect a source downwind of the toe of the slope by working in the lee eddy across the slope or even near the top of the slope.

An isolated tree trunk or one in an open forest traps scent in eddies on the downwind side. Scent accumulates in the eddies and on the bark and dogs typically alert there (Figure 3.14). A high-density shelterbelt is like a ridge; in that similar eddies can be produced on the upwind and downwind sides.

Low density shelterbelts (Figure 3.15), elevated structures, and tractor trailers that are open underneath may prevent scent from reaching the ground for some distance downwind. Starting to search them from downwind rather than close to them may be desirable.

Wind direction in a forest is highly variable, which indicates that a dog that detects a scent plume there and moves upwind at that instant will not likely be moving in the direction of the source (Table 3.4). This makes it more difficult to find sources in forests than in fields and indicates that closer grid spacing is required in forests compared to fields.

A jet of air near the ground level can penetrate a sparse forest almost four times the forest height (Figure 3.16) so that it may be possible to search the area adjacent to the forest edge from well into the forest.

Above-Ground Searches 4

4.1 Search Strategies

4.1.1 Introduction

This chapter is primarily concerned with searching, detecting, and locating sources on the ground or above it. In general, only rough guidelines can be given to handlers because weather, terrain, vegetation, and other factors can be highly variable over time and distance and can act independently and in concert to produce a myriad of confounding effects for the search dog team. The handler needs to be continually alert and flexible to changes in the weather, especially wind and physical settings, while searching to thoroughly cover their search area (i.e. to place their dogs downwind and within scenting range of all potential source locations). These skills need to be developed and maintained during training.

Scent is transported by gravity flow of air, convection, and wind, which are the primary processes of scent transport in the atmosphere. These processes create scent plumes that are thought to behave like smoke plumes from a chimney or camp fire. Scent plume movement from outdoor sources is primarily determined by weather, especially wind, and physical settings (terrain, vegetation) that create and influence air movement. Plumes move by gravity and buoyant flow of the scent molecules when there is no wind. The use of dogs to efficiently detect and locate explosives, drugs, people, cadavers, and other sources requires information on the characteristics of scent plumes and how their movement is influenced by weather, terrain, and vegetation. However, there is a lack of scientific information on plumes from these sources, especially in outdoor settings. Consequently, SD handlers must use information derived from studies of wind and plumes of other sources (e.g. insects, smoke plumes) to infer the probable behavior of scent plumes from the sources they seek.

4.1.2 Searching and Detecting

Evolution has produced dogs with naturally efficient strategies for searching and locating scent sources. A moving dog obviously uses its nose to detect the presence of a scent plume. Moving directly upwind is not efficient since the dog can detect scent only in a narrow corridor close to its line of travel as shown in Figure 4.1. An exception to this occurs when air is channeled into a narrow valley, especially at night when the cool side slopes channel cold air with scent into a plume at the valley bottom. Trained hunting dogs and SDs, when not under the influence of their handlers, will search naturally by moving directly crosswind (quartering the wind) with their heads canted slightly upwind. With this method, dogs can detect scent upwind from as far as conditions allow, which maximizes the area searched from a narrow corridor to a wide swath (Figure 4.1). This is the most efficient method since the greatest area is covered with each pass and fewer passes through the search area are needed. Quartering the wind minimizes the time and energy required to search an area for both the dog and handler, and when properly executed, it results in a high POD. Proper execution requires the handler to have a high level of spatial awareness and changing conditions which must be developed and honed during training.

Quartering the wind is a gridding method. It requires the team to move upwind at the end of a pass through the search area before turning to make another pass. The distance moved upwind (grid spacing or lane width) is left to the judgment of the handlers based on their experience in training and searching with their dogs in similar conditions. The grid/lane width depends on the nature and size of the source, whether it is above or below ground, terrain, and vegetation in the search area; weather (especially wind and air stability); and other factors. Searches for intense above-ground sources (e.g. recently deceased subjects) may have grid lines separated by hundreds of yards. Searches for small above ground but covered sources (teeth, shell cases, cigarettes) may have grid lines separated by a few yards and may even require cross gridding to reliably detect and locate them.

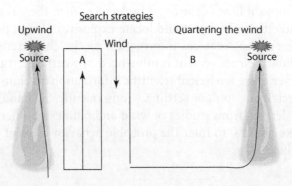

Figure 4.1 Comparison of upwind and quartering the wind search strategies. Up arrows are the paths of dog teams A and B. Team A covers a narrow strip (area A) while moving upwind. Team B covers a strip as wide as the dog can detect the scent plume (area B) and extending across the search area. This maximizes the area covered and minimizes the time and energy required by the team to search their area (Osterkamp 2001).

A few advanced handlers use a modified version of the gridding method for searching (quartering upwind, Figure 4.2) that is used by insects, fish, birds, and dogs when they have detected a source (DeBose and Nevitt 2008). The dogs are taught to move back and forth in front of them (left to right and right to left) using hand signals, voice and/or whistles, while they walk nearly straight upwind (Osterkamp 2001, 2002, 2003). It is a fast and efficient method when conditions allow it to be used. Gridding methods cannot always be used, and it is often necessary to modify them to fit existing weather, terrain, and vegetation.

Large area outdoor searches for live or deceased subjects have identified variations and additions to the grid method that can be used for any large above ground sources. These include hasty searches and hilly terrain searches (along ridges and in valleys and drainages). Hasty searches are often the first method employed by the handler. These are used when limited time is available to conduct the search, the required POD is low, or to delineate the boundaries of the search area prior to conducting a more thorough search. They often follow natural or man-made travel paths such as trails, roads, forest and field boundaries, fences, ridges, or streams. Large slopes that are not too steep can be searched along contour lines working from upslope downward, if possible, to conserve the energy of the team.

4.1.3 Locating Sources

Dogs use the same natural strategy that insects, fish, and birds use to locate a source (Figure 4.2). If the plume is not continuous, they quarter the plume upwind which involves moving across the plume at an angle upwind. When they pass through the edge of the plume, they turn into the wind and go back across it until they re-enter the plume and again quarter upwind.

Locating the source

Figure 4.2 When a source is detected, insects, fish, and birds quarter upwind to locate the source and dogs use the same strategy.

The process is repeated as they advance upwind toward the source. When the plume becomes continuous, they move directly upwind to the source. Continuous plumes usually occur close to the source and are also associated with laminar flow, turbulent flow over relatively smooth surfaces and channeling. Very low velocity winds may produce a meandering scent plume that varies in direction, confusing the direction to the scent source. Strong, swirling, gusty winds may produce gusts of scent that also confuse the direction to the source.

While all the details and implications of this method are not completely clear, it appears that dogs use their wet noses to determine the direction of the wind, then quarter across wind to detect the scent plume and quarter upwind to follow the plume to the source either instinctively or as a learned behavior. Many dogs with experience in hunting, foraging, and searching use the wind naturally in this way. Puppies and young dogs can be readily taught to quarter by the handler (Osterkamp 2001, 2002, 2003). Teaching a dog to quarter at the direction of the handler and, where possible, using this strategy in training and searching exploits the natural behavior of the dog when searching for scent and conserves the energy of the team.

A search dog that is trained to quarter out from the handler in a good search pattern, can be controlled at a distance, and can be directed from a distance to search in a grid/lane or specific areas will be of great value to the team effort (Osterkamp 2001). Some agencies (e.g. FEMA, US military) require dogs to perform these behaviors as part of their training and certifications and bird hunters spend many hours teaching dogs these skills.

4.1.4 Calm and Extreme Turbulence

Calm and extremely turbulent conditions require special methods. Completely calm air is rare; there is usually a slight drift of air that may change direction randomly and repeatedly. This can move and spread scent in all directions from a source so when the dog encounters a meandering plume it may not be able to determine the direction to the source. Low wind speeds can also produce meandering scent plumes. When scent is encountered under these conditions, the dog may start to search randomly, circling and looping while obviously in scent. The handler needs to recognize this behavior and develop a strategy to help the dog. One possible strategy is to search in a spiral out from the point where the scent was detected, and another is to grid and/or cross grid the area. If the search area is small, it may be helpful to place the dog on leash and conduct a precise grid search to find the source. If the source is not found, it may be necessary to wait for wind to develop or to return at a time when there is wind.

Extremely turbulent conditions have the air repeatedly swirling and gusting in different directions, especially when there are large objects in the flow (trees, rough terrain, buildings). These objects create turbulence that fragments and redirects the scent plume and sends scent bearing gusts in all directions. If the dog detects scent and determines the wind direction from a gust, it may not be the direction to the source. Under these conditions, the dog may detect scent from one direction and then another and become confused when trying to move in the direction of the source. One strategy is for the handler to stop, try to determine the prevailing wind direction and then quarter upwind. Spiral and grid searches are options as well as returning when the wind is less turbulent.

These considerations indicate that search dogs can be expected to have difficulties locating scent sources when the wind is nearly calm and when it is extremely turbulent. Therefore, it can be hypothesized that there may be a range of optimum wind conditions at some intermediate velocity where they will be most successful locating a source. It is likely that the size and intensity of the source and the environmental setting (e.g. field or forest) would also be important parameters. There is support for this hypothesis from a study of skunks, foxes, and raccoons (Ruzicka and Conover 2011) that showed these predators were most active when wind speeds were roughly 5 to 10 mph in a field-like setting. This indicates the optimum wind speed for predators searching in a field-like setting is 5 to 10 mph. Optimum wind speeds may be different for SDs but there is no information available.

Search methods can determine whether the dog will get access to the scent plume. Failure to access the plume is often a result of handler error and a common cause of failure for SDs. An efficient method for searching is to first perform a hasty, free search (off leash) around and through the search area and follow with gridding if nothing is found.

4.2 Special Effects

4.2.1 Slope, Valley, and Prevailing Winds

Slope, valley, and prevailing winds can interact to develop a myriad of wind conditions that differ depending on site conditions (Schroeder and Buck 1970). For example, upslope and up valley winds can occur in one part of a valley and downslope and down valley winds in another. Upslope winds usually dominate the ridges and saddles, while upslope and up valley winds combine to define wind speeds and directions at the lower elevations.

With strong heating, late afternoon upslope winds in mountain topography tend to hold weaker prevailing winds above the ridge tops so that surface winds are primarily those associated with thermal convection (Figure 4.3). Later in the day, as the upslope winds weaken, the onset of downslope flow lowers the prevailing wind level back onto the slopes and ridge tops. When

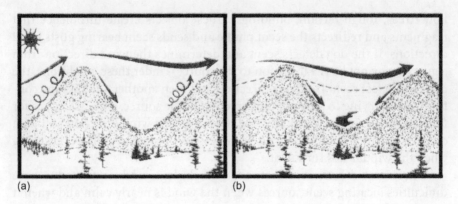

(a)   (b)

Figure 4.3 (a) Late afternoon heating can hold prevailing winds above the ridge tops. If the winds are cool and dense, they may blow up and down slopes when crossing wide valleys and from ridge to ridge when crossing narrow valleys. (b) When inversions form in the valleys, slope and valley winds below the inversion are undisturbed by prevailing winds above. (From Schroeder and Buck 1970.)

inversions develop in the valleys, lower slope and valley winds are not disturbed by the prevailing winds. Below the inversion, winds are cool, gentle, downslope and down valley. Above the inversion, the prevailing wind on upper slopes and ridges is generally warmer, stronger, and more turbulent.

Morning upslope winds begin first on east facing slopes just after the sun strikes the slopes and tend to flow directly upslope and up minor side drainages (Schroeder and Buck 1970). As the up valley winds increase during the day, the upslope winds turn more up valley (Figure 4.4). Daily upslope wind speeds are maximum on south and southwest facing slopes because they receive more sunlight and are minimum on north facing slopes. On densely forested slopes, upslope winds may exist above the tree canopy with a downslope flow in the shaded cooler trunk space below. Where there is dense undergrowth in the trunk space, this downslope flow can be retarded, diverted, or halted.

Prevailing winds in the same direction as slope and valley winds reinforce them, and when opposite to them reduce, cancel, or reverse them. This is especially true for the usually weak downslope and down valley winds at night. Prevailing winds that set up recirculation zones in the valley can enhance, retard, destroy, and redirect slope and valley winds (Figure 4.5) and cause them to be periodic. Periodic winds can be especially difficult to interpret because the source may be in the recirculation zone or the scent may be carried from another direction by the prevailing wind.

Combined slope, valley, and prevailing winds create especially difficult conditions for SD teams because these winds vary with both location and time. Handlers must be continually alert to wind direction and how it influences coverage of the search area. It may be necessary to modify their search plan or to return to parts of the search area to cover missed areas.

Figure 4.4 Upslope winds are directly upslope initially but are turned to a more up valley direction as the up valley wind increases during the day. (From Schroeder and Buck 1970.)

Figure 4.5 Prevailing wind moving into a valley divides at multiple points and creates eddies in a horizontal recirculation zone behind a low ridge (right of center). This wind sweeping over the top of the ridge and the two peaks can create eddies in vertical recirculation zones on their lee sides and channel wind into the valley from the right and left sides. (From Schroeder and Buck 1970.)

4.2.2 Scent Collectors

SDs often show interest in objects (scent collectors) that protrude into the air-flow downwind of scent sources and in recirculation zones. Scent collectors that consist of natural materials such as vegetation (bunches of grass, weeds, bushes, trees), soil, and rock have surfaces that are especially attractive to scent molecules. This allows scent from a plume to collect on them in quantities that dogs can detect. An example is the rough bark on the downwind side of a tree where scent accumulates in the recirculating eddies from an upwind source (Figure 3.15). Scent collects on the bark or is trapped in the dead air spaces of crevasses in the bark. Figure 4.6 shows two large trees separated by about 20 yards with explosives placed about 7 ft high on the tree in the background. With a light wind toward the tree in the foreground, a dozen EDs that worked this setting alerted or stood upright on the downwind side of this tree, indicating that scent was accumulating there. Some dogs were clearly in scent on the upwind side of the tree but moved around to the downwind side where they alerted. When a dog detects scent from a source in a forest, it may show interest or alert on multiple trees while working upwind toward the source, indicating that several trees in the scent plume may accumulate enough scent for them to detect. Rocks, bunches of grass, and bushes that project above surrounding vegetation and lie in the scent plume of a source are other common examples. Cave-like hollows formed by vegetation with the wind blowing into them can also collect enough scent to cause an alert.

Figure 4.6 Explosives placed 7 ft high on the large tree in the background with the wind toward the tree in the foreground caused EDs to alert upward on this tree on its downwind side (shown), which indicates scent was collecting there.

Scent trapped in dead air spaces may eventually collect on surfaces in these spaces. These could include the dead air space near the ground between stems of grass, in folded leaves, and in the duff on a forest floor. Dead air spaces in corners, in tiny recirculation zones (road curbs), and in the large recirculation zones associated with hills, ridges, rocks, forest edges, and in forest clearings may also trap scent molecules that collect on local vegetation and surfaces. Scent collectors and trapped scent may act as secondary sources as suggested in Figure 4.6. Young dogs in training and dogs consistently trained on faint scent may alert on these secondary sources, but should be encouraged to follow the scent plume to the primary source. If the wind changes from the time the scent collected to when the dog detects it, the dog cannot follow the scent plume to the primary source. Handlers must recognize the dog's behavior and use their knowledge of weather, terrain, and vegetation and their effects on local scent movement to help the dog find the source. Grid searches and circling or spiraling out from the alert are common strategies.

An article search study in Florida (Mesloh and Mesloh 2006), which used one dog to search for human scented bottle caps placed on the ground surface in tall grass, suggested that the best time to search was mid-morning after a few hours of sunlight. It was hypothesized that the scent was trapped and collected near the ground surface overnight and that some uplift (convection) was required to bring the scent up and out of the grass to the level of the dog's nose. While plausible, other factors (wind, humidity, barometric pressure, the dog's movement) may have been involved. Not enough information was available to evaluate the hypothesis. For short grass, a forested surface with leaves or needles, or a relatively bare soil surface, the optimum conditions for detection of small articles would be expected to be different, but there is no available information.

4.2.3 Ponding

Scent ponds are depressions in terrain or vegetation that collect scent. Examples (Figure 4.7) are ponds or puddles that have gone dry, depressions,

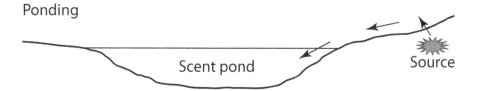

Figure 4.7 Cold air and scent from a surface or buried source flow downslope at night and fill the depression (pond) with scent. Scent remains in the pond until daytime turbulence removes it.

a valley blocked by a dense stand of trees, a length of ditch that has relatively dense vegetation on the downslope end, and depressions over old graves. Syrotuck (1972) and Rebmann et al. (2000) also give examples of ponding (pooling) in these depressions. Ponding commonly occurs at night under relatively calm and clear conditions by gravity flow of cold air and scent into the pond or by gravity flow of heavy scent molecules into a pond under calm conditions. The pond may fill partially or completely with scent that remains trapped until there is enough turbulence to flush it out. This turbulence can be mechanical, produced by the wind interacting with objects in the flow, and/or thermal caused by solar heating in the depression. A cloudy day with little wind may allow the scent to remain in the pond all day.

When dogs enter a pond and detect scent, they usually show a CB while obviously searching for a source. After searching and not finding it in the pond, they may leave the pond and then return to it. This behavior may be repeated a few times, but the dog will eventually give up and leave the area especially if the handler appears to be moving away. It is critical for the handler to recognize the behavior and help the dog find the source. If the ground is sloped, even slightly, the source is likely upslope. If there is no discernible slope, spiraling out from the pond margin may be a useful strategy. For a large pond, scent may have ponded in only one part of it.

4.2.4 Channeling

Anything that channels wind channels the scent it carries. Channels are commonly formed by terrain (valleys, canyons, streams), vegetation (paths, trails, roads in fields, and forests) and structures (berms, walls, houses, buildings). Channels can be one-sided like the edge of a forest with a field, a steep ridge, or the bank of a lake or river. When the wind direction is at an angle to the channel, wind bearing scent can be diverted into the channel and along it. Figure 4.8 is an example of channeled scent from a cadaver. Syrotuck (1972) and Rebmann et al. (2000) also show settings where channeling may occur.

Dogs that detect scent in the channel must follow the scent upwind in the channel to find the source. This process may be confounded by discontinuities in the scent plume, presence of scent collectors in the channel, flow along an outside curve, or sources that are not in the channel but rather some distance off to the side. In these cases, the handler must correctly interpret the dog's actions to help the dog locate the source. For a source off to the side of the channel, the handler needs to use the dog to determine where the scent first enters the channel and then attempt to use their knowledge of local scent movement to locate the source. This is difficult, and it may not always be possible to succeed, especially when the scent comes from a distance.

Scent moving with upslope flow on the side of a ridge may be prevented from entering a road on top of the ridge by a stronger wind that channels

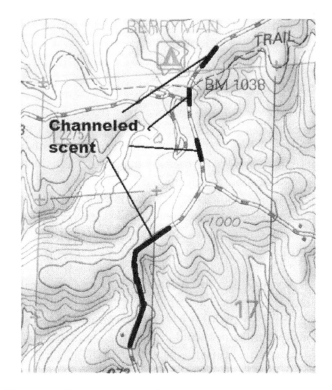

Figure 4.8 CDs and people detected channeled human decomposition scent along a forest road on a wooded ridge with the wind from the northeast.

along the road. Dogs working along the road cannot detect scent from the upslope flow which makes it necessary to work the dog along the edge of the ridge rather than in the road.

4.2.5 Chimney Effect

Schroeder and Buck (1970) noted that the sun shining on the dark surfaces of trees, power poles, vertical surfaces (cliffs, sides of structures), sloping surfaces (hillsides facing the sun), and other surfaces that are dark compared to the surroundings (ploughed fields, dark crops, island of trees in a field) heats the air in contact with them. This causes the air to rise along the heated surface in a kind of "chimney" effect and facilitates the escape of warm air aloft. In the absence of a stronger prevailing wind, this upward convective movement draws air from the area near these features upward (Figures 3.1 and 3.12), which causes it to rise out of reach of a dog. Trees are a common example when scent is drawn to them and upward on their exteriors or interiors. Dogs may alert or show interest at the base of the trees or look upward where scent may have collected on the rough bark or the underside of branches. Isolated features on level ground must be searched by gridding with small spacing, possibly just a few times the size of the source, to detect a source within them.

4.2.6 Ridge to Ridge Scent Transport

Conditions that allow wind to transport scent from ridge top to ridge top (Figure 4.3) occur when prevailing winds are stronger than up valley convective winds, when inversions form in valleys and when downwind ridges are somewhat higher. Winds may or may not pass through the valley bottom in the first case but cannot pass through it when inversions are present. The ridges can range in size from those a thousand feet or higher in mountainous terrain and separated by a mile or more to those several yards high in relatively flat terrain and separated by several tens of yards. If the winds do not penetrate the valley, dogs working along a ridge typically show a CB, turn into the wind, start downslope, lose the scent, and return to the ridge top (Figure 4.3). They may repeat this behavior once or twice, but if the handler continues to move along the ridge, the dog will usually abandon the scent. The handler must recognize this behavior, determine, and correctly interpret local conditions that influence wind direction and devise a way to help the dog find the source. A likely location would be on the adjacent upwind ridge, although this may be influenced by local topography and processes that redirect the wind. Handlers can get experience with ridge to ridge flow by setting up this type of problem at short distances during training.

4.3 Gridding and Detection Distances

4.3.1 Introduction

SD handlers often conduct searches without the benefit of any formal search management and need simplified methods to select grid/lane widths to attain a desired POD. There is little published information that can be used by handlers in the field to choose grid/lane widths for above ground sources except for the empirical stability method of Graham (1994) derived for detecting live persons. For other sources, handlers must rely on anecdotal information and their personal experience.

Searches by SD teams rely on the combined handler and support persons (visual) and canine (scent) searches, and both are strongly dependent on distance. Theoretical calculations beyond the scope of this work show that the distances at which non-detection (misses) occur as well as other quantities are also needed for calculating POD from search theory (Robe and Frost 2002; Chiacchia et al. 2015). The calculated POD depends on factors such as the level of effort, size of the search area, and how easy or hard it is to detect the object of the search. However, this calculated POD based on search theory differs from the POD usually reported (percent of sources in an area that were detected).

There are many factors that influence the calculated POD and detection distances that vary with time and location during a search. The primary factors include the scent flux or intensity (amount of scent from the source), source location, weather, terrain, vegetation, and the amount of effort made by the team. The scent flux depends on the source size, temperature, location, and whether it is contained or not. Weather (wind direction, speed, presence of sunshine, clouds, air temperature, ground temperature, humidity, precipitation) influences the ability of SDs to work and detect sources. Interactions of these weather factors with terrain and vegetation control the movement of the scent plume. The exact characteristics (size, shape, location, pattern) of the terrain and vegetation elements are highly site specific in their effects, which makes it difficult to define detection distances and grid/lane spacing in general.

Experience obtained during training is necessary for developing search strategies and choosing grid/lane widths. The effects of conditions that increase scent concentrations (scent collectors, recirculation zones), decrease scent concentrations (turbulence), cause scent to rise (convection), and prevent scent from reaching the dog's level (inversions) can only be learned by experience. Also, detection is not equivalent to success because the dog must still follow the scent plume to the source and examples of conditions that make this impossible are given herein. In these situations, the handler must learn how to help the dog.

Factors associated with individual dogs that influence detection distances include physiological (health, diet, conditioning), psychological (handler dog interactions), training, motivation to search, threshold for detection, and presence of unfamiliar distractions (scents, sights, and sounds).

4.3.2 Examples

Table 3.3 shows the cumulative POD by air stability class and distance from the source for a dog/handler team searching for a live subject in areas typical of the eastern US (Graham 1994). Additional examples are given below to illustrate PODs for some types of searches and conditions.

Reed et al. (2010) conducted controlled search trials in northern California oak woodlands to assess how scat detection rates of two dogs were influenced by the distance of scats from a search line and by variation in six environmental factors. Both dogs detected >75% of scats (75% POD) located within 11 yds of the line and the dogs' detection rates decreased with increasing distance of scats from the line. Detection rates for the two dogs varied significantly with distance and decreased to about 30% and 40%, respectively, at 27 yds. Among environmental factors, deterioration of scats by precipitation was the most important variable explaining variations in scat detection rates for both dogs.

A detailed study of detection distances for desert tortoises in open shrub desert habitat (Cablk et al. 2008; Nussear et al. 2008), which used two trained dogs, showed that the tortoises could be detected up to about 70 yards. Mean detection distance was about 15 yards. Detection rates were about 70% for relative humidity between 16% and 85%. Wind speeds were up to 20 mph and greater wind speeds resulted in greater detection distances. No relationship was found between detection distances and tortoise characteristics (age, class, sex, or size), environmental conditions (temperature, wind speed, and relative humidity), or other study parameters. Detection distances for knapweed in short vegetative cover on relatively flat ground using three dogs (Goodwin 2010) were up to 68 yds, like the results for desert tortoises.

Cablk and Sagebiel (2011) studied the ability of three certified CDs to detect teeth in Nevada. Handlers were advised that the research trials would focus only on teeth as targets, could train for >2 months prior to the trials, and were required to keep training records. The site of the trials was flat with a pine overstory and a shrub/scrub understory consisting of mountain mahogany, sagebrush, and native grasses. Ten teeth were randomly placed in plots (10.9 × 10.9 yds) on the ground surface or partially buried and were not visible to the handler. The plots were cross gridded with six grid lines in each direction placed at 5 ft 6 in spacing. The dogs were worked along the grid lines on leashes that allowed them to cover one half of the grid spacing, 2 ft 9 in. The teeth recovery rates for the three dogs using cross gridding were 78%, 61%, and 20%. The results showed that dog teams could recover individual human teeth in the field setting with high precision, that the team's capability varied significantly, and that training records supported a team's expected field performance.

Two dogs were used in a study to find brown tree snakes in Guam in a dense tropical forest area about 44 × 44 yds in size during early morning hours only (Savidge et al. 2011). Detection rates for the two teams were 44% and 26% for an average of 35%. Detection distances as indicated by a CB or alert ranged up to 13 yds. About a third of these CBs/alerts were within a yard of the snake. The results were for snakes mainly in trees at an average elevation of 3 yds. Temperatures ranged from 73 to 93°F and humidity ranged from 68 to 100% with a mean of 89%. Wind speeds ranged from 0 to 2 on the Beaufort scale with a mode <0.6 mph (i.e. calm conditions). Success increased with increasing average humidity and decreasing average wind speed. Low wind speed may have allowed scent to pool at ground level in dense vegetation near the snake which enhanced detection.

Relatively long detection distances were found for detecting feces from right whales in the open ocean (Rolland et al. 2006). The dogs were worked downwind of a pod of whales or areas where whales had been previously sighted. When a dog detected scent, the boat was steered in the direction indicated by it or in upwind transects perpendicular to the wind (gridding). Feces were detected at distances that ranged up to 1.2 miles. Finding the feces was not difficult because of their size, good weather, and the absence of any significant thermal or mechanical turbulence over open water. These conditions would be expected to produce relatively undisturbed scent plumes that could be followed upwind to the source.

This study also compared the abilities of humans and dogs to detect the feces. Humans detected seven samples at 61 to 393 yds while the dogs detected the same samples at 164 to 616 yds.

The above examples are not adequate to define grid/lane spacings for desired PODs. They do suggest grid/lane spacings that may result in detection of similar sources under similar conditions and, in some examples, the potential PODs. They also suggest that grid/lane spacing should be much less than maximum detection distances. However, these studies were all limited, and the results are likely to change when more sources, dogs, and a wider range of conditions and study parameters are included.

4.4 Distant Alerts

4.4.1 The Problem

Bryson (1984) noted that their dogs consistently alerted on searchers up to 0.6 miles in mountainous terrain. A distant alert, while not precisely defined, is taken to be an alert or CB offered by a dog in response to the scent from a source that is far away. There is no widely accepted definition of the distance. It could range from a few tens of yards for small or buried sources to much more than a mile depending on the size and intensity of the source, weather, terrain, vegetation, and other factors. Distant alerts are often distinguished by the fact that it is often difficult or impossible for the dog to follow the scent plume to the source. Some of the conditions that favor long distance transport of scent and distant alerts include fanning, looping, large eddies and wind gusts, sweeps and openings in forest canopies, and ridge to ridge scent transport. Large areas of terrain that are flat, gently sloping, open, or water bodies also favor long distance transport. Humans can experience "distant alerts" from large intense sources such as above ground decomposing cadavers. Distant alerts by CDs of a mile or more have been reported in searches for these cadavers and for live subjects (Bryson 1984; Palman 2011; Irwin 2008; McMahon 2014). There does not appear to be any reports of distant alerts by other types of SDs. Wolves have been reported to detect live prey at 1.5 miles (Mech 1970) which is similar to other predators (jackals, hyenas).

With fanning, lack of vertical mixing allows the scent plumes to be transported without much change in concentration at the top of an inversion so that dogs could detect scent from a distance where it contacts elevated terrain by working them at this elevation. Eddies and wind gusts much larger than the scent plume can also transport the plume or large segments of it with little change in concentration. However, once these contact the ground it is common for weather, terrain, vegetation, and other intervening turbulent processes to modify the scent plume (dilute, fragment, redirect, elevate) and generally make it difficult or impossible for dogs to follow the plume to the source. This is also true for sweeps and openings in forests that bring wind bearing scent down below the canopy. When the dog cannot follow the plume to the source, it then becomes a problem for the handler/IC to solve. Knowledge of scent plume movement can help them locate the source or narrow its location so that there is a greater chance of finding it.

Distant alerts are an opportunity for the team to find the source. Difficulties in locating a distant source depend on the distance, number, and characteristics of intervening factors that influence scent plume movement. For example, daytime upslope and up valley flow can redirect scent before it is picked up by prevailing winds. Channeling by valleys, canyons, ridges, rivers, forest edges, trails, and roads can move scent significant distances at angles to the prevailing winds. Forests with a continuous canopy may prevent scent from reaching the ground at the dog's level except in openings and places where sweeps occur. These and other factors may make it difficult to find distant sources by searching upwind. Distant alerts are easier to resolve in sparsely vegetated terrain that often occurs in arid regions, at higher elevations, and in relatively flat or gently rolling terrain.

Distant alerts may involve all the processes that influence scent plume movement such as scent collectors, ponding, channeling, chimney effects, up and downslope flows, thermals, gusting, looping, sweeps and ejections, forest openings, ridge to ridge flow, and recirculation zones. These processes may act independently or in concert to produce scent conditions and concentrations that dogs can detect at a distance. Scent may concentrate on scent collectors in recirculation zones, in the lee of steep changes in terrain, and at forest edges. Scent from a distant source can be brought down to ground level by looping, sweeps, in forest openings, and when wind bearing scent contacts elevated ground. A common and particularly difficult situation in hilly and forested terrain occurs when upslope winds bearing scent encounter stronger prevailing winds that move the scent at a significant angle to the upslope winds.

Scent in a forest can cause dogs to stand on their hind legs or on trees looking up, move around obviously in scent, self-reward (e.g. pick up a stick), whine, or to stand or sit looking upward or at the handler, and appear to be frustrated. A recirculating eddy on the upwind or lee side of a hill or ridge from a source that is far upwind may cause the dog to follow the scent up or down the slope until they lose the scent and then to return to the start. They may repeat this behavior or just move away if the handler moves. Some dogs just stop and stare upwind when detecting the faint scent of a distant source and then may look at the handler. In these cases, the handler should take a few steps toward the dog, an action that seems to give them "permission" to follow the scent plume. Other observed behaviors include chomping grass (nervously), head turns, and stopping to carefully examine common scent collectors (e.g. clumps of grass, bushes, rocks, lee side of trees).

Scent over water that is colder than the air (common during the day over water) is either on the surface or in a thin layer of air above it so that it is useful to get the dogs as close as possible to the water surface. When scent is present, dogs may have their noses almost in contact with the water or even have their lower jaws in it. If the water is flowing, scent collects on anything protruding from the water (logs, brush, sticks, leaves) and on vegetation on the outside of bends. As noted previously, a stream may also channel scent from a distance either on the water surface or just above it.

4.4.2 Locating the Source

CDs that detect scent from a faint source will give a CB/alert that the handler should recognize. However, handlers and dogs both require special training to locate a distant source and only a general outline is given here. Handlers must become more sensitive to often subtle behaviors that show the dog is in scent; to the effects of microscale weather, terrain, and vegetation on scenting conditions; and to the presence of special effects that influence the movement of scent. They must also develop the habit of continually analyzing dog behavior and scenting conditions and adjust their search tactics as necessary. Skill at recording and interpreting observations and data is required. Dogs must gain the experience and confidence they need to follow faint scent for long distances or search for isolated scent on scent collectors. One procedure is to train the dog in trailing before training any other detector skill, especially one that requires nose to the ground searching. This procedure is used to train mine detector dogs (GICHD 2004). Dogs trained to trail on leash or off leash and then cross-trained in cadaver search can be trained to follow discontinuous scent from a distance upwind from both live subjects and cadavers (McMahon 2014). However, it is difficult to apply unless the terrain is relatively open which is characteristic of high altitudes and arid regions.

As in all dog training, simplify the initial conditions to where you know the dog will be successful. Start with short distances, simple terrain, and sparse vegetation. Increase the variables (distance, terrain, vegetation, time) one at a time in small steps that allow the dog to always be successful. Work each step with differing conditions characteristic of your search areas and where special effects may influence scent movement. The goal of this training is to improve the ability of the team to follow scent plumes, continuous and discontinuous, and to locate the paths of scent in scent collectors, when looping conditions are present, and when quartering upwind to detect puffs of scent. When there is no scent or not enough scent available for the team to follow, handlers must use their experience to help their dog.

If a well-trained SD gives a CB/alert but cannot locate or follow a scent plume to the source, it should initially be considered a distant alert. The probability of locating a source that produces a distant alert increases when the handler records data and observations necessary to interpret it. Multiple CB/alerts from other dogs in the area or the same dog can also increase it, assuming the handlers are competent at recognizing them.

Current technology includes GPS and cell phone tracking capabilities that should be used by all SD teams to provide a recorded track of their path through the search area and a record of the position of any CB/alerts. If a dog indicates scent or alerts in a certain direction, the wind direction at the position of the dog or the direction they are pointing should be recorded immediately since wind can be highly variable, especially in forests. If the dog is clearly in scent but not indicating a particular direction, the local and prevailing wind directions should be recorded.

For distant alerts, the handler or their support should record the usual data for any CB or alert (date, time, map or GPS coordinates, and wind direction) supplemented by observations on weather conditions, terrain, and vegetation and their interpretation of the CB/alert. Weather conditions should include air temperature, wind, percent of cloud cover, precipitation, and length of the handler's shadow. Wind data should include the wind direction at the level of the dog, at the tops of any trees near the alert, any obvious indicator of wind (gusts, dust, low cloud movement), and the prevailing wind speed and direction. Weather conditions with the prevailing wind should be recorded hourly by IC for the search area but may not always be done. Prevailing wind could be from the above observations or from a nearby weather station such as an airport or city. Cloud cover and the length of the handler's shadow are needed to provide an estimate of atmospheric stability. Terrain can usually be determined from topo maps but small scale features such as trails, gullies, cliffs, depressions, small ponds or streams, and others may not be apparent. The presence of water bodies and especially flowing water in nearby stream and river channels should be noted. Vegetation characteristics include type, height and density, presence of openings and clearings, and nearby edges of fields and forests. The handler's interpretation should include the presence of special effects (scent collectors, ponding, channeling, chimney effect, up and downslope flows, gusting, looping, sweeps and ejections, ridge to ridge flow) and any other observations of conditions that may influence scent movement.

There are several strategies that may be useful for interpreting distant alerts. For complex terrain and/or vegetation, one strategy is to try to accumulate as many distant alerts as possible in a first attempt to define the general area from which these alerts are originating and then to search for the source in that area. Their nature of being "distant" often means that the usual search boundaries must be expanded. This can be done with daytime searches by taking advantage of upslope winds on sunny days and prevailing winds which can carry scent across ridges, saddles, passes, and hill and mountain tops. If the winds are light and variable in these areas or the areas are forested, the scent plumes may be intermittent. This means that teams moving rapidly may miss the scent plumes, so it is desirable to conduct these searches at a slower pace. Improving POD may also be done by using several teams separated by about 100 yds, moving slowly, one team moving very slowly, or by teams spending more time in saddles, passes, and any place where scent may be channeled or near the tops of hills, mountains, and ridges that intercept the prevailing wind. Distant alerts during daytime searches, when conditions favor upslope flow, may indicate that the source is below the elevation of the alert.

In some searches, it may be possible to box the source (i.e. define the area where the source must be) by using wind from different directions and then concentrate resources in that area. The idea is that alerts with a prevailing north wind usually suggest the source is in that direction. If alerts are then experienced with a south wind but farther to the north than the first alerts, then the source is likely in the area between the two sets of alerts and similarly for east and west winds. This method relies on the presence of favorable winds that may require weeks to occur during which the decomposition scent may become fainter. It is important to conduct as many searches as possible if the subject may still be alive or before decomposition scent of a deceased subject decreases.

Another strategy is to conduct late afternoon to early morning searches in clear, stable weather with relatively calm conditions at the bottom of gullies, valleys, drainages, and slopes, since gravity flow of cool air bearing scent drains downslope in shade and at night. These searches may be more successful than the usual daytime searches because upslope flow in daytime tends to be deep and turbulent and downslope drainage flow tends to be thin, less turbulent and concentrates scent closer to the ground. Downslope drainage flow may start and stop at random times, so teams should pay special attention to the flow, stopping when it stops and continuing after it starts. Alerts in shade during late afternoon to early morning searches in clear stable weather with little or no prevailing wind may indicate that the source is above the elevation of the alert.

4.4.3 Examples of Distant Alerts

It is impossible to give a definitive interpretation of distant alerts since enough information can never be obtained. The necessary information for the search area would include detailed terrain and vegetation maps, maps of wind, air temperature, cloud cover and air stability at times just before and during each alert, presence of special effects, and other information. The interpretations of distant alerts given below are based on written reports and discussions with dog handlers that conducted the searches or were present at them and on an incomplete knowledge of local scent movement. While inadequate, it is hoped that these examples of distant alerts will help improve the ability of handlers and search managers to find the lost and missing. Additional accounts of distant alerts have been given by Irwin (2008) and McMahon (2014).

4.4.3.1 Machias River, Maine, Suicidal Subject

Figure 4.9 illustrates the effects of scent channeling by a river and the use of human and dog alerts to find the subject. The subject's vehicle was found at the location shown on Figure 4.9 in November about 5 to 6 weeks after he was last seen, so there was a long time for scent to spread around the area. Teams from MESARD (Maine Search and Rescue Dogs) searched downstream along the river and the team on the west side of the river had several alerts on small hills. The wind was from the east and the weather cold, cloudy, and foggy. The team on the east side did not work far enough downstream to find the subject. At the same time, a team working the water in a canoe did not have any alerts even though they passed very close to the subject who was lying about 10 yds from the 6 to 8 ft high banks. However, neutral air stability, a recirculation zone on the west slope of a ridge to the east, and other factors may have prevented scent from reaching the canoe level where the dog could have detected it.

A few days later, game wardens reported smelling decomposition scent as they walked a high bank on a bend in the river near the subject's vehicle on a sunny day with wind from the south blowing directly up a long straight portion of the river to the bend. The high bank may have created a recirculation zone or pool of scent that was deflected to the west and north over the bank where the people could smell it.

Several ideas based on the above facts were developed to guide the search. Lines drawn upwind from the human alerts at the bend and east from the dog alerts and the location of the vehicle on the east side of the river suggested the subject was downriver on the east side somewhere near the intersection of the lines. Lack of an alert by the team in the canoe indicated that the body was not in the water. These considerations suggested that the east bank of the river should be searched to or beyond the intersection of the lines. The subject was found by a MESARD dog team on the east side of the river about two-thirds mile south of the vehicle and about a quarter mile north of the dog alerts. On the first day of the search, it appears that the hills on both sides of the river may have channeled the subject's scent to the south where it was picked up by the east wind and transported across the river during neutral

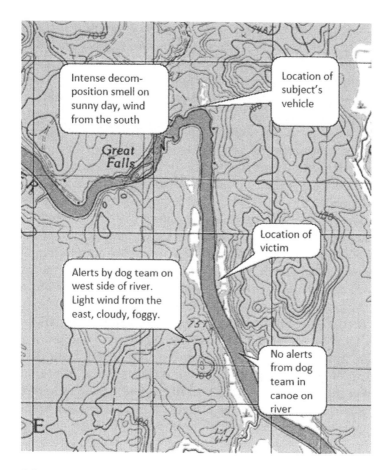

Figure 4.9 Distant alerts by a CD and human decomposition scent detected by people illustrate the effects of scent channeling by the river, possible neutral stability, and the use of the alerts to find the subject. (Map and search information courtesy of Deborah Palman, MESARD.)

stability conditions to the dog team on the west side although other interpretations are possible.

4.4.3.2 Waterville Valley, New Hampshire, Alzheimer's Subject

Figure 4.10 shows CD alerts (including indications and interests) and detection of decomposition scent by people over a 12 week period after a woman with Alzheimer's disease was reported missing. The woman's body was found by a MESARD searcher traveling home on an ATV on a cross country ski trail after a day of searching with her dog. It was located 25 yds off the trail that led back to the woman's house and over 170 yds uphill from Avalanche Brook.

A tremendous effort was made by dog teams and ground searchers over 12 weeks in the fall after the woman disappeared. They searched along every trail plus all the water courses within 1 mile of the place last seen (PLS). Unfortunately, she was over 1.4 miles from the PLS in a place where foliage prevented her from being seen. Dog alerts and indications were up to 1.2 miles from the body as shown on Figure 4.10.

Winds were generally strong from the northwest and would sometimes continue at night. Waterville Valley is bordered to the north and west by peaks and ridges typically 3,000 to 4,000 ft in elevation. Two major valleys, one from the west-northwest and the Mad River valley to the north, channel northwest winds into Waterville Valley. This complex setting created highly variable circulating winds and eddies in the search area which distributed scent throughout the valley and made it impossible to reliably determine the location of any scent detected. The setting was further complicated by Avalanche Brook because the stream has a steep gradient, is set well below the level of the surrounding woods, and is in a valley cut down into the terrain. This suggested that the valley was shielded from higher level circulating winds so that scent could flow downstream, which was verified by observations of the movement of leaves just above the water surface.

The north facing slope where the body was found was partially protected from the wind by the terrain and shaded by the terrain and forest at a time of low sun angles. It appears that scent flowed downhill from the body to the stream channel, was carried by the air downstream, and accumulated in the bend at the junction with the Mad River, where there were three alerts and decomposition smell detected by people. Interest by a dog to the east of the body was likely a direct result of the northwest winds channeled east up

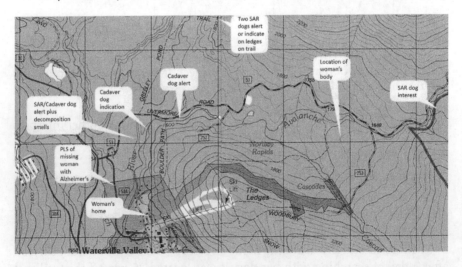

Figure 4.10 Distant alerts and CB by MESARD and New England SAR canine units and detection of decomposition scent by humans over a 12 week period after the woman went missing. (Map and search information courtesy of Deborah Palman, MESARD.)

Avalanche Brook. Alerts by two dogs to the north were possibly a result of high level circulation in the valley.

Interpretation of the effects of the swirling variable winds in the valley was difficult. However, the three alerts near the junction of the river and brook and the interest of a dog farther to the east suggested that the body was in the drainage of the brook. Working out the details of this assumption eventually led to discovery of the body. There is little that can be done under these extremely complex conditions, but accumulating alerts, cataloging and recording observations (like the leaf movement over the water), and persistence in analyzing and searching can lead to finding the source. If it is an option, waiting for different wind conditions may sometimes help.

4.4.3.3 *Clarks Fork River, Wyoming, Missing Person*

A man was reported missing on October 1 and his vehicle was located near the Clarks Fork River on October 4. Canine teams from Park County Search & Rescue and Northwest K-9 Search & Recovery searched over the next 2 weeks and had multiple alerts (Figure 4.11) that eventually led to finding the man's body on October 22 near the river at the bottom of cliffs where he fell.

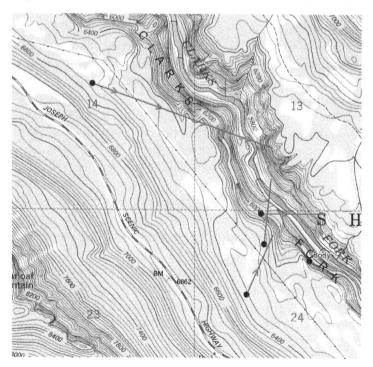

Figure 4.11 Some of the distant alerts by PCSAR (Park County Search & Rescue) after the man went missing. The filled circles, •, are the locations of the alerts and the body. Lines are drawn upwind from the alerts. (Map and search information courtesy of Kris Brock, PCSAR.)

The alert in the upper left quadrant was about 1.4 miles from the body. It appears to be the result of channeling by the wind upstream from the body to where the river turned north and the scent was carried up and out of the canyon. The three alerts in the lower right quadrant are <½ mile from the body. The upper and lower ones may have been the result of channeling by the canyon and terrain near the cliffs. The middle alert is difficult to explain; however, time lapse photographs of clouds in mountains often show extreme variations in wind directions that may have caused it.

4.5 Summary

The primary methods of scent transport in the atmosphere are by gravity flow of air, convection, and wind. These processes create scent plumes that are thought to behave like smoke plumes from a chimney or camp fire. Scent molecules move by gravity and buoyant flow when there is no wind. The use of dogs to efficiently detect and locate explosives, drugs, people, cadavers, and other sources requires knowledge of the characteristics and movement of their scent plumes.

Dogs search naturally by moving directly crosswind (quartering the wind) which minimizes the time and energy needed to search an area and results in a high POD (Figure 4.1). When a source is detected, insects, fish, birds, and dogs quarter upwind to locate the source which involves moving across the plume at an angle upwind (Figure 4.2). When they pass through the edge of the plume, they turn into the wind and proceed back across it in the direction they came from until they re-enter the plume and again quarter upwind advancing them toward the source.

Calm and extremely turbulent conditions require special methods. Under calm conditions, the dog may start to search randomly, circling about. Under turbulent conditions, the dog may detect scent from one gust and then become confused by another when trying to move toward the source. Possible strategies to help the dog include spiral and grid searches and returning when there is wind or it is less turbulent.

Optimum wind speeds in a field are roughly 5 to 10 mph but may be different for other terrain and vegetative conditions. An efficient method is to first perform a hasty search around the borders and through the search area and follow with a grid search if nothing is found.

Late afternoon upslope convective heating can hold prevailing winds above the ridge tops (Figure 4.3). If prevailing winds are cool and dense, they may follow slopes when crossing wide valleys but cross from ridge to ridge in narrow valleys. When inversions form in the valleys, slope and valley winds below them are undisturbed by prevailing winds above. On densely forested slopes, upslope winds may exist above the tree canopy with a downslope flow in the shaded cooler trunk space below. Upslope winds are directly upslope initially but turn to a more up valley direction as the up valley wind increases during the day (Figure 4.4).

Wind in hills and mountains can be channeled by terrain and create vertical and horizontal eddies which result in complex search conditions (Figure 4.5)

Scent collectors consisting of natural materials such as vegetation, soil, and rock have surfaces which are especially attractive to scent molecules. Scent collects on them in quantities that dogs can detect. Examples are the rough bark on the downwind side of a tree and cave-like hollows formed by vegetation with wind blowing into them (Figure 4.6). Scent collectors can act as secondary sources. Young dogs in training and dogs consistently trained on faint scent may alert on them but handlers should encourage and help them follow the scent plume to the primary source.

Scent ponds are depressions in terrain or vegetation that collect scent (Figure 4.7). When scent ponds are encountered, it is critical for the handler to recognize the behavior of the dog and help the dog to find the source.

Anything that channels wind channels the scent it carries (Figure 4.8). Channels are commonly formed by terrain, vegetation, and structures. Channels can be one-sided like the edge of a forest with a field, a ridge, or the bank of a lake or river. Dogs may need help following the scent in the channel and finding where scent entered the channel.

The dark surfaces of trees and any vertical or sloping surfaces in sunlight heat the air in contact with them, which causes the air to rise along the heated surface. This facilitates the escape of warm air aloft. The upward convective movement can draw air from near the base of these features upward. Dogs may alert or show interest at the base of trees or look upward where the scent collects on the rough bark or the underside of branches.

Wind can transport scent from ridge top to ridge top when prevailing winds are stronger than up valley convective winds, when inversions form in the valleys, and when downwind ridges are somewhat higher. Dogs working along a ridge show a CB, turn into the wind, start downslope, lose the scent, return to the ridge top, and may repeat the behavior. The handler must recognize this behavior and devise a way to help the dog find the source.

Distant alerts can occur more than a mile from a strong source. Locating the source of a distant alert is usually difficult because of the distance, number, and characteristics of intervening factors that influence scent plume movement (Figures 4.9, 4.10, and 4.11). These factors often include scent collectors, channeling, up and downslope flows, thermals, gusting, looping, sweeps and ejections, forest openings, ridge to ridge flow, and recirculation zones.

Dog behaviors during a distant alert include looking upward, self-rewarding, whining, staring upwind, biting grass, and others. In dealing with distant alerts, handlers must become more sensitive to often subtle behaviors of their dogs when in scent; to the effects of microscale weather, terrain, and vegetation on scenting conditions; and to the presence of special effects that influence the movement of scent. The probability of locating a source from a distant alert increases when the team records data and observations necessary to interpret the alert.

Strategies for locating the source include trying to accumulate more alerts, working ridges, saddles and hilltops during the day, working drainages and valleys when side slopes are in shade and at night, and boxing the source (i.e. define a smaller area where the source must be) by using winds from different directions.

Several examples of distant alerts are described.

Buried Sources

5

5.1 Introduction

Scent from a buried source moves through the soil, ground cover, scent boundary layer, and into the air where it can be detected (Figure 5.1). The availability of scent in the air above a buried source depends on the properties of the soil and scent molecules and their interactions; on processes that occur in the soil, ground cover, and scent boundary layer; and on the weather. Scent plume movement in air is influenced by terrain and vegetation, and weather influences scent movement through all media between the source and the dog. Scent movement through the soil is constrained because it can move only in the pore spaces between soil particles while in the gas and liquid phases. Scent transport also depends on the rate of movement and on whether the VOCs are in the gas phase or the water phase (i.e. how they are distributed or partitioned between phases). In dry soil, VOCs are adsorbed on the soil particle surfaces as a kind of residue and are not free to move. Our primary interest is in upward movement of scent, but downward movement can be of interest especially in the presence of flowing underground water.

Information on the movement of scent in soils is available from studies of buried explosives and decomposition VOCs, but there does not appear to be any for drugs and other buried sources. Fortunately, there is a substantial literature on the movement of gases, water, fertilizers, pesticides, and other chemicals in agricultural soils and on the movement of hazardous contaminants in soils. This information can be used to develop insights on scent movement in soils that are useful in training and deploying SDs used for detecting and finding explosives, drugs, cadavers, and other buried sources.

The use of SDs to detect buried sources is a difficult task that tests the team's ability to detect and locate the faint scent of a source that may be wrapped or in a container, covered by different soil types, ground surface covers, vegetation, terrain, and in variable weather conditions. The scent molecules available at the soil surface are known for some explosives (Jenkins et al. 2000). Scent molecules for cadavers (Vass et al. 2004, 2008, 2012) have been cataloged, but the specific types used by the dogs to detect cadavers are not generally known. While some information is available, more is needed to determine the quantitative effects of soil, ground cover, and surface environmental conditions (primarily weather, vegetation, and terrain) that influence

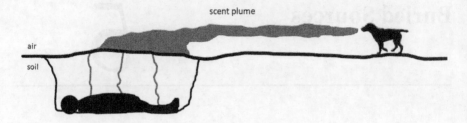

Searching for a clandestine grave

Figure 5.1 Scent from a buried source must pass through soil, ground cover, scent boundary layer, air, vegetation, and over terrain to reach the dog's nose. Weather influences scent movement through all these media.

the success of SDs in finding buried sources. This chapter is an introductory discussion of scent transport in soils and attempts to show how this information can be exploited under certain conditions to increase PODs for buried sources. The results are not completely satisfactory because they are based on anecdotal information, sparse data, limited theory, and untested hypotheses.

5.1.1 Soil and VOC Properties

Soil consists of inorganic particles from weathered rock, organic products from the flora and fauna that exist in or on the soil, and materials transported by water and wind (Marshall and Holmes 1979). Soil particles (grains) vary in size from coarse-grained gravels and sands to fine-grained silts and very fine-grained clays. Soil particles are in contact with each other and have three-dimensional interconnected pore spaces that create channels through the soil (Figure 5.2). These pore spaces contain soil gases (air and water vapor) and soil water or ice. Scent (VOCs) is present as gases, dissolved in water, insoluble liquids (from wet sources), and as source micro-particulates. Soil water also exists as thin water films on soil particle surfaces. Gases and liquids move through the channels formed by the pore spaces in the soil and water films move over the surfaces of the soil particles. Scent can move through soil as gases in the soil pores, solutes dissolved in the water films and pore water, insoluble liquids, and as solids in the form of source micro-particulates much smaller than the pore spaces (Figure 5.2). Scent in all its forms can also enter the groundwater and be transported by it.

Physical properties of interest for scent movement in soils include soil type, porosity, saturation, water content, temperature, and organic content. Soil types include organic and inorganic (gravel, sand, silt, clay) and mixtures of them. Porosity is the fraction of the total soil volume that consists of pore space. Silts and clays have greater porosity (e.g. clays, about 0.6) than sands and gravels (e.g. sands, about 0.4), but sands and gravels have much

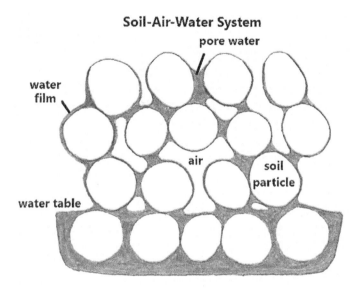

Figure 5.2 A conceptual two-dimensional model of soil containing air and water. Scent can move through soil pores by gas phase diffusion and advection or transported when dissolved in pore water and water films that move through the pores and over the surfaces of the soil particles.

larger interconnected pore spaces which make them much more permeable to the flow of gases and liquids (Table 5.1). The degree of saturation is the fraction of pore space filled with water. Soil is 100% saturated when the pore space is filled with water. A dry soil may have just 1% of its pore space filled with water. Dry soils are common in arid climates but are usually limited to the surface soil in temperate climates. Water content is the fraction of the total soil volume or weight that is water. In some areas, especially lowlands, a water table may exist. Soil is unsaturated above the water table and saturated below it.

Soil temperatures influence all the chemical and physical properties of soils and scent. Temperature influences volatilization rates (availability of scent) largely through its effect on the vapor pressure of VOCs. It also influences the movement of scent molecules in both the gas phase and when dissolved in the water. Organic content is the fraction of the total soil volume

Table 5.1   Relative Values of Porosity and
Flow Compared for Gravel, Sand, Silt, and Clay

Soil Type	Gravel, Sand	Silt	Clay
Porosity	Low	Medium	High
Flow	High	Medium	Low

or weight that consists of organic material and typically ranges from a few per cent to about 80%. Soils with large amounts of organic material adsorb more scent than mineral soils which leaves less available for transfer to the air. This makes it somewhat more difficult for dogs to detect sources buried in soils with large organic contents. Clay content and soil pH influence volatilization through adsorption effects that reduce the solution concentration of dissolved VOCs and VOC concentrations in the gas phase.

The chemical properties of scent molecules that influence scent availability and movement include vapor pressure, phase partition coefficients, diffusion coefficients, solubility, and degradability. Vapor pressure is a measure of the volatility of a chemical and can vary significantly with commonly encountered changes in soil temperature. VOCs with high vapor pressure produce more scent than those with low vapor pressure.

The concentrations of VOCs in soil air, dissolved in soil water and attached to soil particle surfaces, depend on the phase partition coefficients for two phases in contact and at equilibrium. For example, the partition coefficient for a VOC in soil air in contact with soil water containing the dissolved VOC is the concentration of the VOC in the air divided by the concentration in the water. These coefficients are determined primarily by the chemical compound, soil type, water content, and temperature. Phase partition coefficients determine whether scent transport to the soil surface will be in the gas or water phase. For example, the primary chemical components of TNT include TNT, DNT, and dinitrobenzene (DNB). The phase partition coefficients for these chemicals in air in contact with water are small which indicates only a small fraction of a percent exists in the air with about 10% in the water phase and the rest adsorbed on soil particle surfaces that are not free to move (Phelan and Webb 2002). Since the water contains almost all the mobile chemicals, water phase transport dominates scent movement in the soil for these chemicals except at low water contents.

The phase partition coefficients for decomposition chemicals vary considerably. Since it is not known what VOCs are used by dogs in detecting buried cadavers, it is not possible to thoroughly evaluate decomposition scent movement in soil and scent concentrations in air over buried cadavers.

Diffusion coefficients are useful for determining the amounts of VOCs that diffuse in the air and water phases. Diffusion coefficients for VOCs in air are roughly 10,000 times greater than for those dissolved in the water (Phelan and Webb 2002). However, as for explosives, the concentrations of VOCs in each phase that are available to move must be considered and these depend on the phase partition coefficients.

Water solubility is the amount of VOC that can dissolve in water. There are large differences in the solubility of explosives, drugs, and decomposition chemicals. For example, at room temperature, TNT is only slightly soluble (0.13 g/L) while AN is highly soluble (150 g/100 ml). Degradation processes in soils cause source VOCs to change form, chemical properties, and can result in their elimination from the soils (Phelan and Webb 2002). Soil mineral reactions, biological transformations, and plant root uptake are examples of these processes. Degradation rates depend on soil water content, soil type, and temperature and are characterized by their half-life (time required for the VOC concentration to decrease by half). Some VOCs degrade quickly with lifetimes in soils measured in days. For example, the relatively low concentrations of 2,4,6-TNT in soils compared with its other chemicals appear to be attributable to a very short half-life for this compound (about a day) compared to the half-life for 2,4-DNT (about 26 days) under similar conditions, which indicates that 2,4-DNT is more likely to survive passage to the soil surface.

Water contents more than 1% result in fast degradation rates and the effects of clay or organic contents in soils is to reduce the half-life of VOCs. Subfreezing soil temperatures (<32°F) and low water contents, much <1%, limit degradability. Increasing soil temperatures from freezing to about 72°F can decrease the half-life for 2,4-DNT by a factor of 3 or more in a wet soil.

There are significant differences in the chemical properties of VOCs associated with buried sources, especially vapor pressure, phase partition coefficients, diffusion coefficients, and degradation rates. These differences indicate that the concentration of each VOC in the gas and water phases will be different, each VOC will move with different diffusive velocities in soil air and water, and the lifetime of each VOC in the soil will be different. This implies there will be a spectrum of VOCs above buried sources ranging from those that are absent to those with enough concentration to be detectable by dogs.

5.1.2 Buried Sources

Burying a source involves digging a hole, placing the source, filling the hole, disposing of excess soil, and camouflaging the surface disturbance. FBI data (Hoffman et al. 2009) shows that clandestine burial sites were located a short distance from infrequently traveled roads or pathways, approximately 10 ft away from the closest large tree and were typically surrounded by bushes or heavy foliage. Typical burials varied in depth from 1.5 to 2.5 ft and the corpse was usually clothed or wrapped in plastic and faced down. Difficulties associated with digging also suggest that the grave will not usually be placed where large rocks or hard dry clay are found. If the source is heavy such as an adult body, it will usually be brought to a point near the grave by a vehicle and carried not much more than about 100 yds (Rebmann et al. 2000) unless there are multiple people involved or the corpse is light.

The soil placed in the hole will have significantly different properties, especially structure, density, and water content compared to the surrounding undisturbed soil. This indicates that scent movement from the source to the surface in the disturbed fill soil will be modified compared to that in the surrounding undisturbed soil. Scent movement to the surface will likely be enhanced in the fill soil because it is difficult to compact the fill soil to the same degree as undisturbed soil. The characteristics of the scent distribution surrounding a buried source depend on the physical and chemical properties of the soil and VOCs, whether the soil and source are dry or wet and whether the source VOCs are soluble or insoluble. Buried explosives would normally be dry and recently buried cadavers would be wet.

If the soil and source are dry or the source is insoluble, dissolved fluids will not exist. If the soil is wet with water soluble VOCs, soil pore water and soil water films will contain dissolved VOCs. If the soil contains insoluble liquids, their fate depends on whether they are lighter or heavier than water and how they interact with soil particles. Some decomposition fluids are relatively insoluble in water and often lighter. When a cadaver is buried in contact with the soil, interaction of the decomposition fluids with the soil fines can produce a mucus sheath around the cadaver consisting of the fluids and fines soil fraction (Janaway 1997). Little is known about the details of this process.

Figure 5.3 is a conceptual model of the possible scent distribution associated with buried human remains based primarily on studies of explosives and hazardous chemicals in soil. The scent can move through the soil except

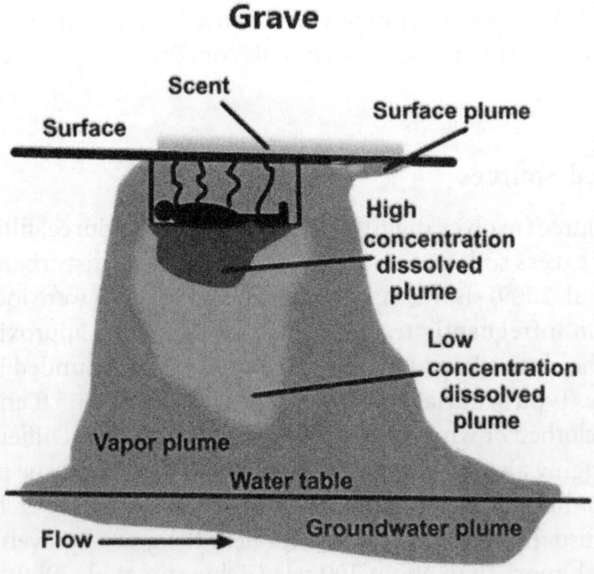

Figure 5.3 A conceptual model of a grave showing the possible scent distribution on a slope. Decomposition fluids occur under the body. The mucous sheath and micro-particulates are not shown.

for that adsorbed on soil particle surfaces, on organics, and that removed from the flow by processes discussed above.

The ground surface and the groundwater table can be level or sloped. If both are level, scent transported to the surface over buried sources can accumulate during favorable conditions and create a surface distribution of scent that is expected to be slightly larger than the source and centered over the source.

On sloped ground, the surface scent distribution would extend downslope from the source as shown in Figure 5.3. Aitkenhead-Peterson et al. (2011) have observed significant downslope movement of decomposition chemicals from cadavers on the ground surface. Figure 5.4 shows the soil surface concentrations of 2,4-DNT downslope from land mines buried under a gently sloping ground surface (Hewitt et al. 2001).

Since 2,4-DNT is the primary chemical in TNT that dogs use for detecting the explosive, the results shown in Figure 5.4 indicate that the spatial distribution of this chemical in the surface soils is a "scent print." The TMA-5 mine is roughly 7 × 8 in and produces a scent print roughly 2 × 2 ft or about 3 times the size of the mine on this slope. The highest values of scent do not occur at the mine but about 6 to 8 in downslope from the mine. The PMA1A is about 3 × 4 in and produces a scent print about 1.7 ft wide, extending 2.3 ft downslope or about 6 to 7 times the size of the mine on this slope. The highest values of scent do not occur at the mine but a few inches downslope from the mine. Reasons for the differences in the results for the mines are unknown but likely associated with mine characteristics, soil properties, surface slope, and other effects.

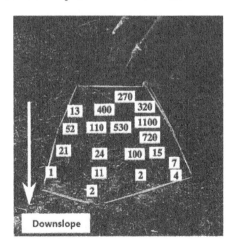 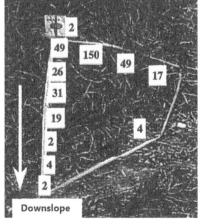

Figure 5.4 Spatial distribution of 2,4-DNT (ng/g) in surface soils downslope from buried land mines, at Ft. Leonard Wood, Missouri. A TMA-5 antitank mine (left) and PMA1A antipersonnel mine (right). (From Phelan and Webb 2002. Data from Hewitt et al. 2001. See also Osterkamp 2020.)

The importance of the observed high surface concentrations of 2,4-DNT associated with mines buried in dry soils is that the concentration available for detection is orders of magnitude higher (thousands of times) on the surface soil particles than in the air. On dry soils, this suggests dogs may be inhaling soil particles suspended by the action of air jets to detect mines and/ or desorbing VOCs on the soil particles with their humid exhalations. While inhalation of surface soil particles over landmines and desorption of VOCs by their humid breath may be alternate mechanisms that dogs use for detection, it is not necessary because of their robust capabilities for trace vapor detection. Nevertheless, these scenting processes may be used during favorable environmental conditions.

It is thought that the size of the surface scent print for a mine that is buried on level ground should be about twice the lateral dimensions of the mine. On slopes, surface runoff can create a scent print for some distance downslope of the source (Figures 5.4 and 5.5). Sargisson et al. (2012) found that scent was transported downslope from buried mines in small eroded surface drainage channels during severe rainfall events resulting in numerous false alerts by EDs in the channels. This is further evidence of a scent print associated with mines. If erosion channels are present on slopes, scent from buried sources may be concentrated in them and these features should be searched carefully. SDs may alert downslope of the source so that an excavation carried out at the point of an alert may not find the source. It is useful for the dog to be trained to find the position of the strongest scent which is most likely close to the source (Figure 5.4). Strategies to narrow the source location are to work the dog from different directions, especially downslope toward the initial alert, use multiple dogs, return under more favorable or different conditions and, if the source is not hazardous, vent the soil by probing upslope of the initial alert.

If a buried source is in unsaturated soil above a water table, the vapor plume, dissolved soil water plume, insoluble liquids, and micro-particulates may eventually penetrate to the water table as shown in Figures 5.3 and 5.5. Insoluble liquids and micro-particulates lighter than water would float on the water table and the dissolved soil water plume would mix with the water. Buoyant and dissolved materials would be transported with groundwater flow. Non-buoyant liquids and micro-particulates would sink below the water table while being carried along by groundwater flow.

If a source is buried below the water table (not common) or the water table rises above the source after burial, buoyant insoluble liquids and micro-particulates would be expected to rise to the water table and be transported downstream by groundwater flow. Non-buoyant insoluble liquids and micro-particulates would move downward by gravity and downstream in groundwater flow. In either case of a source above or below the water table, if there is groundwater flow, scent can be transported underground for long distances.

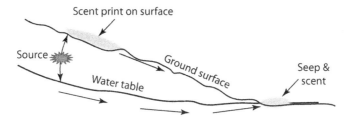

Figure 5.5 Scent print transported downslope of a buried source by surface run off. Underground water flow can transport scent to downslope seeps or springs that are often found at the toe of slopes and along the shores and banks of lakes and rivers.

Vass (2012) reported decomposition VOCs at a distance of 1/2 mile from human remains. Scent can be brought to the surface in seeps and springs that occur on slopes often at the toe of the slope (Figure 5.5) and along the banks of lakes and rivers, usually near the water level. These seeps, springs, and lake and river banks in a search area should be carefully checked by SD teams for the presence of scent.

5.2 Scent Movement in Soils

5.2.1 Processes

Scent movement to the surface from sources buried at shallow depths (typically <2 ft) is complex, involving soil and source properties, a host of processes associated with physical, chemical, biological components, and weather effects. The complexity and level of scientific background required to address these processes and lack of information on buried sources, except for explosives and some contaminants, make it difficult to develop an understanding of scent movement associated with buried sources. The following is an attempt to present scent transport processes in terms that are more accessible and familiar to SD handlers. For the most part, observable information (soil, vegetation, terrain, and weather) is used to evaluate site conditions, potential search times, and search methods. It is a limited qualitative approach that does not address all the processes involved. However, it may allow handlers to develop a better understanding of scent transport in some of the conditions and settings where they work.

For more information, Jenkins et al. (2000) summarized the results of laboratory and field research from an extensive study of buried land mines at Ft. Leonard Wood, Missouri. Phelan and Webb (2002) provided a comprehensive summary of the behavior of TNT, DNT, and DNB from mines in soil which includes laboratory and field research, modeling of scent transport, availability of scent at the soil surface, and the use of EDs. A detailed field study of the effects of environmental and other variables on the detection of mines by EDs in Afghanistan was conducted by Sargisson et al. (2012). Rivett et al. (2011) reviewed the movement of VOCs, primarily contaminants in unsaturated soils. Some of these contaminants are associated with decomposition and other sources.

Transport processes for VOCs in unsaturated soils from buried sources are broadly classified as diffusion and advection in the gas and water phases as shown in Figure 5.6. Diffusion is the movement of VOCs at the molecular level in all directions (radially) away from the source. It is often the dominant mode of scent transport in the gas phase. Advection refers to the bulk movement (currents) of air and water containing scent.

Evapotranspiration refers to evaporation of water at the soil surface and transpiration of water from vegetation. These processes dry the soil at and near the surface and produce a gradient in water content that pulls (wicks) water and dissolved scent upward. Infiltration of precipitation by gravity moves water and dissolved scent downward. Transport of micro-particulates could occur in the water phase and downward by gravity but there is

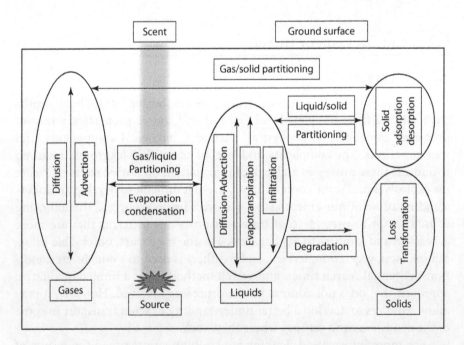

Figure 5.6 A conceptual model of VOC vertical transport processes in unsaturated soil. Vertical arrows represent processes that result in vertical flow upward or downward. Horizontal arrows represent processes that redistribute the phases or remove VOCs from the flow. (Modified from Phelan and Webb 2002.)

no information on this topic. If the source is wet, such as a recently buried cadaver, the possible presence and transport of insoluble liquids would have to be considered.

Horizontal double ended arrows (Figure 5.6) represent reversible partitioning between gas, water, and solid phases because of volatilization/dissolution and adsorption/desorption. There are several degradation processes that remove VOCs from the flow (single ended arrows in Figure 5.6) by transformation and loss by chemical reactions, microbial biodegradation, and plant root uptake. The amount of scent flowing to the surface can be significantly reduced by these processes, especially if the half-life of the VOC is short compared to the time required for it to reach the surface.

On exiting the soil surface, the scent passes through any ground cover and a surface boundary layer into the atmosphere where conditions can vary greatly between day and night and seasonally.

5.2.2 Gradient Transport in Unsaturated Soil

VOCs in the gas phase and those dissolved in pore water and water films on soil particle surfaces can move in the air and water by diffusion and be carried by advection in moving air and water. Computer-assisted modeling is required to predict the complexities of scent movement. A limited understanding can be obtained by considering the effects of changes in quantities that are observable under field conditions. In this simplified approach, scent movement is a result of gradients (differences) in temperature (T), moisture (M), pressure (P), and chemical concentration (C) of VOCs (Marshall and Holmes 1979). Like heat, scent flow is in the direction from high values to low values. The movement is influenced by the magnitude of the gradients, properties of the VOCs, soil properties, and the effects of external conditions, primarily weather. The effects of gravity on micro-particulates and insoluble liquids such as insoluble decomposition fluids depend on whether they are lighter or heavier than water and have been discussed above.

Chemical properties are unique to the VOC, vary significantly between VOCs, and depend on temperature and water content, among other factors. These considerations make it problematic to extrapolate information for one VOC to others. Soil properties are strongly dependent on soil types and water content. Variations in weather can influence scent transport at shallow depths in the soil by causing changes in temperature, water content, pressure, and chemical concentrations over all time scales.

Gradient movement can occur both upward and downward. Our primary interest is in upward movement which requires that surface values be less than those at depth. These gradients are responsible for moving air and water containing VOCs to the surface where they move from the near-surface soil into ground cover and a boundary layer in the air above.

Temperature gradients transport VOCs in air and water from warmer to cooler soil so that cooler surface temperatures compared to the source temperatures result in scent transport out of the soil which creates favorable search conditions. These conditions can be caused by nighttime cooling of the ground surface, short term weather changes, and seasonal effects. If the source is not too deep (about a foot or two depending on soil properties), nighttime surface cooling can cause temperature gradients later at night and during early morning, with source temperatures warmer than the ground surface temperatures. These temperature gradients initially cause water vapor, gas phase VOCs, and water films containing VOCs to move toward the surface and create favorable conditions for scent flow out of the surface in the late night and early morning hours before the sun heats the surface. SD handlers have noted improved detection of buried sources at these times.

Soil temperatures can lead to competing effects in scent transport. For example, an increase in temperature causes an increase in volatilization rates but concurrent soil drying with adsorption of VOCs on soil particle surfaces may not result in an increase in the availability of scent. Degradation rates are greater at warmer temperatures, but at colder soil temperatures volatility is lower and less scent is available. Freezing conditions may halt VOC degradation. Degradation by-products may be detectable by SDs but there is little information on this topic.

Dry soils typically adsorb large amounts of VOCs on soil particle surfaces and leave a residue that reduces available scent levels. As the water content increases, water replaces the VOCs adsorbed on the soil particle surfaces and releases them for possible transport to the surface and atmosphere. As the soil becomes wetter, gas pore space is reduced, gas phase transport decreases, and water phase transport increases.

Laboratory experiments have shown that increasing the humidity of dry soils can release huge quantities of VOCs adsorbed on the soil particle surfaces (Petersen et al. 1996). Surface flux changes of about 3 orders of magnitude (10^3 = 1000 times) for DNT have also been observed during wetting and drying events (Phelan et al. 2001). This indicates that favorable times to search for sources buried in dry soils are late night and early morning when air humidity is high, when dew is present, or after a light rain. Informal experiments have shown that misting a dry soil surface can substantially improve scenting conditions for explosives and suggest that this may also be possible for other buried sources provided that the soil/air partition coefficients are large for the VOCs associated with these sources.

Pressure gradients can transport scent out of the soil surface, provided the pressure at the surface is less than the pressure at the source and the scent is in the gas phase. These pressure gradients can be caused by reductions in barometric pressure, rising tides, wind, and other factors. Consequently, search conditions are more favorable when the barometer is falling or low, tides are rising in tidal zones, and when the wind is strong and variable.

Chemical gradients transport scent in the gas phase and solutes in the water phase from regions of higher to lower scent concentrations (i.e. away from the source in all directions including upward flow toward the surface and downward below it).

In the absence of precipitation, evapotranspiration tends to dry the uppermost soil. The resulting gradient in water content draws water vapor and water in films containing dissolved VOCs to the soil surface where evaporation continues. Evaporation is a distillation process that leaves the VOCs behind where they may volatilize directly into the air as scent or be adsorbed on soil particle surfaces to be released later under favorable conditions. Evaporation may be largely responsible for the surface scent print observed over mines.

VOC half-lives decrease rapidly with increases in soil water content from dry conditions and as soil temperatures increase above freezing. Some hydrocarbons associated with decomposition have half-lives less than a year. If the half-life of source VOCs is much less than the time required for them to move from the source to the soil surface, the amount that reaches the surface may be much less than that available near the source and some VOCs will never reach the surface.

The presence of the soil surface interrupts transport of VOCs upward and can result in accumulation of water and VOCs there. This can modify the gradients in water content and chemical concentrations and even cause them to reverse locally and result in a local backflow downward. Condensation or evaporation at the surface may also occur and modify the gradients and make it impossible to thoroughly evaluate scent transport in the field.

Scent movement can be restricted artificially. Landfills that are compacted daily and then covered by specially designed soil caps that do not allow flow of gases including scent through them are an example. Searches for bodies in these landfills is an almost hopeless task unless the cap is disrupted, the garbage removed in layers and made accessible to the dogs, and the dogs are allowed access to underlying material. This type of search is hazardous to the dogs.

5.3 Soil–Air Interface

5.3.1 Boundary Layers

The boundary layers of interest for buried sources are associated with surface roughness elements such as pebbles and large rocks and vegetation consisting of leaves, grass, weeds, and bushes. These roughness elements produce turbulent boundary layers somewhat greater than their height above the ground surface. There are several types of boundary layers over buried sources including those for water vapor and scent. For smooth, flat, and level bare soil with no wind, and surface temperature less than air temperatures (inversion present), the scent boundary layer thickness for buried explosives is thought to be less than an inch (Phelan and Webb 2002). Boundary layer characteristics are influenced by the ground cover and weather (primarily wind speed and radiation) and possibly by the actions of the dog exhaling (Figure 2.3) and movement that create temporary local air currents just above the surface. Boundary layer thicknesses decrease with increasing wind speed. Solar radiation, when present, warms the ground surface which warms the air in contact with it. Colder air above with warmer air at the surface is an unstable condition that results in small scale thermal convection that mixes scent from the ground surface, with the air above possibly moving it upward out of reach of dogs. The magnitude of this effect depends primarily on the temperature difference between the soil surface and the air.

On bare soil, the effects of air stability and wind on scent from a buried source start to become important as the scent exits the soil and boundary layer and enters the atmosphere (Figure 5.7). For stable conditions with soil surface temperatures cooler than the air and no wind (typical of conditions at night, when the surface is in shade and cloudy days), an inversion may form and scent would be expected to pool over the source in a thin inversion layer. If a small depression is present the thickness of the scent boundary layer may be much greater than that for a flat surface, probably as thick as the depth of the depression. When ground cover is present it would also

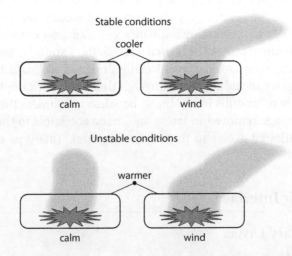

Figure 5.7 Scent movement over bare ground above a buried source showing the effects of solar radiation, air stability, and wind on the scent plume. The surface is cooler than air temperatures for stable conditions and warmer for unstable conditions.

be thicker, probably approaching the thickness of the ground cover. If the ground cover is dense, it may be useful to wait for convective instability or wind that would help move the scent upward so the dog could detect it. With sufficient wind, the scent layer would be disrupted, and a scent plume would form downwind where it would be more easily detected.

Stable calm conditions require the dog to search with its nose close to the ground surface and to be almost directly over the source to detect the scent. These search requirements are similar when a depression exists over an older grave since the depression traps scent in it during the night under relatively calm conditions. The scent remains in the depression until it is removed by wind or convective turbulence. These conditions make it desirable to select search dogs for buried sources that show a tendency for nose to ground searching and to use training methods that produce dogs proficient in this type of searching. Hound breeds and some dogs of other breeds do this naturally.

For unstable conditions with soil surface temperatures warmer than the air and no wind (typical of conditions when the surface is in sunlight with your shadow <1½ times your height), convective instability would form a vertical plume over the source. With wind speed much greater than the rise velocity of air in the plume (typically about 1 ft/sec), the vertical plume would be bent toward the horizontal where it would be more easily detected.

For unstable and calm conditions, the dog's nose could be elevated but it would have to pass through or close to the vertical plume over the source to detect it. The above conditions indicate that search lanes would have to be narrow, perhaps only a few yards for large sources and even smaller for small sources, to obtain a high POD. Stable and unstable conditions with wind that produces a scent plume at the dog's level allow SDs to detect the plume some distance downwind with its head elevated using much wider search lanes.

5.3.2 Ground Covers

Ground cover effects are associated primarily with low lying vegetation in contact with the soil such as live organics (plants, moss, grass, weeds), dead organics (leaf litter, dead plants), and the effects of a transient snow cover. Bare ground is exposed to atmospheric conditions while ground cover mitigates their effects on the underlying soil by shading the soil, insulating it, and reducing the amount of solar radiation that reaches the surface. This results in lower surface temperatures and decreased evaporation from the surface. Ground cover can absorb water, increase surface wetness, and influence water content in the subsurface. It influences scent behavior when scent exits the soil surface and passes through the ground cover into the air.

CDs often show a change of behavior when sniffing grasses, weeds, shrubs, and especially tree trunks near a buried body. There are two hypotheses to explain this behavior. One is that VOCs from the buried source are taken in by plant roots, carried to the stem and leaves, and volatilize into the air where they can be detected. This is a complex process that requires nutrient VOCs from the source to contact the roots, be absorbed, travel through the plant to the leaves, and volatilize into the air. The second is that VOCs present in the air above a buried source collect on nearby plant surfaces where they can be dislodged by air jets from the dog's nose or volatilized and be detected by dogs sniffing these surfaces. While it is known that chemicals can be absorbed through the roots and enter plants (Carter et al. 2014), the second hypothesis is simpler but there does not appear to be any data confirming either hypothesis and one or both may be true.

Information on the characteristics of a scent plume moving from the soil into a surface cover is limited. Sargisson et al. (2012) showed that detection success decreased with increasing vegetative cover near a mine. If the vegetation allowed the surface to dry and was sufficiently sparse so that dogs could get their noses close to the ground, then a mine search could still be done. Spiky plants and plant smells near the mine had no significant effects on detection success for sparse plants.

Informal experiments with a cover of grass suggested that the boundary layer thickness was about the same as the thickness of the grass cover. For article searches in tall grass in Florida, it has been hypothesized that sunlight was needed to produce convective (turbulent) transport out of the grass (Mesloh and James-Mesloh 2006). Convection would facilitate scent movement upward, in and above grass for the dogs to detect scent without having to place their noses deep in the grass. This may also be true for other types of dense vegetation (taller grass, weeds, small shrubs). Scenting conditions with little or no wind and vegetation higher than the dog's head are very difficult. Experience with hunting dogs suggests that a dog must almost step on a bird to find it under these conditions. There does not appear to be any information on the boundary layer associated with leaves or needles on a forest floor.

Snow covers can be classified for our purposes as wet or dry, windblown or not, and compacted snow. Wet snow covers are associated with snow that falls under warm conditions, with daily warming, or warming weather events that cause internal and surface melting. In some regions, melting during daylight hours and refreezing at night is common. This can produce impermeable ice lenses in the snow that retard or prevent flow of scent to the snow surface.

Dry snow covers are associated with cold climates and/or high elevations where subfreezing temperatures are common and continuous. It is a low-density snow that favors scent movement. Dry snow is such a good insulator that a thickness of 2 ft can cause ground surface temperatures to rise to a few degrees below freezing with subzero air temperatures. This creates a large temperature gradient that favors scent transport out of the snow. Windy conditions cause snow to drift. The action of wind on snow is to fragment snow crystals into tiny particles that bond together to form a hard, dense surface layer of snow (wind slab) that retards the movement of scent.

Compacted snow includes avalanched snow, ploughed snow berms along roads, and snow dumps that result from clearing travel routes and other areas in northern cities. Snow dumps can be dangerous to search because chemicals, needles, broken glass, and other hazardous materials are collected with the snow. Compacted snow severely retards scent transport. However, dogs have demonstrated the ability to find live people and cadavers in avalanched snow within minutes of being buried. It is proposed herein that this ability is a result of the settling that occurs when a flowing avalanche consisting of snow and a large volume of air stops moving. On settling, most of the air would be forced out of the snow to the surface carrying the scent of a buried victim with it. The expired air would leave a trapped scent plume in the snow above the victim and scent on the surface of the snow that dogs could detect. This process would not apply to slab type avalanches.

Generally, subfreezing air temperatures cause the soil water in pores to freeze from the surface downward. Except for dry soils, freezing partially or completely blocks the movement of scent. Moss, vegetation, and dry snow are good thermal insulators, and act like a blanket that tends to keep the soil surface warmer than the air temperature. Consequently, soil under a layer of moss, vegetation, or snow may be unfrozen even when air temperatures are below freezing so that searches for buried sources in these conditions can sometimes be successful. Probing the soil is the only sure way to determine if the soil is frozen or not.

When there is little or no snow cover with subfreezing air temperatures, fine grained frozen soils tend to contract and crack. Contraction cracking can allow scent to escape directly to the atmosphere provided that the cracks penetrate to the buried source. Cracks deeper than 3 ft have also been observed to form in agricultural soils under hot and dry conditions, and when they occur in a search area, they should be checked for scent. If source scent is detected above a crack, the source may be directly below the alert or some distance from it because of possible lateral movement of scent in the crack.

5.4 Searching for Buried Sources

This section examines the effects of soil, vegetation, and weather on searches for buried sources and compares conditions that would result in lower or higher PODs. The effort is hampered for at least two reasons. First, except for some explosives and drugs, it is not generally known what chemicals are used by the dogs to detect specific sources. Since the chemicals are unknown, their physical and chemical properties that influence scent movement cannot be determined. For example, phase partition coefficients determine the relative quantities of the chemicals in each phase (gas or liquid) and adsorbed on soil particles. If the chemicals are unknown, the coefficients are unknown so that scent movement and adsorption effects in soils cannot be evaluated. Second, the influence of different types of ground cover, vegetation, and small-scale thermal turbulence on scent movement and plume behavior are not well known which makes it difficult to evaluate scent movement from the soil surface to the dog's nose. Consequently, the following comparisons on the effects of soil, weather, and vegetation on detector dog searches may change as more information becomes available. The information used in these comparisons is partly anecdotal (primarily from K9 handlers), a result of laboratory and field research, and from modeling studies.

Jenkins et al. (2000) have shown that the chemicals associated with TNT in mines are distributed unevenly around the mine, decrease rapidly in concentration upward, and some may not reach the ground surface. The gradient processes described above are responsible for upward movement of the chemicals through the soil. Degradation processes cause decreasing concentrations upward that can prevent some chemicals from reaching the surface. These gradient and degradation processes are controlled by the properties of the soil and scent and by the weather which collectively determine the type, amount, and rate of chemical movement to the ground surface. Consequently, it is necessary to consider these processes, properties, and weather effects to understand how source chemicals move from the source to the ground surface.

The results of Jenkins et al. (2000), Hewitt et al. (2001), and Sargisson et al. (2012) indicate that DNT from buried mines is concentrated in the surface soil, forming a scent print. The sources of VOCs evolving into the air above buried sources are the VOCs adsorbed on the surface soil particles (i.e. in the scent print), VOCs in the gas phase that transit to the soil surface from below, and VOCs produced by volatilization of soil water at the soil surface. The relative importance of site and environmental conditions on these processes that produce detectable scent for SDs are not well known which makes it difficult to evaluate the best times to perform searches.

It has been noted (Chapter 2) that the scenting methods used by SDs to detect sources involve direct sniffing of source VOCs and actively using exhalation air jets to extract VOCs from surfaces and particulates. Exhalation air jets on surfaces that are dry and dusty or have loose particulates on them disturb the surface materials so that dogs can inhale them and extract adsorbed VOCs. It is not likely that this process would be efficient on moist surfaces. This implies that soil, weather effects, and other factors determine the amount of scent available for detection. These considerations may hold for other sources but there is little information available except for some hazardous chemicals that are also associated with decomposition.

5.4.1 Searching

Searches for buried sources are usually planned, except for the military, and a common strategy is to select a time when conditions would be optimal for dogs to detect and locate the source. In addition to the difficulties noted above, others exist partly because of a lack of quantitative information on what constitutes optimal conditions and partly because of uncertainty in predicted weather conditions at the time of the proposed search. For the most part, we can only define search conditions qualitatively: those that have a lower probability of success and those that have a higher probability. We cannot state a reliable value for those probabilities.

Favorable times to detect a buried source are when working and scenting conditions are good and when the scent is likely to be available to detect. Working and scenting conditions are good when the dogs do not become physically or mentally stressed and poor when they do. Examples of poor conditions include high temperatures, dusty conditions, muddy ground, thick or thorny vegetation, steep terrain, and too much interference by the handler while the dog is searching. The availability of scent above the surface of a buried source depends on its movement through the soil, ground cover, and as a plume in the atmosphere. If scent has accumulated in a scent print at the surface, its availability would depend on conditions favorable for volatilization at the surface (Cousins et al. 1999).

Scent from a shallow buried source spreads laterally in the soil as it rises to the surface where it can create a surface scent print somewhat larger than the source. The size of the surface scent print is of interest to SD handlers since it helps to define the width of the search lanes to be used. If the search lanes are too wide, POD for the source will be reduced. Lane widths for shallow buried sources appear to depend primarily on the horizontal dimensions of the source and weather (especially atmospheric stability and wind, see Figure 5.7). As the density of surface vegetation (grasses, weeds, prickly vegetation), depth of burial, and desired POD increases, lane widths should decrease. Wind makes it possible to use a greater lane width for a given set of conditions. The experience and reliability of the team can also be important in selecting lane widths.

Lane widths for SDs used in demining operations are set by the agency or country that oversees these operations (GICHD 2004). The dogs are trained to work on long leads (about 9 to 12 yds) or on short leads. Long lead dogs work in lanes about 1.5 yds wide although the handler has some discretion in choosing the width. They are taught to go out from the handler to the end of the leash in the lane being searched, return in the previously searched lane, and move to the next unsearched lane. Short lead dogs work in lanes about 0.5 yds wide. The handler walks in the previously searched lane while the dog on lead searches the next lane. The handlers attempt to work the dogs in lanes across the wind and may change the direction with changes in wind direction. Each lane is searched by 2 dogs. Other patterns include circular, semi-random, and free ranging.

Limited information on lane widths for buried bodies and other large sources appear to range from about 2 to 10 or more yds depending on conditions. Searches for bones, teeth, fired shell cases, and other small sources need smaller lane widths. In searches for teeth placed on the ground surface, 3 dogs searching on leash using a lane width just under 2 yds, and with cross gridding on a windy day (16 mph average speed) recovered a maximum of 78% of the teeth (Cablk and Sagebiel 2011).

Linear searches (along paths, trails, roads, edges of structures, or natural features like vegetation, fields, shorelines, etc.) are best done on the downwind side of the feature being searched. If there is a steep nearly vertical wall (formed by vegetation, terrain, or a structure), searches on the downwind side should be close along the wall. On the upwind side, they should be some distance away from the wall.

Sun shining on a wall, steep surface, or vertical vegetation (e.g. trees, Figure 3.1) heats the surface which heats the adjacent air and causes it to rise along the surface. Under calm conditions, this effect carries scent near the wall upward and out of reach of a dog. For windy conditions, sun and wind produce opposing air currents on the upwind side and reinforce air currents on the downwind side which makes it difficult to evaluate the resulting scent movement.

A method often used in area searches by CD handlers is to first do a free-ranging search through the area. The team starts on the downwind side with a coarse grid and checks any likely places for a burial. If nothing is detected, the handler then uses a fine grid with lanes running crosswind.

Searches for some sources (e.g. explosives) can be extremely hazardous and require special methods.

5.4.2 Soil Conditions

Environmental conditions such as soil, weather, vegetation, and terrain are site specific and the availability of scent depends on the chemicals (VOCs) in the scent and how these interact with the local environmental conditions. This implies that results from field studies and modeling will be site specific and will depend on the type of source. Care must be taken when extrapolating results from one site to another and for results from one type of source to another when attempting to define optimum times and conditions for conducting searches. For example, computer modeling results and the conclusions of field studies for one type of source may not hold for different locations and climates or for VOCs associated with different sources. These characteristics, especially partitioning between phases, diffusion rates, evaporation, degradation, and loss in the soil, influence VOC movement in soils and the availability of scent in the air above the soil. Consequently, while the results shown in Tables 5.2 to 5.4 are based on general conditions, some may not hold for all sources in all places. Table 5.2 compares the effects of soil conditions, source size, and depth of burial on PODs for buried sources.

Gravity is always present and would move scent downward, especially during infiltration. Lighter than air scent molecules in unsaturated soils and buoyant materials in saturated soils would move scent upward.

Large chemical concentration gradients exist near a source that can move scent rapidly by diffusion over short time periods (Rivett et al. 2011). Vertical movement as a result of chemical gradients will be upward above the source and downward below it. Above the source, movement by concentration gradients may be changed or temporarily reversed by temperature, moisture, and pressure gradients that move scent toward the source.

Weather conditions for shallow burials are important in determining whether the net movement will be upward or downward. Consider the gradients to result from the difference between the values at the buried source and at the ground surface. Maximum upward scent flow occurs when all the gradients near the surface cause upward flow (T, M, P at the surface are less than at the source) and minimum when all the gradients cause downward flow (T, M, P at the surface are greater than at the source).

These relatively simple conditions can become complex because of transient effects produced daily and by changing weather conditions that modify the near-surface gradients. During the day, solar radiation increases soil surface temperature and evaporation. At night, radiation to space decreases soil surface temperature and may result in condensation (dew). In addition, changing weather (barometer, wind, rain) can modify the near-surface gradients which can change near-surface scent concentrations. Scent movement is extremely difficult to determine when the separate gradients cause flow in different directions and computer-assisted modeling is required to evaluate it.

Table 5.2 Comparison of the Effects of Soil Conditions, Source Size, and Depth of Burial on PODs for Buried Sources

Soil	Lower POD	Higher POD
Gradients	T, M, P at surface > at source	T, M, P at surface < source
Type	Clay or silt	Sand or gravel
Water content	Dry	Moist
Organic content	Large	Small
Thermal condition	Frozen	Unfrozen
Source size	Small source	Large source
Source depth	Deep burial	Shallow burial

Lower PODs do not mean that the source cannot be detected but that detection is less likely than for higher PODs. Water content is that between the source and surface.

Increasing organic contents of soils increases the amount of scent adsorbed and leaves it less available for detection. However, the level of scent removed may not make it impossible to detect a source. Information on soil types can be obtained from agricultural soil maps and can be helpful in planning a search and interpreting the results. Fine-grained soils such as clays and silts are less permeable to scent flow than coarser soils like sand and gravel. Where soil types vary locally or are intermixed, this knowledge may be less useful. Ice in frozen soil can block the scent flow, as noted, unless the soil is dry.

Sargisson et al. (2012) have shown that detection success increases with increasing size of mines containing TNT and decreases with increasing depth of burial. The latter result may be attributed to degradation processes in the soil. Both results appear to hold for other buried sources.

5.4.3 Weather Conditions

Weather conditions that influence scent transport from buried sources to the atmosphere include wind, barometric pressure, air temperature, radiation, humidity, and precipitation including snow (Table 5.3). These conditions are important because they influence scent transport processes through their effects on soil conditions at depth, at the ground surface, in ground cover, and in the air above.

Table 5.3 Comparison of the Effects of Weather Conditions on PODs for Buried Sources

	Lower POD	Higher POD
Wind	Calm or strong, gusty wind	Light wind (5 to 10 mph)
Air pressure	Barometer rising	Barometer falling
Air pressure	Falling tide	Rising tide
Temperature	<32°F or >80°F	>32°F or <65°F
Sun	Sunny	Cloudy
Sun (stability) and wind	Sunny, wind <4 mph, unstable air (shadow <1½ h)	Partly cloudy (cc >4/8), light wind (5 to 10 mph), stable air (shadow >1½ h)
Humidity	Low (<20%)	Higher (>20%)
Precipitation	Heavy rain	Dew or light rain
Precipitation	Wet snow, melted and refrozen, wind slab, or >1 ft deep	Dry powder snow, never melted, no wind slab, or <1 ft deep
Timing	Summer, afternoon	Summer, late evening, night, or early morning or fall, winter, or early spring

Lower PODs do not mean that the source cannot be detected but that detection is less likely than higher PODs. Note: h is not hours, it is the handler's height.

5.4.3.1 Wind

Consider the effects of wind only. Calm (no wind) means there is no scent plume. Fortunately, this condition is rare. There is usually a slight wind drift with low wind speed and random direction that produces a meandering scent plume which makes it somewhat easier to find the source. Strong winds with swirling and gusting elements that distort, fragment, dilute, and redirect the scent plume make it difficult to find the source. Light winds (5 to 10 mph) produce a well-defined scent plume that make it easier to find and follow the plume to the source (France et al. 1997; Ruzicka and Conover 2011).

5.4.3.2 Pressure Gradients

Both diffusion and advection may be important in moving soil gases and scent to the surface. An increased outflow of soil gases (air, water vapor, scent) is expected with decreasing air pressure at the ground surface and increasing air pressure at the water table. Decreasing air pressure at the ground surface can result from a falling barometer and wind (Bernoulli effect). Increasing air pressure at the water table can result from a rising water table such as that caused by a rising tide. Whatever the cause, if there is little scent in the gas phase (as with TNT), additional scent flow due to advection would be small. Since the VOCs used by dogs to detect buried cadavers are unknown, partitioning between gas, water, and soil phases cannot be determined. This makes it impossible to evaluate the effects of air pressure in transporting scent to the soil surface over buried cadavers and many other sources.

Considering only wind and barometric pressure, if there is little or no wind, decreasing barometric pressure would dominate movement of scent in the gas phase to the surface. If there is constant barometric pressure with significant wind, wind effects would dominate, and if there is decreasing barometric pressure coupled with strong wind, pressure effects for bringing scent to the surface would be optimal but not necessarily significant.

It appears that wind dominates where significant wind occurs over agricultural soils. This may be due to tillage in these soils which makes them more permeable to the flow of soil gases. Soil permeability is also greater over buried sources because of the disturbed soil so that windy conditions may help bring scent to the surface over them. This also suggests that wind over coarse sands and gravels may be effective in bringing scent in the gas phase to the surface.

5.4.3.3 Air Temperatures

5.4.3.3.1 Warm Temperatures When scent concentrations are low and scenting conditions poor, panting may reduce the ability of SDs to detect a source. However, experience has shown that they can still find a buried source if they are close to it (within about a yard) and if the soil is moist (France et al. 1997; also see Figure 5.7).

Lasseter et al. (2003) conducted a study of CDs in Alabama during July and August when air temperatures ranged from 82°F to 93°F with humidity of 55% or more. Results showed that hot weather and high humidity always influenced the performance of the dogs even with multiple breaks and water available. Handler experience suggests that at temperatures <65°F, dogs can do light work without thermal stress.

Handlers can cause emotional stress in SDs and reduce their performance by using too many commands, getting irritated with the dog, and failing to let the dog work.

5.4.3.3.2 Cold Temperatures and Snow   Results from France et al. (1997) are that temperatures limit the ability of dogs to detect scent at a distance if the source is buried in soil. For sources buried in snow with air temperatures that allow little or no melting, the dogs had to be within a yard of the source to detect and find it. If there was significant melting, the dogs could locate the source from a greater distance. With sources buried in snow or in soil below snow, and air temperatures below freezing, the dogs may not be able to locate the source. While the details and data of this study are not fully known, it appears likely that snow thickness and the permeability of the snow to scent (determined by snow type and age, internal structure, previous melting and refreezing events, presence of ice layers) may have influenced the results. Air temperatures below freezing are not always sufficient to freeze the ground since undisturbed snow is such a good insulator.

Aspnes and Aspnes (1998) conducted a study in Interior Alaska where snow is typically less dense (powder), not refrozen, has no ice lenses, and is more permeable. The results showed that dogs could locate a cadaver source on the ground surface buried in snow at temperatures of −25°F and at distances of 25 yds or more. Handler experience with SDs in Interior Alaska indicates that dogs have no difficulty performing scent work with sources buried in snow at temperatures less than −30°F.

The study of Komar (1999), which tested the ability of CDs to detect cadaver sources on the ground surface covered with litter, showed that temperatures warmer than −22°F and snow depths up to a foot had no effect on performance. Familiarity with sources and experience in these terrains and conditions did influence performance.

If the soil is moist and frozen from the surface downward, the presence of ice in the pore spaces would generally block scent from moving upward and make it difficult to impossible for dogs to detect a buried source. If the soil is dry and frozen, the pore spaces would not be blocked by ice and it may still be possible to detect a buried source.

5.4.3.4 Wind and Sun (Air Stability)

The effects of wind and atmospheric stability on scent plumes have been noted previously. France et al. (1997) found if there was no wind, dogs had difficulty detecting a source unless they were within about a yard of it. This result is expected when there is no wind for both stable and unstable conditions (Figure 5.7) and suggests that the scent print at the ground surface was about 1 to 2 yds across for the buried pigs used in the study. With enough wind (perhaps 3 to 5 mph) and a stable atmosphere, the layer of scent at the surface would be disrupted and form a scent plume downwind (Figure 5.7) which makes it more likely that the dogs would detect it. If the air is unstable with no wind, the scent plume would rise vertically and carry the plume out of reach of the dogs. The dogs would have to pass through or close to the plume to detect it. Detection is easier if the wind speed is sufficiently large to force the plume down near the level of the dog's nose. The study suggested that a wind speed of >5 mph is desirable although this result may be due to site conditions such as vegetation height and density that require a certain level of turbulence to move scent from the ground cover into a plume. When wind speed is high and the wind is gusting, extreme turbulence near the ground may distort, redirect, dilute, and fragment the scent plume and make it more difficult to detect it and to follow it to the source.

The length of a person's shadow is a rough measure of the air stability as discussed in Chapter 3. Stable air with no wind allows scent from a buried source to concentrate near the ground and stable air with wind produces a scent plume. Unstable air with no wind causes scent to rise vertically over the source and with wind produces a scent plume. Wind velocity much greater than the convective rise velocity can cause a vertical plume to be forced down to the level of the dog.

5.4.3.5 Humidity

Relative humidity depends strongly on temperature. Maximum relative humidity occurs about daylight when air temperatures are minimum and reaches a minimum about the time of maximum temperatures. Relative humidity near the ground surface can be dramatically different from that measured at chest height. If the relative humidity at chest height is 30% and the surface is 20°F warmer, the relative humidity just above the surface will be roughly half or about 15%. This makes it difficult to evaluate the impact of humidity and temperature measured at chest height on scenting conditions near the ground surface.

Studies on the effects of humidity on the ability of dogs to detect a buried source have produced complex and seemingly different conclusions. France et al. (1997) suggested that the humidity should be about 20% or higher for optimal scenting conditions in Colorado. Sargisson et al. (2012) conducted a detailed study of weather factors that influenced the ability of EDs to detect and find buried mines in Afghanistan for 5 periods during a year. Searches were conducted during the morning daylight hours only. For the conditions unique to this region, it was concluded that wind speed, air temperature, and relative humidity had no overall significant effects on detection success although humidity was deemed the most important.

The results indicated that high humidity produced somewhat poorer detection in this arid environment, except in the early daylight hours, when high humidity and dew on the ground surface appeared to facilitate detection (possibly by releasing adsorbed VOCs from the dry surface soil). The cool surface also favors upward scent movement in the soil. Detection success typically decreased with decreasing humidity until about 9 a.m. and then increased with decreasing humidity until midday when testing was halted for the day. The initial decrease in detection in early morning may have been caused by drying of the soil surface as it was warmed by the sun. A reduction in the availability of scent would have been caused by readsorption of VOCs and by reversal of the temperature gradient near the surface. Increased detection during later morning is thought to have been the result of the dogs actively desorbing surface scent molecules with their warm and humid breath. Another possibility is that the unstable air near the surface, as a result of solar heating, may have facilitated convective movement (thermal turbulence) upward of air and scent where it would be more accessible to the dogs.

The reasons for these apparently different results between the Colorado and Afghanistan studies have not been addressed. They could be due to the different physical and chemical properties of the VOCs associated with decomposition and explosives, presence of vegetation, small scale convective turbulence near the ground, scenting method used by the dogs, or the wicking effect associated with evaporation at the surface. It is known that humidity influences the availability of scent from explosives but there is a lack of quantitative information on the effects of humidity on other sources.

Humidity does not appear to have a significant effect on the scenting ability of the dogs over ranges encountered in the field (about 20 to 80%). Some handlers mist their dog's noses when humidity is low to improve their scenting ability, an untested hypothesis.

5.4.3.6 Precipitation

High humidity, dew, and light rain on dry soils release the adsorbed VOCs on the surface soils into the atmosphere which increase the availability of scent there by orders of magnitude as noted. Heavy rain dilutes the concentrations of near-surface VOCs, moves them downward as it infiltrates the soil, decreases availability of scent, and lowers POD. Light powder snow is permeable to scent while dense, wet snow, especially that which has been refrozen or contains ice layers, has low permeability to scent.

Table 5.4 Comparison of the Effects of Vegetation on PODs for Buried Sources

	Lower POD	Higher POD
Vegetation	Dense grass, weeds, brush	None or sparse
	Higher than a dog's head	Lower than a dog's head
	Cacti, thorns, prickly vegetation	None or sparse

5.4.4 Vegetation

Table 5.4 compares the effects of vegetation on POD for buried sources. Mesloh and James-Mesloh (2006) found that mid-mornings were the most productive time of day to search tall grass in Florida and hypothesized that the effect of dense vegetation on scent coming from articles on the soil surface was to allow scent to remain in the vegetation until wind and convective instability caused it to move upward and out of the cover. Typically, wind and instability do not develop until about mid-morning so this hypothesis suggests that in searches of areas that contain a significant vegetative ground cover, there should be an improvement in PODs during the morning.

If the ground cover is much higher than the dog's head, it may not be possible for the dog to detect a plume above the cover. Sargisson et al. (2012) concluded that the spikiness of plants surrounding a mine had no significant effect on detection success. When vegetation is dense and contains prickly types such as cacti, thorns, or briars, dogs and handlers may be reluctant or not able to penetrate them and leave these areas unsearched.

5.5 Summary

Scent from a buried source moves through the soil, ground cover, scent boundary layer, and into the air as a plume where it can be detected by a dog (Figure 5.1). The availability of scent in the air above a buried source depends on the properties of the soil and scent molecules and their interactions; on processes that occur in the soil, ground cover, and scent boundary layer; and on weather which influences scent movement through all media between the source and the dog's nose. Scent movement through the soil is constrained because it can only move in the pore spaces between soil particles while in the gas and water phases. Scent transport also depends on the rate of movement and on whether the VOCs are in the gas phase or the water phase (how they are distributed or partitioned between phases). In dry soil, VOCs are adsorbed on the soil particle surfaces as a kind of residue and are not free to move.

Scent is present as gases, dissolved in soil water, as insoluble liquids (from wet sources), and as source particulates. Soil water exists in soil pores and as thin water films on soil particle surfaces. Scent can move through soil as gases in the soil pores, as solutes dissolved in water films and pore water, as insoluble liquids, and as solids in the form of source particulates much smaller than the pore spaces (Figure 5.2). Physical properties of soils that influence scent movement include soil type, water content, temperature, organic content, and others.

Soil temperatures influence the chemical properties of soils and scent volatilization rates (availability of scent) largely through their effect on the vapor pressure of VOCs. Temperatures also influence the transport of VOCs in both the gas phase and when dissolved in the water. Soils with large amounts of organic material adsorb more scent than mineral soils which reduces the amount of scent available to move and makes it more difficult for dogs to detect sources buried in these soils.

The chemical properties of VOCs that influence scent availability and movement include vapor pressure, phase partition coefficients, diffusion coefficients, solubility, and degradability. Phase partition coefficients determine whether scent transport to the soil surface will be in the gas or water phase. For example, the primary components of TNT include TNT, DNT, and DNB. The phase partition coefficients for these chemicals in air in contact with water are small indicating that only a small fraction of a percent exists in the air with about 10% in the water phase and the rest adsorbed on soil particle surfaces that are not free to move. Since the water contains almost all the mobile chemicals, water phase transport dominates scent movement for TNT in dry soils.

Degradation processes in soils cause source VOCs to change form and chemical properties and can prevent them from reaching the soil surface. Soil mineral reactions, biological transformations, and plant root uptake are examples of these processes. Some VOCs degrade quickly with lifetime in soils measured in days. For example, the concentration of 2,4,6-TNT in soils is reduced by one half in about a day compared to about 26 days for 2,4-DNT indicating that 2,4-DNT is more likely to survive passage to the soil surface.

FBI data indicates that clandestine graves typically varied in depth from 1.5 to 2.5 ft were located a short distance from infrequently traveled roads or pathways, about 10 ft away from the closest large tree, surrounded by bushes or heavy foliage, and the corpse was usually clothed or wrapped in plastic and faced down. A conceptual model of the scent distribution associated with a grave is shown in Figure 5.3.

Since 2,4-DNT is the primary chemical in TNT that dogs use for detecting the explosive, Figure 5.4 indicates that the spatial distribution of this chemical in the surface soils is a surface "scent print" (Osterkamp 2020). If the ground surface over a buried source is level, the scent print is roughly circular, larger than the source and centered over it. On sloped ground, the scent print extends downslope from the source as shown in Figures 5.3 and 5.4. Figure 5.4 shows measured scent prints on gently sloping ground for antitank and antipersonnel land mines. The TMA-5 mine is roughly 7 × 8 in in size and produces a scent print roughly 2 × 2 ft in size or about 3 times the size of the mine. The PMA1A is about 3 × 4 in and produces a scent print about 1.7 ft wide and extends to 2.3 ft downslope or about 6 to 7 times the size of the mine. This scent print from a buried mine is unevenly distributed, and, on slopes, the highest values occur several inches downslope from the mine with the scent print extending 2 ft downslope within a year of burial. It is hypothesized herein that a similar scent print may exist for other buried sources.

If erosion channels are present on slopes, the surface scent from buried sources may be concentrated in them and these features should be searched carefully. These channels may cause EDs to alert significantly downslope of the source so that an excavation carried out at the point of an alert may not find the source. It is useful for the dog to be trained to find the position of the strongest scent which is most likely close to the source. Strategies to narrow the source location are to work the dog from different directions (especially downslope) toward the initial alert, use multiple dogs, return under more favorable or different conditions, and vent the soil by probing upslope of the initial alert. A dog should be present during the excavation of an alert site to provide direction for the digging effort.

Scent that penetrates downward to flowing underground water can be transported long distances underground (at least ½ mile for human remains). It can be brought to the surface in seeps and springs that often occur at the bottom of slopes and along the banks of lakes and rivers, usually near the water level (Figure 5.5). These seeps, springs, and lake and river banks in a search area should be checked by SD teams for the presence of scent.

Scent movement to the surface from sources buried at shallow depths is complex and involves soil and source properties and a host of processes associated with physical, chemical, biological, and weather effects (Figure 5.6). This requires computer modeling. A simplified approach is developed that uses handler observable information (soil, vegetation, terrain, and weather) to evaluate site conditions, potential search times, and search methods. In this approach, scent movement in unsaturated soil is a result of gradients (differences) in temperature (T), moisture content (M), pressure (P), and chemical concentrations (C) of VOCs. Like heat, scent flows from high values to low values and upward movement requires that surface values be less than those at depth (Table 5.2).

Temperature gradients transport VOCs in air and water from warmer to cooler soil so that cooler surface temperatures compared to the source temperatures result in scent transport upward, which creates favorable search conditions. These conditions can be caused by nighttime cooling of the ground surface, short term weather changes, and seasonal effects. Temperature conditions are usually favorable for scent flow to the surface in the early morning hours, during cold spells, and during seasonal cold weather.

Pressure gradients can transport scent out of the soil surface, provided the pressure at the surface is less than the pressure at the source and the scent is in the gas phase. Pressure conditions are more favorable when the barometer is falling, tides are rising in tidal zones, and the wind is strong and variable.

In the absence of precipitation, evapotranspiration tends to dry the uppermost soil. The resulting gradient in M draws water vapor and water in films containing dissolved VOCs to the soil surface where evaporation continues. VOCs on the surface may volatilize directly into the air as scent or be adsorbed on soil particle surfaces to be released later under favorable conditions. Informal experiments have shown that misting a dry soil surface can dramatically improve scenting conditions for explosives and suggests that this may also be possible for some other buried sources. This indicates that a good time to search for sources buried in dry soils is early morning when air humidity is high, when dew is present or after a light rain.

Chemical gradients transport scent in the gas phase and solutes in the water phase from regions of higher to lower scent concentrations (i.e. away from the source in all directions including upward flow toward the surface).

The effects of air stability and wind on scent from a buried source become important as the scent enters the surface boundary layer (Figure 5.7). For stable air conditions with soil surface temperatures cooler than the air and no wind (typical of conditions at night, when the surface is in shade and cloudy days), an inversion may form, and scent would be expected to pool over the source in a thin inversion layer. With these conditions, dogs need to search with their noses close to the ground. For unstable conditions, soil surface temperatures warmer than the air, and no wind, convective instability would form a vertical plume over the source. Dogs can search with their heads up. For both stable and unstable conditions with no wind, dogs must pass very close to or over the source to detect it. When wind is present, dogs can detect the source in the downwind plume.

Snow can be wet or dry, windblown or not, and compacted. Wet snow that refreezes at night usually has ice lenses that retard or prevent flow of scent to the snow surface. Dry snow favors scent movement to the surface. Windy conditions produce a dense surface layer (wind slab) that retards the movement of scent. Compacted snow from some types of avalanches severely retards scent transport.

Dogs can find live people and cadavers in avalanched snow within minutes of being buried. It is hypothesized herein that this ability is a result of the settling that occurs when a flowing avalanche consisting of snow and a large volume of air stops moving. On settling, most of the air would be forced out of the snow to the surface carrying the scent of a buried subject with it. The expired air would leave a trapped scent plume in the snow above the subject and scent on the surface of the snow that dogs could use to detect and locate them.

Frozen soils partially or completely block the movement of scent. When snow is present, probing the soil surface is the only sure way to determine if the soil is frozen or not. Contraction cracking caused by freezing or drying soils can allow scent to escape directly to the atmosphere provided the cracks penetrate to the buried source.

In addition to the difficulties noted above, others exist partly because of a lack of quantitative information on what constitutes optimal conditions and partly because of uncertainty in predicted weather conditions at the time of the proposed search. For the most part, we can only define search conditions qualitatively: those that have a lower probability of success and those that have a higher probability. We cannot state a reliable value for those probabilities.

The sources of VOCs evolving into the air above buried mines are the VOCs adsorbed on the surface soil particles (i.e. in the scent print), VOCs in the gas phase that transit the soil from below, and VOCs produced by volatilization at the soil surface of soil water. When scent reaches the ground surface, weather effects and other factors that influence volatilization at the ground surface and in ground covers determine the amount of scent available for detection by SDs (i.e. favorable search strategies, times, and conditions for searching for buried sources).

Favorable times to detect a buried source are when working and scenting conditions are good and when the scent is likely to be available to detect. Working and scenting conditions are good when the dogs do not become physically or mentally stressed and poor when they do. Examples of poor conditions include high temperatures, dusty and windy conditions, muddy ground, thick or thorny vegetation, steep terrain, as well as too much interference by the handler while the dog is searching. The availability of scent above the surface of a buried source depends on whether enough scent can survive passage through the soil and ground cover.

The size of the surface scent print is of interest to SD handlers since it helps to define the width of the search lanes to be used. Search lanes too wide reduce POD and search lanes too narrow expend more of the team's energy and time than necessary. Lane widths for shallow buried sources appear to depend primarily on horizontal dimensions of the source and weather (especially atmospheric stability and wind, Figure 5.7). As the density of surface vegetation (grasses, weeds, prickly vegetation), depth of burial, and desired POD increases, lane widths should decrease. Wind makes it possible to use a greater lane width for a given set of conditions. The experience and reliability of the team is also important in selecting lane widths.

SDs used in demining operations are trained to work on long leads (about 9 to 12 yds) or on short leads. Long lead dogs work in lanes about 1.5 yds wide although the handler has some discretion in choosing the width. Short lead dogs work in lanes about 0.5 yds wide. The handlers always attempt to work the dogs in lanes across the wind and may change the lane direction with changes in wind direction. Other patterns that are used include circular, semi-random, and free ranging.

Limited information on lane widths for buried bodies and other large buried sources ranges from about 2 yds for poor conditions to about 10 yds or more for good conditions. Searches for bones, teeth, fired shell cases, small IEDs, and other small sources need smaller lane widths.

Linear searches (along paths, trails, roads, or natural features like vegetation, fields, shorelines, etc.) are best done on the downwind side of the feature being searched. A method often used in area searches by CD handlers is to first do a free ranging search through the area maximizing use of the wind and the team's experience. Start the team on the downwind side, use a coarse grid, and check any likely places for a buried source. If nothing is detected, set up a fine grid with lanes running crosswind.

The properties of soils and VOCs and interactions between them indicate that care must be taken when extrapolating results from one site to another and from one type of source to another.

Table 5.2 compares the effects of soil conditions, source size, and depth of burial that result in lower or higher PODs for buried sources. Lower PODs do not mean that the source cannot be detected but that detection is less likely than higher PODs. Higher PODs occur when T, M, and P at the surface are less than at the source, in sand, or in gravel soils that are moist, with low organic contents, unfrozen, for large sources, and shallow burial.

Weather conditions that influence scent movement from buried sources to the atmosphere include wind, barometric pressure, air temperature, radiation, humidity, and precipitation, including snow (Table 5.3). These conditions are important because they influence scent transport processes through their effects on soil conditions at depth, at the ground surface, in ground cover, and in the air above. Higher PODs occur when winds are light (5 to 10 mph); barometer is falling; tide is rising; $32°F < T < 65°F$; it is cloudy or sunny with light wind; humidity is >20%; there is dew or light rain; snow is dry powder, has never melted, has no wind slab, or is <1 ft deep; it is during summer in late evening, night, or early morning, or fall, winter, or early spring.

Table 5.4 compares the effects of vegetation on PODs for buried sources. Higher PODs occur when there is no vegetation; when it is sparse, lower than the dog's head; and when there is no prickly vegetation. Detection success in searches by EDs decreased with increasing vegetative cover near a mine. If the vegetation allowed the surface to dry and was sufficiently sparse so that the dogs could get their noses close to the ground, then a mine search could still be done.

Water Searches 6

6.1 Introduction

Dogs have been successful in detecting swimmers and cadavers underwater (Eisenhauer 1971; Stanley 1981), but there does not appear to be any published information on the use of dogs to search for explosives, drugs, and other materials in water. This chapter will focus on the use of dogs to detect scent from bodies underwater although the information would also be useful when searching for other underwater sources. Much of the material in Sections 6.1 through 6.2 has been extracted from Osterkamp (2011).

Water search dog teams are used to narrow the search area for recovery operations. The information the handler needs to provide to recovery agencies is the most likely location of the body based on the training, experience, and competence of the team. Information obtained with a water search dog team is not exact because of water depth, movement, and turbulence of the water; presence of an extended scent print (oily film) on the surface; and movement of the scent plume by wind. What is usually provided by the team is the location of a small area likely to contain the body. Scent from the body is transported to the water surface primarily by buoyancy and from the water surface to the air by volatilization and bubble bursting. It appears that these processes create a scent print on the water surface and scent plume in the air above the water surface. The handler's job is to use the dog to detect the scent plume and find the area on the water where the scent first comes to the surface. This information must then be interpreted by the handler to provide their best estimate of the location of the body.

Our understanding of the nature of scent, scent-bearing materials, and scent movement in water is incomplete. Consequently, it is not possible to state with certainty the nature of all scent sources, scent movement to the water surface, behavior of scent on the surface, how the scent gets into the air, and what it is that the dog smells. However, there is extensive literature on the behavior of gases, liquids, and solids in water that can be used to improve our current understanding. This chapter uses that literature to identify likely sources of scent and scent-bearing materials from submerged bodies, to suggest potential scent transport processes from bodies through the water to the air–water interface and thence into the air. The information is used to examine hypotheses about human scent in water, scent movement, and implications for water search dog training and deployment. Realistically, it can serve only in the interim until the necessary data from research specific to submerged human bodies is available.

6.1.1 The Body in Water

Drownings are classified as wet (water in the lungs) or dry (no water in the lungs). Dry drownings (<15% of drownings) may occur because the subject is dead on entering the water or because of the mammalian dive reflex which excludes water from the lungs. This dive reflex is associated with cold water and is more common in infants <1 year old (Teather 1994).

The body in water experiences forces that cause it to weigh less than in air, change shape and density, and move about in three dimensions. One cubic foot of freshwater weighs about 62.4 lbs at 32 to 60°F (64.1 lbs for seawater) and the pressure on its bottom surface is 0.433 psi (62.4 lbs/144 in^2) and 0.445 psi for seawater. For a column of water of depth, d (ft), the pressure at its bottom is 0.433 times d (0.445 times d, for seawater). At depth, d, this pressure acts equally in all directions. There is a misconception that water pressure "holds a body down" (i.e. there is a net downward force on the body). The above discussion indicates that the pressure at the top of a horizontal body is less (the depth is less) than at the bottom where depth is greater. This means that the body experiences a net upward pressure or force that is equal to the weight of the water it displaces. Thus, the effect of pressure on the body is to buoy it up rather than to hold it down. However, the body of a person who has just drowned is typically heavier than the water it displaces, so the body continues to sink until it reaches the bottom.

Another effect of pressure on a body is to compress it into a smaller volume, increasing its density. The reduced body volume displaces less water which decreases its buoyancy so that body weight increases with depth. About 100 bodies were weighed underwater to depths of 100 ft, and the results verified that there was an increase in weight with depth (Teather 1994). The experiment also showed that adults who weighed from 110 to 200 lbs weighed 7 to 16 lbs underwater. This weight was sufficient to resist movement by currents <1.5 mph (2.2 ft/sec). However, water velocity decreases close to the bottom and the depth where the velocity was measured was not stated. It is assumed herein that it is the velocity at the top of the body, roughly 1 ft above the bottom. Dry drownings would have air in the lungs, be more buoyant, move with less current, and may float earlier than wet drownings.

Generation of decomposition gases in the body causes its volume to increase which displaces more water and increases its buoyancy. The expanding body may eventually attain neutral buoyancy (zero weight) and then positive buoyancy causing it to rise. As it rises, decreasing pressure allows the body to expand more which increases its buoyancy and accelerates its ascent to the surface. For the subjects in the above experiment, neutral buoyancy requires decomposition gases to expand the body volume by about 190 to 440 cubic inches (Osterkamp 2011).

As the depth increases, the pressure on the body increases so that more gas is needed to expand the body against the increased pressure and attain positive buoyancy (i.e. more gas is needed to make the body float). Deep lakes tend to be cooler, and cool temperatures reduce decomposition and gas production which increases the time required to float and reduces the likelihood that the body will float. Recovery operations for drowned subjects show that some bodies in deep cool water never float. Divers experienced in body recovery estimate this depth at <100 ft where the pressure is on the order of 40 psi, experienced water search dog handlers put it at about 100 ft, and theoretical calculations suggest about 180 ft. Variations in water temperature and other factors that influence gas production in the body can probably account for these differences.

In lakes with currents and in streams, a body may move before neutral buoyancy has been attained. For currents <1.5 mph (2.2 ft/sec) at about 1 ft above the bottom, some buoyancy must be attained before the body moves, but for higher velocities the body can move without an increase in buoyancy. Observations of the movement of ice on stream bottoms weighted with sediment and almost neutrally buoyant (Osterkamp 1977) suggest that the body would be expected to bump along the bottom until buoyancy is neutral and then rise as the buoyancy increases. This is supported by observations of body damage caused by scraping and collisions with the bottom attributed to body movement by currents or wave action (Teather 1994).

Water temperature controls water density, and therefore buoyancy, but its primary effect is to influence buoyancy through decomposition. Decomposition gas production does not significantly influence buoyancy of bodies submerged for <12 hours at 60 to 65°F, <24 hours at 50 to 60°F, or <48 hours at temperatures colder than 50°F (Teather 1994). It is not possible to use these results to predict the time to float since other factors may be involved including both physical (clothing, shoes, amount of weight carried for activities, weight carried by homicide or suicide victims) and biological ones (composition of last meal or drinks, amount of body fatty tissue, decomposition stage, presence of scavengers).

6.1.2 Body Scent Source

The body is the source of a host of scent materials. Dogs cannot smell a body through the water, but scent and scent bearing materials from the body enter the water and rise through it to the surface and into the air to be detected. There does not appear to be information on the nature of the scent or scent-bearing materials emanating from submerged decomposing bodies. Consequently, this information must be inferred from studies of living humans, decomposing bodies in the terrestrial environment, bodies recovered by divers in recovery operations, those found floating or washed ashore, submerged pig carcasses, and water search dog training aids. VOCs from buried decomposing bodies have been identified (Vass et al. 2008). These compounds may be soluble or insoluble in water and lighter or heavier than water. Water may modify them and accelerate or retard decomposition depending primarily on its temperature, availability of oxygen, and whether it is salty or fresh, moving or still, or differs from normal pH. The presence of scavengers and other factors can also be important (Teather 1994).

Observations are difficult to find but decomposition studies suggest that bodies may be submerged twice, once on drowning prior to bloating and once after floating when decomposition gases have been released. Some bodies never float and some never sink, especially individuals wearing life vests or other buoyant material and infants. The post-drowning timeline for scent sources is strongly influenced by water temperature through its effect on decomposition. At water temperatures in the 30s°F, decomposition is so slow that internal gas production may not be enough to float a body for weeks, if at all. At water temperatures in the 80s°F, a body may float in a day or two.

Consideration of training aids that dogs are known to detect can aid in the identification of potential scent sources from a submerged body. SD handlers know that dogs can detect submerged clothing and shoes, possibly from VOCs in the items (e.g. from sweat, secretions) as a result of contact with the skin. Handlers also use human hair that has glandular secretions on it as a training aid. Fingerprints consist of water soluble compounds and insoluble compounds modified by hydrolysis and bacterial degradation that include VOCs that have been implicated in human scent (Ramotowski 2001). A single fingerprint on a slide immersed in water can produce an oil film on the water surface within a few minutes (Pearsall and Verbruggen 1982), and hair submerged in calm water quickly produces an oil film on the surface (Osterkamp personal observations). Human bones produce VOCs and have been used as training aids for end stage decomposed bodies in water. In a study of submerged pig carcasses, the odor of bones with greasy decomposed tissue has been noted (Anderson and Hobischak 2004).

This discussion of potential scent sources from submerged bodies starts with the time of drowning. For searches conducted soon after the event, dissolution of VOCs from the skin (sweat) and insoluble oily residues from secretions would be important. Vomitus, feces, urine, and existing intestinal gases purged as a result of muscle relaxation have been implicated (Teather 1994). Injuries to skin, tissue, and bones (from homicides, suicides, propellers, body movement as a result of currents or wave action, and scavengers) can produce body fluids and particles of skin, tissue, and bones. Studies of pig carcasses show that scavengers may cause body fluids and particles to be released throughout the period of submergence especially when the body rests on the bottom. Blood, foam, and blood-stained foam have been observed coming from the mouths and nostrils of recent drowning victims, apparently due to lung damage caused by agonal gasps during drowning. A bubbly, malodorous, brownish green, blood-stained fluid has been observed coming from the mouths of drowning victims as a result of pulmonary autolysis (Teather 1994).

Microorganisms associated with putrefaction convert soft tissue to simple molecules, gases, and liquids. Gases produced in the bowels and other parts of the body during putrefaction include hydrogen sulfide, carbon dioxide, methane, ammonia, sulfur dioxide, and hydrogen (Vass 2001). Tissues are converted to volatile fatty acids and other compounds including putrescene and cadaverine that have been used to train cadaver dogs. Gases and fluids in the intestines and lungs purge from the mouth, nostrils, and rectum. Accumulation of decomposition gases in body cavities and in soft tissues lead to flotation. The remains float until they lose their putrefaction-produced buoyancy and then sink.

Shedding of hair and nails and skin sloughing occurs. Saponification (formation of adipocere, a malodorous, cheesy, compound of fatty acids) retards decomposition. It can persist for long times, particularly where the body is covered (clothes, dive suit). A diver recovered from a depth of 886 ft after 10 years had skeletonized hands and head that were exposed to the water, but the body inside the dive suit had saponified, appeared almost fresh, and produced a strong smell (Zimmermann 2006). Internal organs may remain in a semi-liquid state. Eventually the body will be skeletonized with the remains often partially covered by clothes and flesh and partially held together by greasy connective tissue. Disarticulation follows with the potential for separation of bones by currents, wave action, and scavengers (Teather 1994).

The above limited survey of the fate of submerged human remains indicates that scent sources from submerged bodies include gases (dissolved and in bubbles), liquids (plumes and droplets of body fluids, secretions, and decomposition fluids), and solids (particles of skin, tissue, bones, feces, vomitus) that may be encountered in a search for the remains. These materials have been shown to consist of or have associated VOCs that can be detected by search dogs. It seems clear that the training of a water search dog should include scent sources covering the full range of decomposition and fate of these remains (Table 6.1). It also appears that exposing a dog to remains at the proper stage of decomposition before a search (prescenting) may improve their detection capability. Common deployment times for water search dogs range from a few hours to a few days after a known drowning and at random and sometimes much longer times for missing persons, homicides, and suicides. There are observations of the successful use of dogs many years after the occurrence of a drowning (Graham and Graham 1987).

Table 6.1 Potential Scent Sources for Training Water Search Dogs Based on the Decomposition Stage of the Body

Stage	Potential Scent Sources
Fresh, up to 2 days (no bloating, rigor mortis may be present)	Hair, sweat, fluids from lungs, fluids and particles from fresh tissues (when injuries are involved)
Early decomposition, 2 days to 1 week (bloating present, discoloration)	Decomposition fluids and gases, decaying tissue, and skin
Advanced decomposition, 1 week to 1 month (sagging, bleaching of soft tissue, erosion of surface tissue, adipocere formation begins)	Decomposition fluids and gases, decaying tissue, and skin, adipocere at late stage
Skeletonization, 1 month or longer (skeletal elements exposed, adipocere present)	Bone, skin, connective tissue, cartilage, adipocere

Stage durations vary substantially depending on water depth and temperature, presence of scavengers, and current among other factors.

6.1.3 Scent Movement in Water

The above considerations indicate that the body produces scent materials in all the common phases of matter (gases, liquids, and solids) and the physical characteristics of these materials, including solubility, phase, and density (buoyancy) suggest specific scent transport processes. Local hydrodynamic conditions, especially currents and turbulence in rivers, also play a role. Studies of hydrocarbon seeps in the seabed, gas transfer at air–water interfaces and ice formation in freezing streams provide insight into the characteristics of these processes. Potential transport processes available to move scent from the body to the water surface and into the air above the water are examined below.

6.1.3.1 Gases

There do not appear to be any measurements or observations of the gases emanating from a submerged decomposing body, but it is likely that these would be much the same as those from a decomposing body in the terrestrial environment. Decomposition gases, foam, and bubbly fluids observed coming from the mouths and nostrils of bodies, and bubbles released from clothing, are examples. Since decomposition gases are soluble in water (Gill-King 1997), potential gas sources are dissolved VOCs and gas bubbles.

Potential scent transport processes for dissolved VOCs to the water surface include molecular diffusion, vertical turbulent diffusion, and entrainment in an upward flow of bubbles, buoyant liquids, and solids. Molecular diffusion is too slow which leaves turbulent diffusion and entrainment. When the dissolved gases reach the surface, volatilization is the most likely pathway for scent transport into the air above the water surface (Cheng et al. 2005).

Investigations of submerged hydrocarbon seeps (<230 ft. water depth) provide some insight into the nature of gas bubbles and their transport to the water surface. The seeps release gases as bubbles that may be oil coated as well as oil droplets that rise to the surface because of their buoyancy and local water conditions. The gases released are primarily methane but also include carbon dioxide and trace gases such as hydrogen sulfide, some of the same gases produced during decomposition. As methane bubbles rise, they exchange gases with the surrounding water, dissolve as methane out-flows, grow as dissolved air (nitrogen and oxygen) inflows, and expand due to decreasing water pressure. Bubble rise velocities typically range up to ~1 ft/sec for large bubbles (MacDonald et al. 2002).

When gas bubbles reach the surface, bursting occurs. Upon bursting, the bubbles leave an oil sheen on the water which indicates that they contained oil. Bursting gas bubbles can eject bubble contents (gases and water drop-lets with oil from the inside surface of the bubbles) into the air to a height of ~1 ft above the water surface (MacIntyre 1974) as shown in Figure 6.1. Breaking waves, splashing, and wind spray can enhance gas transport from the water into the air.

The above studies suggest that decomposition gases and some fluids may be transported to the water surface by bubbles. Bubble bursting at the sur-face, enhanced by breaking waves, splashing, and wind spray, would eject gases and water droplets with fluids into the air above the water surface and

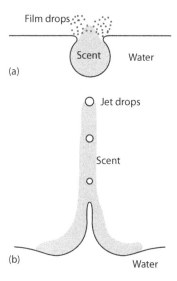

Figure 6.1 When a bubble containing scent reaches the surface, the film on top in contact with the air bursts and creates tiny film drops (a). Water surface forces act like a slingshot that ejects a jet of water and scent into the air (b). The jet breaks into drops that also contain scent from the inside surface of the bubble. The drops frequently evaporate, leaving their dissolved scent in the air.

leave a film of volatile fluids on the water surface. It would be possible for dogs to detect the gases in the air and VOCs from the films as long as gases are available from the decomposing body.

6.1.3.2 Liquids

Urine and blood consist of organic and inorganic solutes dissolved in water with some volatile compounds and platelets indicating they are heavier than water and would sink in still water. These considerations suggest that urine and blood may not be significant scent sources except in turbulent streams and when entrained in a buoyant flow.

Studies of submerged seeps give some insight into transport processes for buoyant, insoluble body and decomposition fluids to the water surface and for their volatile components into the atmosphere just above the surface. Oil released from seafloor vents breaks into plumes and droplets that rise to the surface. Droplet rise velocities are much slower than bubbles unless entrained in an upwelling with gas bubbles. As oil droplets rise, the more volatile components dissolve in the water, and on reaching the surface the oil spreads in a thin film.

Skin secretions, body and decomposition fluids, and other fluids (from the lungs and gastrointestinal tract, broken skin blisters, other skin ruptures, greasy bones, and other remains) are generally lighter than water. The seep studies indicate that oily fluid plumes and droplets would rise to the surface because of buoyancy and spread there in a thin film. Dissolved gases may rise to the surface by turbulent transport and by entrainment when in close proximity to the buoyant droplets and plumes. Scent can be transported into the air by gas bubble bursting, volatilization, breaking waves, wind spray, and splashing at the surface.

6.1.3.3 Solids

Particles of vomitus, feces, skin rafts, skin, bone, and tissue may be transported to the surface because of their buoyancy and turbulent diffusion. These particles typically have secretions, bacteria, and various body fluids on them that produce VOCs. Dissolution of the VOCs in the water, transport to the surface by entrainment and turbulence, and volatilization at the surface would create a gas flux into the air. Some of the secretions and body fluids may be transported to the surface as plumes or droplets and into the air by volatilization. When they reach the water surface, the associated volatile components on the surfaces of the particles can be transported into the air by volatilization. Larger particles have faster rise velocities because of their larger buoyancy but the rise velocity also depends on the shape of the particles. For particles with a disc-like shape, about 0.04 to 0.2 in in diameter and density about that of ice, the rise velocities would be expected to range from0.1 to 0.8 in/sec, and for skin rafts, <0.04 in/sec (Gosink and Osterkamp 1983). Transport of volatiles into the air would be enhanced by surface water dynamics (breaking waves, wind spray, splashing).

In summary, buoyancy is the primary method for transport of scent materials to the water surface with gas bubbles rising at relatively fast rates and other materials rising more slowly. Entrainment in an upward buoyant flow can enhance the relatively slow rate of less buoyant materials. Turbulence may be effective when present in streams and rivers and may bring materials that are slightly heavier than water to the surface. Volatilization from oily films on the water surface and from solids floating there puts VOCs into the air, and VOCs in the gas phase can be ejected into the air when bubbles burst. Wind spray and breaking waves enhance these processes. An airborne scent plume would develop from these sources.

6.2 Use of Dogs for Water Searches

6.2.1 Scent Displacement

Buoyant scent materials rise through the water to the surface where the emergent materials generate a scent plume primarily by volatilization and bubble bursting. Dogs detect the plume in the air above the water surface after it has been subjected to prevailing winds and atmospheric conditions. Search teams (dog, handler, and boat pilot) attempt to detect and follow the scent plume to the area where the scent materials emerge from the water. The question remains about the body location in the water. In lakes with no current, buoyant scent materials can be expected to rise vertically from the body to the water surface (Osterkamp 2011) so the body should be directly under where the scent emerges (Figure 6.2).

In lakes with through flow, rivers, and tidal areas, scent materials would be carried some distance downstream before they reach the water surface. The distance carried depends on the turbulence, current velocity, and water depth (Osterkamp 2011). Laminar flow (current <2 mph, relatively smooth channels, no obstructions in the flow and a smooth water surface) is not common in rivers but can be found in lakes with through flow and tidal areas close to the time that the tide reverses. It would typically carry scent material some distance downstream underwater before the scent emerges for even shallow water depths. Irregularities in the banks and river bed, objects protruding into the flow, flow velocities >3 mph and variable channel width commonly produce turbulent flow adjacent to shore, in the main channel, behind obstructions, and downstream from dams. Turbulent flow is visible as swirls, eddies, bubbles in the water, and a rough water surface. For these common flow conditions, scent is carried to the surface primarily by turbulence and reaches the surface much closer to the source than for laminar flow (Figure 6.3).

Scent movement in lakes

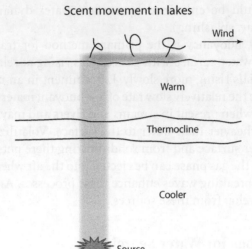

Figure 6.2 A schematic profile of buoyant scent materials rising in a lake. These buoyant materials rise vertically from the source to the water surface through the thermocline. Bursting bubbles eject scent into the air. The bubbles and other scent materials produce an oily film that would spread on the surface and volatilize into the air.

Scent movement in turbulent flow

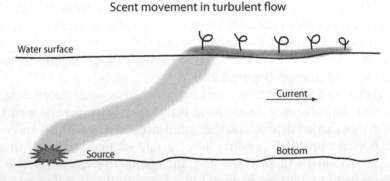

Figure 6.3 A schematic illustration of scent movement in turbulent flow (rivers, tidal areas with incoming or outgoing tides). The bubbles and other scent materials produce an oily film that spreads on the surface downstream and downwind and volatilizes into the air.

6.2.2 Thermoclines

A thermocline is a thin horizontal zone of water found in a lake during the summer stratification that separates warm well-mixed water near the surface from cooler stagnant water below. It was formerly believed that scent from a submerged body on a lake bottom was transported to the surface by diffusion and therefore could not penetrate the thermocline (Hardy 1992). This belief led to the idea that it was best to search for submerged bodies when a thermocline was not present (winter and part of fall and spring) and was also used to explain failures of dogs to detect bodies in the presence of thermoclines. However, the transport processes for gases in bubbles, liquid plumes, droplets of oily secretions, and buoyant particulates are driven by buoyancy (Osterkamp 2011), which would readily transport scent-bearing material through the thermocline to the surface (Figure 6.2). Problems with the performance of water search dogs where thermoclines exist must be a result of other factors.

6.2.3 Scent Pooling at the Surface

There is anecdotal evidence that if the air temperature is colder (35°F or below) than the water, scent pools at the water surface and does not get airborne, which requires dogs to swim or get their noses close to the water surface to detect it (Hardy 1992). However, air in contact with the water under these conditions would be warmed by the water, making it lighter and unstable and cause convection in the air above the water surface. The convective layer would mix air, water vapor, and scent from the water surface into the atmosphere (this can sometimes be observed as a layer of fog with a thickness of several feet or more). Also, gas bubbles that burst at the water surface eject their contents (water droplets with oily scent and gas) into the air with water droplets reaching heights of about 1 ft. Wind (even a light breeze) would enhance volatilization and further mix scent into air near the water surface. Thus, the thickness of the scent plume above the water surface is likely to be on the order of feet or more which would make it possible for a dog to detect it from a boat under the above conditions (Osterkamp 2011).

6.2.4 Natural Decomposition Gases

Methane, hydrogen sulfide, and carbon dioxide are decomposition gases that can also be produced by decaying organic material in wet environments like lakes, swamps, landfills, septic tanks, drainfields, and outdoor toilets. CDs often show an interest in them and even alert on them. These gases are often called "swamp gas". There are examples of lakes drained because of alerts by CDs on swamp gas. It requires considerable time, money, and energy to drain a lake. When nothing is found, it detracts from the reputation of CD teams and uses resources that could have been used elsewhere. Consequently, it is desirable to train dogs not to alert on gases from these areas. This can be done by training CDs in these areas, ignoring any interests and alerts, and rewarding for cadaver sources only. Landfills, septic tanks, drainfields, and outdoor toilets are common in rural areas and ponds and lakes with shallow water over mud bottoms and organic materials produce swamp gas and these places can be used for training.

6.3 Tactics for Water Searches

6.3.1 Introduction

Water searches bring new challenges to canine teams. Searches for drowned subjects are different from other types of searches because the dog's movements are usually restricted to a boat. The dog cannot choose how it moves to detect a scent plume and follow it to the source and must rely on the handler and boat pilot. They become an integral part of the scenting team and are directly involved in locating the source. The handler must continually read the dog for information on the absence or presence of scent, the direction the scent is moving, and communicate this information to the pilot who is responsible for driving the boat. It is easier and more efficient when the handler and pilot are used to working together.

Usually the dog cannot see or contact the body so it must perform its alert based on the presence of scent only. There are also new and unfamiliar hazards that the handler and pilot must be able to recognize such as the effects of waves, currents, hidden obstructions, sweepers, eddies, low head dams, tides, presence of an ice cover downstream of the search area, and more. The pilot, handler, and dog should always wear life vests when working near and on water. It is recommended that the handler take a water safety class before beginning water search work.

An examination of the scent materials from a decomposing body and movement of these materials to the surface indicates the scent plume consists of decomposition gases from bubble bursting and gases volatilized from an oily film on the water surface and from any solids floating there. The primary sources appear to be the oily film and airborne scent (Figures 6.2, 6.3, and 6.4) that are produced as a result of bubble bursting, oily secretions from the body, and oily decomposition material. Bubble bursting is only important as long as gases are available from the decomposing body. The oily film varies in composition depending on the decomposition stage of the body.

The concept of a "scent print" is introduced herein to describe the high concentration of scent on the water surface from a drowned subject or body part in analogy with observations over buried explosives. This scent print must begin where bubbles from the body gases first reach the water surface with additional oils added as other scent materials reach the surface over the body in lakes or further downstream in rivers. It extends downwind and/ or downstream where the material is carried by wind and/or current while emitting scent into the air by volatilization and other processes (Figure 6.4). Volatilization of the oily film which spreads on the surface and fragmenting

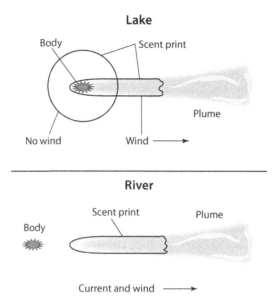

Figure 6.4 Plan views of surface scent prints and scent plumes on a lake with no wind (circle) and a lake and river with wind. In a lake, the body is located under the upwind end of the scent print, and in a river it is located upstream of the upstream end of the scent print.

by surface turbulence and waves is expected to reduce the film thickness to the point where the scent print becomes discontinuous and eventually disappears downstream and/or downwind. The oily film from secretions and gas bubble bursting may be very thin so it would disappear quickly, implying the scent print may be relatively short while the film from fatty decomposition fluids may be thicker and last longer. The location of the scent print in rivers depends on the rise velocity of the scent material, flow velocity and depth, and whether the flow is laminar or turbulent as noted above. There is support for the presence of a surface scent print since oily films have been observed on the surface of calm water over a cadaver source and in laboratory settings. This scent print and airborne scent from bubble bursting are thought to be the sources of the scent plume sought by the team.

While the presence of the scent print is very likely, there are no direct observations of it from submerged bodies and no information on its characteristics (length, width, thickness, volatilization rate of the film, presence of insoluble materials, etc.). This lack of information contributes to the difficulty of locating bodies in water.

6.3.2 Search Tactics

There are several search methods and patterns that are commonly used in water searches with dogs which are primarily based on the type of search, wind direction, and current, if any (Bryson 1984; Graham and Graham 1985; Hardy 1992; Barton and Clemmo 1997; Koenig 2000). Usually, they involve gridding across wind and moving each grid line upwind with the dog always on the upwind side of the boat. The boat should turn into the wind at the end of each grid line and the dog should switch to the upwind side. Once the scent plume is detected as indicated by the dog's alert or CB, the patterns diverge. One pattern (Figure 6.5) is to continue gridding the plume but with shorter grid lines noting the position of each alert as the dog passes through the plume. Eventually, the boat will pass upwind of the scent print with no alert by the dog. On lakes, the body is between the last two grid lines and roughly on a line plotted through the alerts. A fine grid through that area (Figure 6.6) can help to locate the emergent scent print more precisely and the body will likely be under the upwind side of the scent print. If the gridlines are advanced downwind (not recommended), when the first alert occurs the body is upwind between that gridline and the previous one and a fine grid upwind of the alert as above should help to locate it.

Figure 6.6 shows how to locate the upwind end of the scent print more precisely. Divide the area between the alert and no alert grid lines in half and pilot the boat along this line. An alert indicates it is upwind of that line and no alert indicates it is downwind of that line. Next, divide the appropriate half of the area in half again and pilot the boat along this line. Repeat until satisfied (as indicated by prior discussion with the IC) with the precision of the results. The independent use of a second dog can help to define the upstream end of the scent print. The handlers must then estimate its location using the dog's behavior, wind, current, water depth, and other factors (location of CB, alerts, and boat paths) as noted previously.

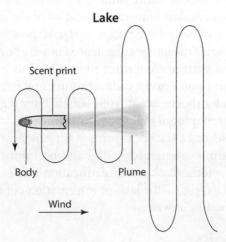

Figure 6.5 Plan view of a lake search with wind illustrating gridding with the first method which is to continue gridding with shortened grid lines after scent is detected.

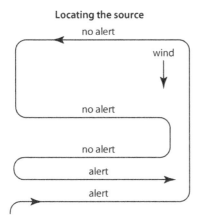

Figure 6.6 Gridding to locate the upwind end of the scent print. The lower and upper lines are part of the initial grid. No alert on a line indicates the source is downwind and an alert indicates it is upwind putting it between the two lines. This distance can be quickly reduced by making repeated passes half-way between the alert and no alert lines.

The second pattern is to mimic the natural tendency of the dog to quarter the wind (grid across wind) to detect the scent plume and to quarter upwind in and out of the scent plume to locate the source (Chapter 3). Close to the source, dogs turn into the wind and follow the plume upwind to the source. Dogs seem to know when to do this but the handler may not. When the dog first alerts or indicates it is in scent, the handler should have the boat turn sharply, about 30° to 45°, into the wind (quarter upwind) and follow the scent plume by watching the dog's head for direction (Figure 6.7). If the dog indicates it is out of scent, the handler should turn back into the wind at about 30° to 45° upwind and attempt to reacquire the scent plume. The procedure is repeated until the dog no longer detects scent or the dog leads the boat directly upwind and then alerts or is obviously out of scent. A fine grid downwind of the position where the dog no longer detected scent (Figure 6.6) can then be used to better define the scent print. If the decision is made to grid downwind, not recommended but sometimes necessary, once the dog alerts on the first encounter with scent, the handler should turn back into the wind and proceed as before.

A third pattern is to turn the boat into the wind when the dog first detects scent and attempt to follow the plume to the upwind end of the scent print. If the plume is lost it can be reacquired by gridding upwind from the point where the dog last had scent. While this can work well for an experienced handler and boat pilot used to communicating with each other, many handlers must work with a new pilot each time they search which can be difficult.

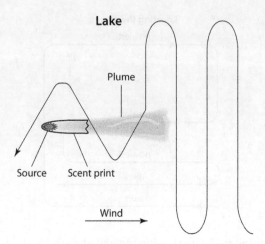

Figure 6.7 Plan view of a lake search with wind illustrating the second pattern which is to quarter upwind after scent is detected.

The patterns increase with difficulty and efficiency from the first to the third; however, on searches there is often little difference between them. Perfect grid patterns are easier to make on paper than in a boat on a lake or in a current. Do not worry about this; the object of gridding is to put the dog downwind and within scenting range of all the parts of your search area.

There are no guidelines on boat speed although most teams work very slowly, perhaps too slowly, especially for large area searches. It is recommended to move at about the speed the dog naturally uses when searching an open field; although some dogs move fast, and a slower speed may give the handler and pilot more time to react to the dog's CB or alert.

Observations of water search dogs during training and searches suggests that some dogs can discern the upwind edge of the scent print which appears to be the area of greatest scent intensity. These dogs show that they are obviously in scent when gridding but do not give their alert until a point where they become much more animated and may try to jump into the water. Possibly, the additional scent put into the air by bubbles bursting stimulates the dogs to alert. Dogs that are excitable, young, novices, or inadequately trained may offer their alerts immediately on encountering the scent plume which is a training problem.

In all boat searches, a handheld or boat -mounted GPS should be used to record the path of the boat and to mark whether the dog is in or out of scent. Using more than one competent K9 team is desirable to confirm the alerts and to further define the scent print. The position of the body must be estimated taking into account the dog's behavior, wind, water depth, and other factors (location of CB, alerts, and boat paths). These quantities should be plotted on a map of the search area and used to estimate the location of the body. Experience in training and searching under similar conditions and discussions with local recovery units and bystanders about any past finds in the search area help to locate the body.

6.3.3 Shoreline Searches

Water searches for bodies near a shoreline are possible when the wind is at least partially onshore. For these searches, the wind direction and channeling by the shoreline are important. Wind blowing directly onshore is the simplest case since the body must be offshore and directly upwind. Dogs may alert at the shoreline or face offshore while staring or whining and some dogs may swim following the plume part way or all the way to the scent print. Wind blowing at an angle to the shoreline is a more difficult case since when the dog offers a CB or alerts, the handler must then carefully determine the wind direction because it is the direction to the body. This is something that is best learned during training. If the shoreline consists of a bank with a sharp change in elevation (even just a few feet) or a sharp change in vegetation (common conditions), wind and scent may be channeled along them making the problem more difficult (Figure 6.8). These changes may also cause

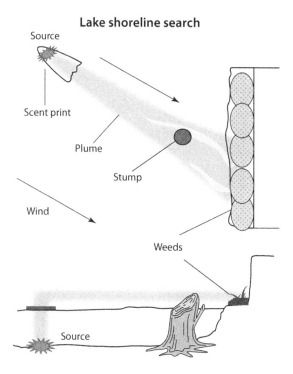

Figure 6.8 Lake shoreline search with wind blowing at an angle onshore. Scent collects on anything above the water surface (e.g. stump) and channels along shore where it collects on vegetation.

scent to collect at the water's edge or on shoreline vegetation. If dogs are not trained to follow scent upwind past scent collectors, they may alert on them.

Dogs can search a limited distance offshore by wading or swimming when the wind is offshore. However, this method should not be used when offshore winds are strong, when there are strong currents, or an outgoing tide since dogs have difficulty swimming against a current of several mph or strong winds. Dogs can be trapped and drowned in rivers by strainers, sweepers, log jams, and the presence of a downstream ice cover. A few advanced handlers train their dogs to take hand signals for direction while swimming offshore which allows these teams to search a hundred yards or more offshore under safe conditions. This method is especially effective in small bodies of water. The dog's alert may consist of swimming in circles, twisting and turning in the scent, looking down into the water, biting the water, or allowing surface water to flow into their mouths and out the side.

The presence of banks, bluffs, and vegetation on land may create turbulent eddies (Chapter 4) in the air near-shore that bring scent a short distance shoreward when the winds are offshore. Lake, pond, and river breezes are like sea breezes but form on lakes, ponds, and rivers during the day and offer the possibility of searching near-shore water from the land. Land breezes from sunset to sunrise make it possible to search difficult shorelines from a boat moving along the shore. These breezes are subject to the prevailing winds that may enhance or destroy them.

6.3.4 Boat Searches

6.3.4.1 Lakes

On lakes with no through flow and little wind, lateral spreading as the scent material rises is expected to be small (Figure 6.2). The initial surface scent print should be larger than the size of the body and increase slightly in width on the surface as the depth increases. The oily scent material on the surface would be expected to spread in a thin film and significantly increase the size of the scent print. Wind would elongate the surface scent print downwind (Figure 6.4), and VOCs from bubble bursting and volatilization would produce a scent plume that moves downwind. The source is always directly below the scent print when the wind is calm and under the upwind end of the scent print when wind is present.

Search tactics on lakes under calm conditions (Figure 6.4) are to grid the search area closely (a few tens of yards or less), and it may be better to wait for wind if the search area is large. If the lake surface is smooth, it does not necessarily mean there is no wind. So be sure to check for wind with a wet finger, surveyors tape, powder puff, or wind gauge. When wind is present (almost always), initial grid lines should be perpendicular to the wind (Figure 6.5 and 6.7). Grid line spacing before the dog has an alert depends on conditions. A rough estimate of grid line spacing with light wind would be about 50 to 150 yards. The handler needs to determine the effects of wind, decomposition stage, and water temperature on grid spacing during training. For a given wind and water temperature, searching for bones associated with an old drowning will be much different from searching for a body when decomposition is at a maximum.

Water turbulence may increase close to shore due to the presence of an irregular shoreline or in shallow water with obstructions. If the shore has a high bank, bluff, or tall vegetation, turbulent eddies may form in the air near the shore as noted for these features in Chapter 4. The presence of hills, bluffs, and tall forests on the shore can modify the wind some distance offshore and in nearby bays. Lakes and reservoirs with through flow appear to behave like slowly flowing rivers, possibly with laminar flow.

6.3.4.2 Creeks and Rivers

Small creeks can often be searched from their shores, but those with shores that are high and steep, covered by dense vegetation or rocks, usually need to be searched with boats. These creeks often have strainers (e.g. brush piles, fallen trees) in the flow that can trap bodies, typically on their upstream sides, and sweepers (trees growing almost horizontally from the banks with limbs partially in the water) that can trap floating bodies. Some creeks have an alternating rapid, pool flow so that scent from a body trapped in rapids upstream or at the head of a pool may be carried downstream below the pool which can be searched by working the dog in riffles at the downstream end. Mountain creeks and those with very steep gradients are dangerous to search. Drainage ditches and canals, especially those that flow only at certain times, often have smooth grass covered beds and banks that favor movement of bodies over large distances. If there are dams, bodies may be trapped against their upstream sides. Schematic illustrations of scent movement in lakes with through flow, tidal areas, and rivers are shown in Figure 6.4. In tidal areas, scent can be carried one direction with the incoming tide and the other direction with an outgoing tide. The scent material always emerges downstream from the source (both directions for tidal areas). The scent print starts where the first gas bubbles reach the surface. It extends downstream an unknown distance while releasing scent into the air. The source is always upstream of the upstream end of the scent print in creeks and rivers.

Tactics to detect the scent plume and locate the surface scent print are similar for both types of flow. Rivers channel air as well as water so that air flow is frequently up or downstream, especially in rivers with high banks or dense and tall shoreline vegetation. While the point where the scent material reaches the surface does not depend on the wind direction, an upstream wind would retard the movement of the scent print downstream and a downstream wind would elongate it somewhat.

Barton and Clemmo (1997) and Koenig (2000) discuss search tactics to locate bodies when the current and wind are in the same direction and in opposite directions. For wind blowing downstream, it is recommended to grid back and forth across the river starting on the downwind side of the search area unless conditions do not allow it. The pilot can angle the boat slightly into the wind with the dog always on the upwind side of the boat which keeps the dog out of fumes from the boat motor. Once the plume is detected, use one of the search patterns described previously (Figure 6.5 and 6.7). The first pattern is described below for all river searches but either of the patterns described above can be used. Continue to grid upwind in and out of the plume (Figure 6.9) until a pass does not yield an alert. When this occurs, the upstream end of the scent print will be between that pass and the previous one and can be defined by a fine grid there (Figure 6.6). The alerts can be used to define an approximate line and the body will be roughly along this line and upstream of the upstream end of the scent print. Divers often work downstream off a tether to a boat anchored upstream of the scent print and along the line of alerts to find and recover the body. The downstream end of their search area is the upstream end of the scent print. Experience in training and searching in rivers will help handlers estimate the position of the body.

When the wind blows upstream (Figure 6.10), the scent print will begin downstream from the body and be carried downstream retarded somewhat by the upstream wind while releasing a decreasing amount of

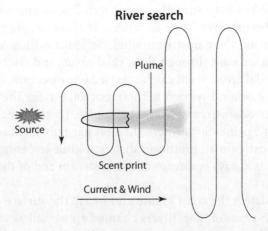

Figure 6.9 River search with wind and current in the same direction. The upstream end of the scent print is between the last two grid lines. Use the method in Figure 6.6 to determine its location. The source in a river is always upstream of the scent print.

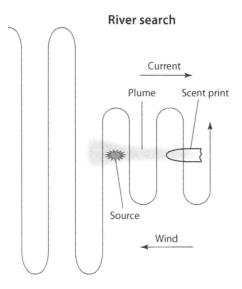

Figure 6.10 River search with wind and current in opposite directions.

scent into the air. With wind and current in opposite directions, the scent plume moves from the scent print back upstream over it and the body which creates a scent plume upstream and downstream of the body. A grid (Figure 6.10) that starts on the downwind and upstream side of the search area would result in a line of alerts downstream in the plume, over the body, and toward the end of the scent print. The dog should give its strongest CB or alert as it passes the point where the scent is maximum. Maximum scent is likely to be the upstream end of the scent print and the dog should be trained to offer its alert there. The body would be upstream from that point and along the line of alerts. If the dog does not offer an alert there, the situation is not hopeless because divers can search along the line of alerts by working downstream off a tether to a boat anchored upstream along the line of alerts.

There is no information for wind that is blowing at an angle to the current. For wind blowing primarily downstream or upstream at a small angle to the current, scent materials will emerge directly downstream of the body. The plume will be carried downwind at the same angle to the current and will be wider than previous examples. As the angle increases, the plume will increase in width. The width will be defined by lines drawn downwind from the upstream and downstream ends of the scent print and increase with distance downwind. A line through the CBs or alerts will also be at about the same angle to the current. Grid upwind across the current as shown in Figures 6.11 and 6.12 or across the wind to detect the plume and define the scent print. The body will likely be directly upstream of the scent print.

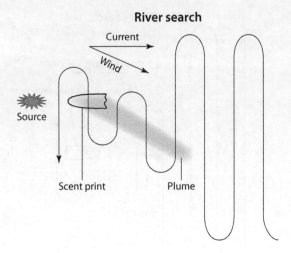

Figure 6.11 River search with wind blowing primarily downstream at an angle to the current.

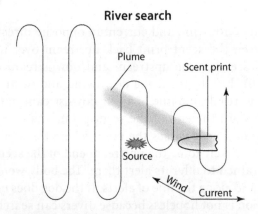

Figure 6.12 River search with wind blowing primarily upstream at an angle to the current.

When the wind blows directly across the river at a right angle to the current (Figure 6.13), scent materials would emerge downstream from the body and form a downstream scent print that would be elongated somewhat downwind. A scent plume would develop that would be as wide as the scent print is long and would move directly across the river. Gridding should start on the downwind side of the river and move up and downstream to advance the grid upwind (across the river). Once the plume is detected, continue gridding upwind in and out of the plume (Figure 6.13) until a pass does not yield an alert. When this occurs, the upwind side of the scent print will be between that pass and the previous one. The alert and path of the boat define an area as shown in Figure 6.13, and gridding this area should help to improve

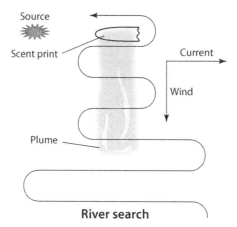

Source

Scent print

Current

Wind

Plume

River search

Figure 6.13 River search with wind and plume moving across the current.

the position of the upwind side of the scent print. The body will likely be upstream of the upwind side of the scent print.

For wind blowing primarily at a large angle across the current, the scent material will emerge directly downstream of the body and form a downstream scent print. The plume will be carried downwind at the same angle to the current. Grid upstream and downstream as shown in Figure 6.14 or upwind and across the wind to detect the plume and to locate and define the scent print as before. Again, the body will likely be directly upstream of the scent print.

Water and air turbulence can be greater close to riverbanks because of the presence of shoreline vegetation, banks, bluffs, and irregularities along the shore. These features may also deflect and channel wind and require closer spaced grids to detect the scent plume and define the scent print.

6.3.4.3 Scent Collectors and Miscellany

Scent collectors in the water include eddies, strainers, sweepers, buoys, docks, wharves, barges, bridge abutments, and other objects in the flow that can trap scent and bodies. Those that extend above the water behave like similar structures on land and their effects on wind and scent are described in Chapter 3. These features should be checked for scent when gridding the search area or be checked from shore, if possible. Eddies are commonly formed wherever current flows around, through, and over objects (rocks, logs, trees) in the water. Bubbly foam sometimes forms in these eddies and should also be checked for scent. Faint scent near the water surface may be enhanced by bubbles produced by the boat's motor that break on reaching the surface, especially when shifting the engine between forward and reverse.

Rising water levels in large drainage ditches, rivers, and an incoming tide can cause backflow into connected lakes and tributaries and cause a body to

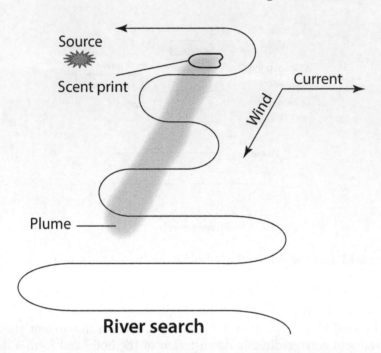

Source

Scent print

Current

Wind

Plume

River search

Figure 6.14 River search with wind and plume moving primarily across the river.

be carried into them. When water levels drop, the body may be trapped in the lake or tributary.

Depressions in a stream bed are stagnant flow areas that can trap bodies until they gain sufficient buoyancy to float. Changing flow conditions and increasing current associated with rising water levels can redistribute bed material (silt, sand, gravel) into the depression covering the body and trap it there. Dogs may still be able to scent the body, but sonar scans of the bed may not show that the body is there.

6.4 Summary

This chapter focuses on the use of dogs to detect and locate bodies underwater and the information would also be useful when searching for other underwater sources. Dogs cannot smell a body through the water but can detect scent from the body which enters the water rises to the surface and into the air. Handlers use the dog to detect the scent plume, find the area where scent first surfaces, and provide their best estimate of the location of the body.

The body in water weighs less than in air, changes shape and density, and moves about in three dimensions. Pressure increases with depth so that the pressure on the top of a body is less than at the bottom. Thus, the effect of pressure on the body is to buoy it up rather than to "hold" it down.

Adults who weighed from 110 to 200 lbs weighed 7 to 16 lbs underwater. Decomposition gases cause the body to increase in volume which displaces more water and increases its buoyancy. The body eventually attains neutral buoyancy (zero weight) and then positive buoyancy, which causes it to rise. Decomposition gas production does not significantly influence buoyancy of bodies submerged for <12 hours at 60 to 65°F, <24 hours at 50 to 60°F, or <48 hours at temperatures colder than 50°F.

Deep lakes are cooler which reduces decomposition and gas production. At temperatures in the 30s°F, decomposition gases may not float a body for weeks, if at all. At water temperatures in the 80s°F, a body may float in a day or two.

Dogs can detect submerged clothing, shoes, human hair, and bones in addition to bodies and body parts. Scent from submerged bodies includes gases (dissolved and in bubbles), liquids (plumes and droplets of body fluids, secretions, and decomposition fluids), and solids (particles of skin, tissue, bones, feces, vomitus). Training aids should include scent sources covering the full range of decomposition and fate of human remains (Table 6.1). Prescenting the dog on remains at the pertinent stage of decomposition before a search may improve their detection.

Buoyancy transports scent to the water surface with gas bubbles rising at relatively fast rates and other materials rising more slowly. Volatilization from oily films on the water surface and from floating solids puts scent into the air and scent can be ejected into the air when bubbles burst (Figure 6.1). An airborne scent plume develops from these sources. Turbulence is effective in bringing scent-bearing materials to the surface. In tidal areas, lakes with through flow, and rivers, scent materials would be carried some distance downstream before they reach the water surface (Figure 6.3).

Thermoclines are not a barrier for scent movement to the surface because buoyancy moves bubbles, liquid plumes, droplets of oily secretions, and buoyant particulates through the thermocline to the surface (Figure 6.2). Detection problems where thermoclines exist must be a result of other factors.

Air temperatures colder (35°F or below) than the water do not cause scent to pool at the water surface, and dogs do not have to swim to detect it. The thickness of the scent plume above the water surface is likely to be on the order of feet or more which makes it possible for dogs to detect it from a boat.

Methane, hydrogen sulfide, and carbon dioxide are decomposition gases that can also be produced by decaying vegetation in water bodies, septic tanks, drainfields, and outdoor toilets. Training dogs in these areas, ignoring any interests and alerts, and rewarding for cadaver sources only helps the dogs distinguish cadaver scent from these gases.

The concept of a "scent print" is introduced to describe the high concentration of scent on the water surface from a drowned subject. This scent print begins where bubbles from the body gases first reach the water surface. Liquids and particulates reach the surface later over the body in lakes or farther downstream in rivers. The scent print is the source of the scent plume sought by the team. It extends downwind and/or downstream where the scent material is carried by wind and current while emitting scent into the air. If wind is present on lakes, the body is located under the upwind end of the scent print and, in a river, it is located upstream of the upstream end of the scent print (Figure 6.4). When the scent plume has been detected, the next step in finding the body is to find the upwind or upstream end of the scent print.

Search tactics and patterns involve gridding across the wind and moving each grid line upwind with the dog always on the upwind side of the boat. The boat should turn into the wind at the end of each grid line and the dog should switch to the upwind side. When the scent plume is detected, three different patterns are used to locate the scent print. A fine grid through that area (Figure 6.6) helps to locate the emergent scent print more precisely.

Boat speed should be about the same as the dog uses naturally when searching. In all boat searches, a handheld or boat mounted GPS should be used to record the path of the boat and to mark where the dog is in or out of scent. The position of the body must be estimated considering the dog's behavior, wind, water depth, current, and other factors (location of CB, alerts, and boat paths).

Water searches can be done alongshore when the wind is onshore. Wind blowing at an angle to the shoreline is a difficult case. If there is a bank with a sharp change in elevation or vegetation, scent can be channeled along it (Figure 6.8).

Dogs can search a limited distance offshore by wading or swimming when the wind is offshore. This method should not be used when offshore winds are strong, when there are strong currents, or an outgoing tide. A few advanced handlers train their dogs to take hand signals for direction while swimming offshore, which allows these teams to search a hundred yards or more offshore under safe conditions. A dog can be trapped and drowned in rivers where there are strainers, sweepers, log jams, or a downstream ice cover.

Lake, pond, and river breezes (like sea breezes) may form on lakes, ponds, and rivers, respectively, during the day and offer the possibility of searching near-shore water from the land. Land breezes from sunset to sunrise make it possible to search difficult shorelines from a boat moving along the shore.

Initial grid lines on lakes should be perpendicular to the wind. Grid line spacing depends on conditions, and with a light wind it would be about 50 to 150 yds. The handler needs to determine the effects of wind, decomposition stage, and water temperature on grid spacing during training. Searching for bones associated with a very old drowning is likely different (less scent) than searching for a recently drowned body.

Creeks that have alternating rapids and pools can be searched by working the dog in riffles at the downstream end of pools. Drainage ditches and canals with smooth grass covered beds and banks allow bodies to move large distances. If there are dams, bodies may be trapped against their upstream sides.

Search patterns are recommended for lakes with through flow, tidal areas, and rivers. These include patterns for wind and current in the same direction, opposite directions, and at angles (Figures 6.9 through 6.14). In each, the most likely location of the body is discussed.

Scent collectors in the water include eddies, strainers, sweepers, buoys, docks, wharves, barges, bridge abutments, and other objects in the flow that can trap scent and bodies. Foam sometimes forms or is trapped in eddies and should also be checked for scent.

Rising water levels in large drainage ditches, rivers, and an incoming tide can cause backflow into connected lakes and tributaries and cause a body to be carried into them. When water levels drop, the body may remain in the lake or tributary.

Depressions in a river bed are stagnant flow areas that can trap bodies, and changing flow conditions (e.g. flooding) can redistribute bed material into the depression covering the body. Dogs may still be able to scent the body, but sonar scans of the bed may not show that the body is there.

Trails and Trailing

7

7.1 Introduction

7.1.1 Trail Scent

This chapter is concerned with scent from a moving person, its characteristics, how it gets to the ground, how the local environment influences this "ground" or trail scent, and how this scent may be used by dogs to follow the path (trail) of the person. No distinction will be made between tracking and trailing since the dogs follow the same scent, and the differences appear to be a result of their natural tendencies and training methods.

Early ideas about the ability of dogs to trail a person involved shoe odor, crushed vegetation (footprints), and scurf. The scurf hypothesis is similar to Syrotuck's (1972), which identified the scurf as rafts (skin flakes). Syrotuck (1972) thought that the ground disturbance (footprints) and gases produced by bacteria acting on the skin flakes were used by dogs to follow the trail of a person. Footprints produce scent from bacteria acting on crushed vegetation and in disturbed soil. Since this scent is not specific to an individual, it will not be considered here because TDs are scent specific.

Scent from the human body appears to consist of gases produced by bacteria acting on the skin and skin flakes (including skin flakes from breath), volatilization of secretions on skin and skin flakes, and VOCs from breath. This scent is specific to an individual and has two components: particulates (skin flakes and bacteria) and gaseous VOCs from all the sources. Dogs can trail and discriminate scent on hard surfaces, which suggests they are using scent from skin flakes and/or VOCs. Human scent may be modified by race, diet, disease, toiletries, and contaminants in the environment.

Lidwell et al. (1959) showed that airborne particles found in hospitals carried an average of about four microbes on particles with a median diameter of 13 μm. These particles were identified as fragments of human skin (Davies and Noble 1962). Particle sizes ranged from 12 to 22 μm (Noble and Davies 1965) and weighed about 2.5E-8 oz.

Syrotuck (1972) assumed a flake size of 14 μm and two billion cells on the skin surface with 1 in 30 shed daily to calculate that about 40,000 full size cells were shed by the body each minute or roughly 700/sec. However, Clark (1974) showed that when a person entered a small room and walked slowly around it for 28 min, the number of particles smaller than 10 μm in the air increased about the same as the number of the much larger skin cells that would have been shed. Many of the recovered particles appeared to be fragments of skin. These particles would have been coated with skin secretions and some would have carried bacteria to contribute to the human scent picture. It is not known if these small skin flakes were part of the larger shed skin flakes or were in addition to them.

7.1.1.1 Human Thermal Plume

Understanding trail scent requires information on how scent from a person reaches the ground. Skin is normally warmer than the adjacent air so that the skin heats the air which produces thermal convection from the body to the surrounding air (Figure 7.1). This results in a human boundary layer next to the skin that flows upward from the ankles to the top of the head. It is about 8 in thick around the upper body, moves at a speed of about 1 ft/sec, leaves the body in a plume at the shoulders and top of the head, and may extend up to about 6 ft above the head (Settles 2005). Every location on the body contributes scent to the human boundary layer so that all types of scent released by the body or on the body are in the upward moving layer and plume. This includes skin flakes, VOCs, explosives, drugs, disease carrying bacteria, and scent from disease. Clothing is not an impediment to the shedding of skin flakes because the pores in the weave of almost all fabrics are much larger than the average flake. However, the bellows action of pant legs and shoes while walking may be responsible for some of the skin flakes and VOCs deposited on the trail as shown in Figure 7.2 (Clark and de Calcina-Goff 2009).

Figure 7.1 Schlieren image of the rising boundary layer and human thermal plume from a person. (Courtesy of Dr. G.S. Settles 2020c.)

Syrotuck (1972) suggested that this body air current was responsible for projecting scent into the air above the head of a person, which would fall to the ground along the path of the person. However, settling velocities are so low for skin flakes (0.04 to 0.4 in/sec) and scent molecules that they would be carried far downwind (hundreds of yards) before contacting the ground. Since TDs generally follow much closer to the trail, some other process must bring the scent to the ground.

If a person is standing still in calm air, the human thermal plume carrying scent over the person's head would slowly settle around the person and deposit on the ground. In wind, the plume that is not deposited would be carried downwind and would be detectable by SDs. If a person is walking in calm air, the plume would be incorporated into a turbulent wake with eddies behind the person (Figure 7.3, Edge et al. 2005). If a person is walking in wind, Figure 7.3 indicates that the location of the wake relative to the

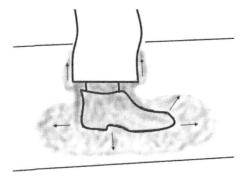

Figure 7.2 Bellows action of a shoe and pant leg, which would be expected to deposit skin flakes and VOCs on a trail. (Modified from Clark and de Calcina-Goff 2009.)

Figure 7.3 Sketch of the wake produced by the thermal plume behind a walking person shows the wake contacts the ground where skin flakes and VOCs would be deposited. This creates the trail of the person. (Based on photography produced by Settles 2020b, courtesy of Dr. G.S. Settles.)

person will be determined by the wind speed and direction. The pattern of the deposited scent is unknown but probably covers much more area on the ground than footprints. These considerations indicate that trail scent is a kind of long, more or less continuous scent print.

Figure 7.3 shows that the eddies in the wake contact the ground and would be expected to deposit scent there. This indicates that trail scent on the ground in the immediate vicinity of the path of the person is a result of the thermal scent plume and eddies in the turbulent wake associated with the moving person and wind. Scent that is not deposited on the ground would be carried downwind. A trail that is in the same direction as the wind or opposite to it would result in maximum scent on the ground and one that is perpendicular to the wind would result in minimum scent.

Since most of the trail scent appears to originate in the human boundary layer, it is derived from every location on the body, contains all types of human scent, modifications to that scent, and all non-human scent carried by the body. The presence of a wake associated with a moving person that contains non-human scent (explosives, drugs, other contraband and hazardous materials) is the basis for wake trailing dogs.

The surfaces where flakes and VOCs are deposited on the trail and downwind of it include soil, water, vegetation (blades of grass, stalks of plants, leaves), and hard surfaces (rock, asphalt and concrete). It is thought that vegetation plays the most significant role (collects the most scent). Deposition is determined by the properties of the VOCs, flakes, surfaces, temperature, humidity, and other factors (Simonich and Hites 1994). Deposition of VOCs (partitioning between the gas and solid surface) depends on temperature, but deposition of flakes does not. Once deposited, sunlight may degrade flakes and some VOCs.

It is known that VOCs move to the earth's surface at lower ambient temperatures and to the atmosphere at higher ambient temperatures. This suggests that there is a daily cycle in the concentrations of VOCs deposited on surfaces and that concentrations should be higher during the night and for surfaces in shade, compared to those surfaces in sunlight (Simonich, personal communication).

Hot and dry air and surfaces can dehydrate the skin flakes to the point where bacterial activity almost ceases (Syrotuck 1972). Surfaces cool when they go into shade and at night. This increases humidity and dew, which causes them to rehydrate and again produce VOCs.

Observations of TD handlers are consistent with this behavior of VOCs. Generally, it is easier for dogs to trail when the air is moist and cool, in shaded areas, at night, and when handlers cast their dogs into shade to recover or start a trail.

When flakes are deposited on surfaces, they continue to emit VOCs from the bacteria and secretions. Each flake would produce a tiny discrete plume

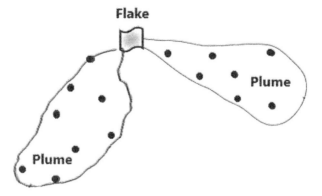

Figure 7.4 Schematic drawing of a skin flake attached to a surface. It continues to emit VOCs (dots), which may also attach to surfaces. Changes in wind direction and turbulence would produce multiple plumes and, in a short time, a cloud of VOCs around each deposited flake.

of VOCs that would move downwind (Figure 7.4), where some VOCs would attach to surfaces.

Changes in wind direction and turbulence near the surface would produce multiple plumes for each flake resulting in a cloud of VOCs in the area of each deposited flake. Movement of the flakes would increase the size and concentration of the scent cloud.

After a short time, the trail would consist of clouds of multiple overlapping plumes of VOCs from each flake in the immediate vicinity of the path of the person. This could produce a continuous distribution of scent on the ground provided the flakes and VOCs could attach to the available surfaces. Variations in surface properties would be expected to result in patches of variable scent concentration. VOCs and skin flakes in the wake that are not deposited would be carried some distance from the path.

This explanation of trail scent is supported by the available evidence and provides a process by which trail scent can be deposited on the ground along the path of a person (Figure 7.3) and a process that can increase the coverage of scent along that path (Figure 7.4), perhaps like Figure 7.5.

This behavior of sources that emit VOCs has been described in field studies of pheromones that emit VOCs (Karg et al. 1994). It is hypothesized herein that it would also apply to the emission of VOCs by skin flakes although with some modifications.

7.1.2 Effects of Environmental Conditions

The effects of surfaces, sun or clouds, weather (temperature, moisture, wind), terrain, vegetation, and turbulence on scent and scent plume movement have been discussed in Chapters 2, 3, and 4. Trail scent consists of gases produced

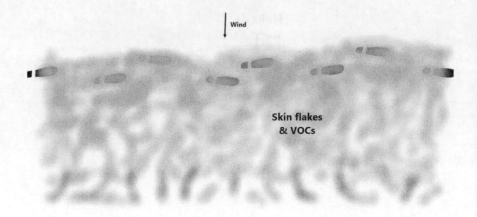

Figure 7.5 Schematic of trail scent deposited along the path (trail) of a person based on Figures 7.3 and 7.4.

primarily by bacteria acting on skin and skin flakes, volatilization of secretions from skin and skin flakes, and VOCs from breath. These bacterial gases and VOCs are the components of trail scent. Bacterial gases are produced while the bacteria remain active. Bacterial activity requires favorable conditions which include food, acidity, time, temperature, oxygen, and moisture. Assuming other conditions are present and favorable, temperature and moisture are the primary conditions which influence activity with warm and moist the most favorable.

7.1.2.1 Temperatures and Moisture

Environmental conditions can interact individually and in concert to create a myriad of different settings for trails. For example, the temperature of a surface depends on slope, orientation, sun or clouds, air temperatures, vegetation, moisture, wind, and other factors. We are concerned with the temperature range where trailing dogs usually work. Generally, this range is from freezing to about 100°F. When considering the effects of temperature on trail scent, it is the temperature of the surface where the trail exists that is more important than the air temperature. Surface temperatures in shade and at night are generally cooler than the air temperature and, in sunlight, are generally warmer than air temperature.

Extremely high or low temperatures influence the ability of bacteria to produce gases. The availability of bacterial gases and VOCs would be expected to increase with increasing temperatures. Although the amount of scent available increases when temperatures increase into the 90s°F and higher, the dogs usually find it difficult to continue working. If high temperatures are associated with low humidity, skin flakes would be expected to dry which would reduce availability of bacterial gases.

This situation can also develop at relatively low air temperatures (70s°F) since dark surfaces (e.g. asphalt) can be 50°F above air temperatures and dry. If the surface is dry bare soil, VOCs may adhere to the soil particles, which leaves less trail scent. Flakes may also adhere to concrete and asphalt or be trapped in tiny holes in the surface, but there is no information on this.

At temperatures like those in a refrigerator (typically <40°F), bacterial activity slows and almost ceases below freezing. At temperatures like those in a freezer (<0°F), bacterial action ceases. This does not mean that TDs cannot trail, since VOCs from the trail scent are still present and can also continue to volatilize from secretions on the flakes although at much reduced rates. Also, skin flakes can be inhaled and produce detectable VOCs in the warm and humid environment of the nose. Experience with TDs in Interior Alaska has shown that they can successfully trail at temperatures of −30°F on frozen surfaces, ice, and hard packed snow.

The type of snow and its thickness determines whether dogs can trail when snow has fallen on the trail. Experience suggests that dogs can still trail with ½ ft of new powder snow on the trail, but a few inches of wet snow that has frozen makes trailing difficult to impossible. Most dogs learn to follow visible footprints in the snow, but others seem to trail as if the footprints were not there.

7.1.2.2 Wind, Terrain, and Vegetation

Wind speed and direction determine where the scent in the wake will contact the ground, but there is no information available. For wind speeds much greater than the speed of the subject, the scent would contact the ground near their footprints and just downwind of the subject. TDs usually trail on the downwind side of the track. Movement of the scent that does not contact the ground will be determined by the interaction of the wind with terrain, vegetation, obstacles, and by thermal turbulence in the same way as a scent plume (Chapters 3 and 4). Vegetation typically has 6 to 14 times more surface area than the land on which it is growing.

This provides a lot of surface area to intercept flakes and VOCs and may enhance trail scent as noted. Observations of TDs trailing in deciduous forests suggest that the dead leaf surfaces appear to hold scent well, possibly as the combined result of shade, increased moisture, and the presence of cavities formed by the leaves.

7.2 Training and Deployment

7.2.1 Scent Articles

Scent articles can be anything the subject has touched or worn. Since trail scent originates from all locations on a body, a scent article from any location would be useful, but areas that produce more scent would be preferable. Bacterial populations are large in areas on the body where the skin is moist, primarily the armpits, genitals and groin, head, soles of the feet, and palms of the hand. Underwear, used baby diapers, hats, pillows, shoes, socks, and gloves that have been in contact with the subject for extended periods of time are desirable scent articles. The handler should personally collect the scent article. If this is not possible, everyone who may have been in contact with it must be present when the dog is scented. Use of the scent inventory method (Mark Holmes, trailing seminars) is desirable if the scent article is contaminated.

Objects that the subject has touched may include burglary tools, bomb fragments, rocks, letters, notes, coffee cups, and blood, among others. Wiping surfaces that the subject has touched can also be used to obtain a scent article. These include steering wheels, door handles, windowsills, and other items.

Footprints are commonly used scent articles. A scent article from the driver's seat of a vehicle can be obtained by placing an absorbent paper or cloth on it for 10 to 15 min. Some handlers recommend covering the article while it is absorbing scent.

Scent articles can be obtained using noncontact methods such as the STU-100 unit (Eckenrode et al. 2006), which is used to vacuum scent from the subject or from objects that the subject has touched. Since the human scent plume contains scent from every part of the body, a more complete scent profile of a subject may be obtained by vacuuming at the top of the head. Another method is to use the human scent plume that exits the body above the head and shoulders in places that the subject frequents. An example is the headliner in an automobile above the driver's seat, which can be wiped with an absorbent paper or cloth that becomes the scent article of the driver (Burt Crawford, personal communication).

Scent articles can be obtained from firearms, bows, knives, and other weapons and from projectiles such as bullets, pellets, arrows, and rocks. Fired shell casings can also be used. The body of an assault victim has been used as a scent article. Another possibility would be to wipe the skin of a victim that has been assaulted, although this does not appear to have been done.

Scent articles stored in airtight containers appear to lose some scent initially, but then level off after the first 2 weeks and are still usable months later (Prada et al. 2015). Fired shell casings stored in a freezer bag for over a year have been successfully used by dogs to trail. These results and others have verified that human scent is stable and reproducible over long times.

7.2.2 Turns and Wind

TD handlers should be constantly aware of the wind direction on trails. Whatever channels the wind, channels scent and may be a barrier to the dog. If the channeled wind and scent are in the same direction and the trail turns out of the channel, the dog tends to significantly overshoot the turn. Typically, wind direction is at some angle to the trail other than 90°, but considering these turns (Figure 7.6) can help to understand what to expect. TDs usually trail somewhat downwind of the trail, depending on their inclination and training. For a crosswind leg with an upwind turn, the dog encounters a lot of scent at the turn from the trail upwind and should immediately turn with the trail. For a crosswind leg with a downwind turn, the scent decreases quickly as the dog passes the turn and it should give an indication of it (e.g. head turn).

A downwind leg with a crosswind turn carries a lot of scent downwind past the turn. The tendency of the dog is to continue past the turn in decreasing amounts of scent until they realize they are getting out of scent. If the dog has been trained using a line (leash) check, apply it about a leash length past

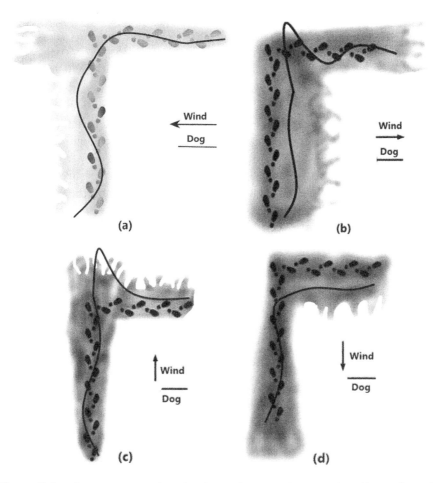

Figure 7.6 Schematic examples of right-angle turns showing the effects of wind direction on the dog's behavior.

the turn in training and periodically on a blind trail. A turn off a downwind leg is especially difficult in a channel. On an upwind leg, the dogs seem much more animated. If the wind is slightly variable, the dogs tends to quarter the trail, or they carry their heads high which causes them to scent the turn and cut off the corner in the trail. If they pass the turn, the scent decreases sharply, and they usually give an indication. If not, apply leash tension.

For the scent collectors (grass, curbs, barriers), dogs usually trail on the grass, along curbs or along a barrier some distance from the trail if the wind is significant.

Trails that are laid primarily upwind are likely to result in the dog air scenting the subject. Trail patterns that begin and end near the same location (letter C or U shape) should not be used regularly. Some dogs quickly learn that the trail always goes back to the area of the start and a variable wind may allow the dog to scent the end of the trail near the start. Different legs of a trail should be far enough apart so that the dog cannot scent an upwind leg, or the trail should be laid so that the upwind leg is run before the downwind leg.

7.2.3 Buildings and Wind

The effects of buildings on wind are to cause the wind to flow over and around them, creating 3 dimensional eddies on the ends and sides that are difficult to predict. For the special case of wind nearly perpendicular to the sides of buildings, the behavior is like that of ridges and islands. Away from the ends of the buildings, vertical two-dimensional eddies occur (Figure 7.7) which produce ground level circulation away from the building on the upwind side and toward the building on the downwind side. For a trail along the building on the upwind side, scent will be carried away from the building and

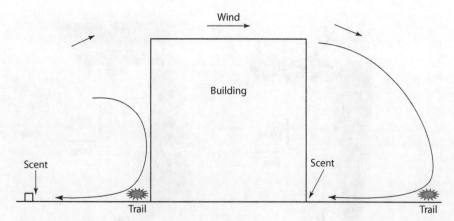

Figure 7.7 Vertical profile of air passing over a building away from the ends. Scent from the trail (🌟) on the upwind side collects against the barrier and on the downwind side, against the building.

dogs will trail there, especially when scent collectors are present within a distance about the height of the building (e.g. curb, vegetation). For a trail on the downwind side and less than the height of the building downwind, scent will be carried to the building and the dogs will trail close to it.

7.2.4 Air-Scenting Trails

TDs that carry their heads high tend to air scent trails when the wind from a leg that has not been run blows across or toward the leg being run. On fresh trails, the distance between the legs can be a city block which indicates that the scent is likely an airborne scent plume. However, air scenting has been observed on trails aged 24 hrs with legs 200 yds apart. This suggests that the airborne scent may be coming from the bacteria on skin flakes, secretions on the flakes, and/or VOCs from surfaces, although there are no observations to confirm this hypothesis.

7.2.5 Direction of Travel

The behavior of TDs when encountering a track with an unknown direction is of interest to all handlers. Three phases of behavior by TDs have been identified (Thesen et al. 1993): searching, deciding, and tracking. Frequency of sniffing was about 6/sec in all three phases. Once the track was found, the deciding phase began. This was clear because the dogs usually halted for a moment. The dogs moved more slowly, had longer sniffing periods, and often slowed or stopped when they passed a footprint. The deciding phase lasted 3 to 5 sec while the dogs sniffed with their noses close to the ground. They needed 2 to 5 footprints to determine the track direction, and once the decision was made the tracking phase began.

Since dogs can determine the direction of an odor trail left by a human, it is of interest to determine the length of the trail needed for them to do it. Six dogs, able to determine direction of travel, were tested on a 21-footstep trail laid on 21 individual carpet squares (Hepper and Wells 2005). The dogs correctly determined direction 1 hr after the trail was made but were unable to do so when the order of the footsteps was randomized by rearranging the order of the carpet squares. Sealing the feet of the trail layer prevented any foot or shoe odor from being deposited but retained any scent made by the carpet disturbance. The dogs could not reliably determine direction of the trail which indicates that they used the individual's odor deposited in or near a footstep rather than any effects related to compressing the wool carpet squares. When the carpet squares were removed, it was shown that the dogs were able to determine direction from 5 footsteps which required about 2 sec to make. At normal walking speed, these dogs could determine the difference in scent between two positions on the trail separated by about 6 ft.

These studies did not investigate the influence of the age of the trail. It does not appear that the dogs in these studies were trained using scent articles, which may have influenced the results. TDs that are trained with scent articles can usually determine direction of travel and, with some testing standards, are required to do this for trails 24 hours old.

7.2.6 Car Trails

There is often doubt expressed about the ability of dogs to follow a person in a moving car. However, skin flakes and VOCs are exhausted from the car vents so that trailing should still be possible. The following examples, which are only a few among many, show that car trails are possible. The question is not whether dogs can do them, but "Under what conditions can car trails be done?"

7.2.6.1 Missing Child

In 1993, a child was reported missing near Denver, Colorado. Three days later a 4 yr-old bloodhound named Yogi was scented with a pair of the child's underpants by his handler, police officer Jerry Nichols, and began a trail near the child's home. The team trailed from W. Grand Ave., near Belleview and South Broadway, continued along Broadway to C-470, exited at Kipling Street, and then west to the mouth of Deer Creek Canyon (Figure 7.8). The length of the trail was about 14 mi and it was done in about 7 hrs. This trail was exceptional because of its age, length, extensive hard surfaces, and vehicle and personnel distractions. The next day, searchers picked up where the team left off, and while searching Deer Creek Canyon, discovered the child's body. Later, Yogi led investigators from Deer Creek Canyon back to the apartments where the murderer lived near W. Grand Ave.

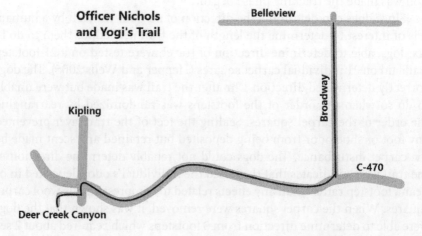

Figure 7.8 Approximate trail of Officer Nichols and Yogi from near Belleview and Broadway to Deer Creek Canyon, a distance of about 14 miles.

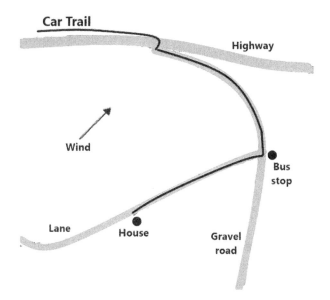

Figure 7.9 Car trail of a kidnapped boy. Scent collected on weeds, grass, and leaves on the side of the trail which made the trail easier for the dog and she clearly preferred trailing on them.

7.2.6.2 *Missing Boy*

A car trail involving scent collectors (weeds, grass and leaves) occurred when a boy was kidnapped in a rural area between his house and school bus stop (Figure 7.9). The trail was started at his house at 10 p.m., about 6 hrs after he was abducted, and went up the gravel lane to the bus stop where he caught the bus to school in the morning. It turned left on a gravel road, and the dog trailed on the right side of the road along and in weeds to a paved highway, crossed the highway, and trailed west on grass in a shallow ditch along the north side of the highway. After more than 100 yds, she left the ditch and moved farther away from the road along a fence where the leaves were piled a foot or so deep next to a tree line. After another 100 yds, the handler called a halt to the trail since it was obviously a car trail implying that the boy had been abducted.

The trail was about 14 hrs old from the house, 6 hrs old from the bus stop, with the wind from the southwest at about 20 mph, and with a total length about ½ mile. It is not likely that the car exceeded 45 mph on the highway. Three days later the abductor was apprehended and the boy rescued. He verified that the trail the dog followed was the direction he was taken by vehicle.

7.2.7 Aged Trails

The stability of human scent has been widely studied but there does not appear to be any information on the stability of trail scent. Handlers have observed that trail scent is stable over time frames of several weeks when conditions are good (warm and moist), like those that occur near sea coasts. However, scenting conditions can vary with time of day and weather. For example, it is known that trails made in the morning on an asphalt surface can be extremely difficult for dogs to run during the afternoon on a sunny, hot summer day. However, when the surface goes into shade and at night, it cools, and the trail becomes much easier for the dogs. Syrotuck (1972) believed that the difficulty was a result of drying skin flakes and reduction of bacterial activity on them but did not consider VOCs from other body sources. There does not appear to any further analyses of trail scent, especially of the relative roles of VOCs produced by bacteria acting on skin flakes and those produced by other sources.

There are many reliable reports by handlers of TDs working aged trails up to a month old but it is not usually possible to obtain an independent verification. A verified trail involved a man thought to be suicidal who was trailed 16 days after he had disappeared in a shipyard in the Pacific Northwest. The age of the trail was verified by police report and a surveillance camera. Daytime temperatures were in the 60s and 70s°F. The trail started at a railroad station, was about ¼ mile long, and led to a locked gate at a shipyard which he apparently crawled under or over it (Figure 7.10). Trail surfaces consisted of cut grass, railroad tracks, covered walk, and paved parking lot. In the shipyard, the surface was gravel and only parts of the trail could be found there, but it

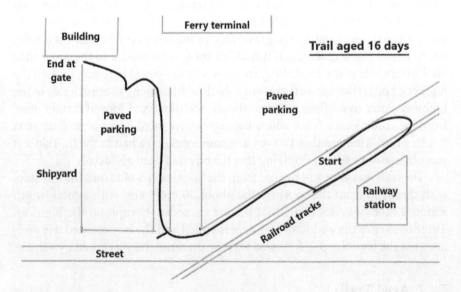

Figure 7.10 A trail aged 16 days near the Pacific Northwest seacoast verified by police report and security camera. The trail was heavily contaminated by cars and pedestrian traffic.

appeared that the man was moving toward the dock after leaving his belongings in a shed.

This trail was heavily contaminated since it crossed the entrance to a busy ferry terminal. It is estimated that hundreds of cars, several hundred trains, and more than a thousand people crossed the trail before it was run.

There does not appear to be any information on the characteristics and behavior of aged trail scent. Does the scent remain on the ground, linger in the air, move daily between the ground and air? Is scent from the feet made by the bellows action of walking in pants and shoes important? What is the relative importance of VOCs from bacteria and from other sources? Can bacteria survive weeks or a month and, if so, under what conditions? What scents do dogs trail on asphalt surfaces weeks after the trail was made? What are the effects of various surfaces and environmental conditions?

7.3 Summary

Scent from the human body appears to consist of gases produced by bacteria acting on the skin and skin flakes (including skin flakes from breath), volatilization of secretions on skin and skin flakes, and VOCs from breath. This scent is specific to an individual and consists of particulates (skin flakes) and gaseous VOCs from all the sources.

Skin is normally warmer than the adjacent air and heats the air, which produces thermal convection from the body to the surrounding air (Figure 7.1). This results in a human boundary layer next to the skin that flows upward from the ankles to the top of the head. Every location on the body contributes scent to the human boundary layer so that all types of scent released by the body or on the body are in the upward moving layer. This includes scent from skin flakes, VOCs, explosives, drugs, disease carrying bacteria, and disease. The boundary layer exits the body at the top of the shoulders and head which produces a plume (Figure 7.2).

A walking person produces a turbulent wake with eddies behind them, and the plume is incorporated into this wake. Eddies in the wake cause part of the plume to contact the ground and deposit scent there (Figure 7.3). Scent from a walking person may also be deposited by the bellows action of the pant legs and shoes (Figure 7.2). Consequently, trail scent consists of the skin flakes and VOCs deposited in the path of the person and downwind. Scent not deposited would be carried away by the wind.

Deposition of VOCs depends on temperature, but deposition of flakes does not. Once deposited, sunlight may degrade flakes and some VOCs. Trail scent can be enhanced by changes in wind direction and turbulence on the surfaces where the flakes are deposited, which would produce multiple mini plumes for all the flakes (Figure 7.4) and result in a cloud of VOCs in the area of each deposited flake (Figure 7.5). There is a daily cycle in the concentrations of VOCs deposited on surfaces, and concentrations there should be higher during the night and for surfaces in shade compared to these surfaces in sunlight. This may be the reason that dogs can trail better on surfaces in shade and at night.

When considering the effects of temperature on trail scent, the temperature of the surface where the trail exists is more important than the air temperature. The availability of bacterial gases and VOCs would be expected to increase with increasing temperatures. Although the amount of scent available increases as temperatures increase into the 90s°F and higher, the dogs usually find it more difficult to continue working. If high temperatures are associated with low humidity, skin flakes would be expected to dry, which would reduce availability of bacterial gases.

At temperatures like those in a refrigerator (typically <40°F), bacterial activity slows and below freezing it almost ceases. At temperatures like those in a deep freeze (<0°F), bacterial action ceases. Experience with TDs in Interior Alaska has shown that dogs can still successfully trail at temperatures of −30°F on frozen surfaces, ice, and snow. This may be a result of inhalation of skin flakes and VOCs. Experience suggests that dogs can still trail with ½ ft of new powder snow on the trail, but a few inches of wet snow that has frozen makes trailing difficult to impossible. Some dogs learn to follow visible footprints in the snow, but others seem to trail as if the footprints were not there.

Vegetation typically has 6 to 14 times more surface area than the land on which it is growing. This provides a lot of surface area to intercept flakes and VOCs and may help enhance trail scent. In deciduous forests, dead leaf surfaces appear to hold scent well, possibly as the combined result of shade, increased moisture, and the presence of cavities formed by the leaves.

Scent articles can be anything the subject has touched or worn. Since trail scent originates from all locations on a body, a scent article from any location would be useful, but areas that produce more scent would be preferable. Underwear, used baby diapers, hats, pillows, shoes, socks, and gloves are desirable scent articles.

Wiping surfaces that the subject has touched can also be used to obtain a scent article. These include steering wheels, door handles, and windowsills among others. Footprints are commonly used. A scent article from the driver's seat of a vehicle can be obtained by placing an absorbent paper or cloth on it for 10 to 15 min. The headliner in an automobile above the driver's seat can be wiped with an absorbent paper or cloth which becomes the scent article.

Scent articles can be obtained from firearms, bows, knives, and other weapons and from the projectiles such as bullets, pellets, arrows, and rocks. Fired shell casings can also be used. The body of an assault victim has been used as the scent article.

The effects of wind direction on trail scent (Figure 7.6) and on turns in the trail, trails near buildings, channeling, and scent collectors are discussed (Figure 7.6 and 7.7). TDs that carry their heads high tend to air scent trails when the wind from a leg that has not been run blows across or toward the leg being run. The distance between the legs can be a city block and air scenting has been observed on trails aged 24 hrs with legs 200 yds apart.

Trails that are laid primarily upwind are likely to result in the dog air scenting the subject. Trail patterns that begin and end near the same location (letter C or U shape) should not be used.

Dogs can determine the direction of a trail left by a human and they have a distinctive behavior when acquiring it. When an hr old trail was detected, it required up to 5 sec and 5 footprints to decide on the direction. It was shown that the dogs used trail scent rather than ground disturbance to determine direction of travel.

Dogs can do car trails. Two car trails are described including one 3 days old and 14 mi long (Figures 7.8 and 7.9). There are reliable reports of TDs working aged trails up to a month old (Figure 7.10). It is not known what components of trail scent are used nor how the dogs can follow these very old trails.

There does not appear to be any information on the characteristics and behavior of aged trail scent. Does the scent remain on the ground, linger in the air, or move daily between the ground and the air? Is the scent from the feet and legs made by the bellows action of walking in shoes and pants important? What is the relative importance of VOCs from bacteria and from other sources? Can bacteria survive weeks or a month, and, if so, under what conditions? What scents do dogs trail on asphalt surfaces weeks after the trail was made? What are the effects of various surfaces and environmental conditions?

Appendix 1: Abbreviations

~	approximately
<	less than
>	more than
μg	microgram
μliter	microliter
μm	micrometer
1.9E-1	the number with the decimal point moved one place left (0.19)
ft/sec	feet per second
ft^3	feet cubed (to the 3rd power)
ft	foot/feet
g/mol	grams per mole
Hg	mercury
hr	hour
in/sec	inch per second
in^3	inches cubed
in	inch
lb	pound
lbs/ft^3	pounds per cubic foot
min	minute
ml	milliliter
m	meter
mph	miles per hour
ng/g	nanograms per gram
oz	ounce
PMA1A	personnel mine
ppm	parts per million
psi	pounds per square inch
sec	second
TMA-5	tank mine
yd	yard

Appendix 2: Acronyms

BADD	burial accumulated degree days
CB	change in behavior
CDs	cadaver dogs
COMPS	controlled odor mimic permeation system
DNB	dinitrobenzene
EDs	explosive dogs
GPS	global positioning system
HHRDs	historical human remains dogs
HRDs	human remains dogs, also called forensic search dogs
IC	incident command
IEDs	improvised explosive devices
MRI	magnetic resonance imaging
NORT	national odor recognition test
PC	potassium chlorate
PLS	place last seen
POD	probability of detection
SDs	search dogs
STU-100	scent transfer unit 100
TDs	trailing dogs
VICs	volatile inorganic compounds
VOCs	volatile organic compounds

Appendix 3: Questions and Needs for SD Training and Deployment

The following questions and needs have been formulated based on the book chapters and references cited therein. Surveys of the literature indicate there is a need for reviews and analyses by experts in diverse scientific fields (weather, biology, organic chemistry, physiology, fluid dynamics) of a wide array of questions involving the use of SDs. These have the potential to improve the training and use of canines in their roles as SDs, specifically, to find the lost, to bring closure to the families of the missing, to aid law enforcement in their pursuit and prosecution of criminals, to secure the borders of our country, and to aid the military in engaging our enemies.

Many of the statements and ideas presented in this book are based on research or handler observations of a few dogs which may change as more dogs are evaluated. Quantitative measurements are sorely needed to substantiate them. The following questions and needs have been selected, but have not been prioritized.

Chapter 2 The Dog's Nose and Scent

- Retrievers used in duck hunting, dogs following a trail through water, and water search dogs have been observed "tasting" the water. The process is different from drinking because the mouth is partially opened and water flows through it and out the sides. Retrievers can also dive under water and find a duck. While there are other possibilities, this may suggest that the dogs are using the vomeronasal organ to detect scent in or on the water. Is it possible for dogs to "taste" scent?
- McLean and Sargisson (2005) have proposed a variation of the effects of the air jets observed by Settles et al. (2002) and Settles (2020). When sniffing dry soil surfaces, the dog's moist exhaled air jets may cause VOCs adsorbed on the disturbed dust particles to be replaced by water molecules and be released into the air where the dog can inhale and detect them directly. While this hypothesis is plausible, it should be confirmed by experiments.

- Training and using SDs efficiently requires an understanding of scent characteristics and movement and interaction of scent with the environment. While information on scent characteristics has been scant in the past, there has been a rapid expansion of information over the last two decades. On the other hand, information on scent movement and the interaction of scent with the environment is sparse. A thorough review of this topic is needed to identify research needs and directions.

- Surfaces in contact with airborne VOCs can interact with the VOCs and modify the concentration of VOCs available to SDs. While some information is available, much more is needed to define the adsorption (stickiness) and desorption (volatilization) of scent molecules associated with explosives, drugs, humans (alive and deceased), on natural and artificial surfaces and for various environmental conditions.

- When a source is placed at a site and removed later, VOCs, microparticles, and liquid residuals may be left behind. A definition of residual scent needs to be developed for several reasons and especially so that everyone can be "on the same page" when discussing it. The amount of time residual scent can be detected by SDs on different surfaces and under various environmental conditions needs to be determined.

- CD handlers typically use cadaver materials as training aids. There are nearly 500 VOCs from decomposing bodies (Vass et al. 2004, 2008), but the specific compounds that elicit an alert by CDs are unknown. Not enough is known about the effects of age, storage conditions (temperature, humidity, aerobic or anaerobic decomposition), and other factors on training aids to predict the suitability of the aids for training CDs. CD handlers must obtain and store many training aids, and information is needed that will allow them to reduce the number of aids required to train the dogs.

- Dogs appear to be able to recognize when a person is dead, but it is not known how they do this. Some nurses report that people who are about to die have a certain smell, but this does not appear to have been studied. Carrion flies, when present and under favorable environmental conditions, have been observed to appear on a corpse in a matter of minutes after death (Haskel et al. 1997). Is there a scent associated with death, an "odor mortis", that appears within minutes of dying or possibly before?

- Decomposition scent differs from live scent since it is thought to be generic. However, each living person's scent is unique, specific to the individual, which indicates that some of the chemicals that make up scent may be controlled by the individual's genetics. It is also known that dogs can detect bones, teeth, and hair in older burials and that these materials retain their DNA. This raises the possibility that dogs may be capable of distinguishing between individual cadavers (skeletons) by the unique scent of their bones, teeth, and hair. Is it possible to train CDs to discriminate between cadavers?

- Blood is commonly found at crime scenes and figures prominently in investigations. CDs are used to detect blood in houses (carpets, beds, sink drains, walls), vehicles (seats, trunks, truck beds), outdoors (grass, forests, pavements), and in many other places. While some information is available (Chilcote et al. 2017), more information is needed on the ability of dogs to detect blood on various substrates and conditions, especially weather conditions.
- Two distinct methods have been developed for introducing sources to EDs and DDs (Goldblatt et al. 2009). One combines sources to produce a scent mixture that is introduced to the dogs. Once the dogs recognize and alert on the mixture, the sources are separated for the rest of the training and never recombined. However, Goldblatt et al. (2009) recommend introducing each source separately either sequentially or during the same time frame. Is one method better than the other?

Chapter 3 Scent and Wind

- Smoke plumes appear to be a good substitute for scent plumes. Releasing smoke plumes under known or controlled conditions in structures, vehicles and outdoors could provide valuable information for SD handlers for training and deploying their dogs. Instructional videos could be made available on smart phones and would help to reduce the time needed for handlers to become competent and help current handlers become more efficient and successful. The effects of stability, instability, turbulence, terrain, vegetation and others could be brought to life in these videos for handlers of SDs.

Chapter 4 Aboveground Searches

- Limited results suggest that the best time to search for articles on the ground surface in tall grass is mid-morning after a few hours of sunlight. It was hypothesized that the scent was trapped and collected near the ground surface overnight and that some uplift (convection) was required to bring the scent up and out of the grass to the level of the dog's nose. It is desirable to test this hypothesis because of its importance for detecting surface and buried objects (e.g. articles, explosives, graves).

- It is hypothesized that there may be a range of optimum wind conditions at some intermediate velocity between calm and strong turbulence where SDs will be most successful locating a source. Optimum wind conditions will be influenced by the characteristics of the source, whether it is above or below ground, weather, and the environmental setting. What are these optimum wind conditions?
- SD handlers often conduct searches without the benefit of any formal search management support and need simplified methods they can use in the field to select grid/lane widths to attain a desired POD for the sources they seek.
- Distant alerts are difficult to resolve (i.e. find the source), especially in hilly terrain. A comprehensive review of conditions that can cause long distance transport of scent plumes and bring them in contact with the ground is needed. It may be possible to use this information to improve our ability to find the sources.

Chapter 5 Buried Sources

- The scent distribution around buried sources, especially human remains is unknown. Relocation of old cemeteries would provide opportunities to map the scent distribution in the soil around graves.
- The presence and pattern of high concentrations of DNT in a thin layer at the ground surface over buried TNT in mines is a "scent print" (Osterkamp 2020 and unpublished notes 2020) that dogs likely use to detect the mines. Additional studies are needed for other explosives, different soil types and conditions, weather conditions and elapsed time after burial.
- Similar studies for graves are needed to determine the potential existence of "scent prints" over graves that CDs use to detect them. The size of the scent print can be useful in selecting grid/lane widths for searches. Information on the decomposition chemicals in the surface soils may help develop training aids or those parts of cadavers most useful in training CDs to find clandestine graves. Would it be possible to bury different cadaver parts in various soil types and soil and weather conditions to narrow the list of VOCs used by the dogs to detect graves?
- The influence of different types of ground cover, vegetation and small-scale thermal turbulence on scent movement and plume behavior are unknown which makes it difficult to evaluate scent movement from the soil surface to the dog's nose.
- If scent has accumulated in a scent print at the ground surface, its availability would depend on conditions favorable for volatilization

at the surface. Field studies of select VOCs for different soils and conditions may help to quantify the availability of scent from the surface which would determine the best times to search.

Chapter 6 Water Searches

- There does not appear to be studies on the scent or scent-bearing materials emanating from submerged decomposing human bodies. VOCs from decomposing buried bodies have been identified (Vass et al. 2008). These compounds may be soluble or insoluble in water and most are heavier than water. Water may modify them and accelerate or retard decomposition depending primarily on its temperature, availability of oxygen and whether it is salty or fresh, moving or still, or differs from normal pH. The presence of aquatic scavengers and the type of scent transport to the surface may also be important (Teather 1994, Osterkamp 2011).
- While the vertical transport of scent and scent-bearing materials to a stream surface can be estimated using advanced methods, handlers need simplified methods that can be used in the field. These methods would help them determine the position of the body for recovery efforts.
- It was hypothesized that a scent print consisting of an oily film exists on the water surface near a submerged decomposing body. Information on its presence, extent, and characteristics is needed. This lack of information contributes to the difficulty of locating bodies in water.

Chapter 7 Trails and Trailing

- Several ideas about trail scent are presented including the source, how it gets to the ground, and a potential process for spreading. These ideas need to be confirmed and quantified by experiments. Questions include the role of small skin fragments, effects of the bellows action of pant legs and shoes while walking, and the continued emission of VOCs from bacteria and secretions when flakes are deposited on surfaces.
- The interactions of trail scent with common trail surfaces need to be investigated, particularly, the partitioning of VOCs between the gas and solid phases and the daily cycle of VOC concentrations. This may not be possible since the specific VOCs used by dogs to follow trails are unknown. Does the scent remain on the surface, linger

in the air, or move daily between the ground and air? However, a
careful review of the subject may yield some information useful to
handlers.

- VOCs and skin flakes may be trapped in the surface pores of hard
  surfaces, such as asphalt and concrete, which may explain the ability
  of dogs to trail on these surfaces. Do skin flakes also stick (adhere)
  to these surfaces? How long can bacteria survive on the flakes? How
  long can VOCs adhere to these surfaces or linger in the pores?
- What factors allow dogs to follow (scent) trails aged for several
  weeks?
- How does the age of the trail influence the ability to determine direction of travel?
- Under what conditions can car trails be done?

References

Aitkenhead-Peterson, J.A., Owings, C.G., Alexander, M.B. et al. 2011. Mapping the lateral extent of human cadaver decomposition with soil chemistry. *Forensic Sci Int* 216:127–134.

Altom, E.K., Davenport, G.M. and Myers, L.J. 2003. Effect of dietary fat source and exercise on odorant-detecting ability of Canine Athletes. *Res Vet Sci* 75(2):149–155.

Anderson, G.S. and Hobischak, N.R. 2004. Decomposition of carrion in the marine environment in British Columbia, Canada. *Int J Legal Med* 118:206–209.

Aspnes, J. and Aspnes, J. 1998. Cold weather searching. Response. *J Nat Assoc Search Rescue* 16(3):1–7.

Barton, B. and Clemmo, L. 1997. *Water search with dogs: A program for training a dog to locate drowning victims.* Stroudsburg: Rescue International.

Belcher, S.E., Harman, I.N. and Finnigan, J.J. 2012. The wind in the willows: Flows in forest canopies in complex terrain. *Annu Rev Fluid Mech* 44:479–504.

Bierly, E.W. and Hewson, E.W. 1962. Some restrictive meteorological conditions to be considered in the dsign of stacks. *J Appl Meteorol* 1:383–390.

Bryson, S. 1984. *Search dog training.* Pacific Grove, CA: The Boxwood Press.

Cablk, M.E. and Sagebiel, J.C. 2011. Field capability of dogs to locate individual human teeth. *J Forensic Sci* 56(4):1018–1024.

Cablk, M.E., Sagebiel, J.C., Heaton, J.S. et al. 2008. Olfaction-based detection distance: A quantitative analysis of how far away dogs recognize tortoise odor and follow it to source. *Sensors* 8:2208–2222.

Cardé, R.T. and Willis, M.A. 2008. Navigational strategies used by insects to find distant, wind-borne sources of odor. *J Chem Ecol* 34:854–866.

Carter, L.J., Harris, E., Williams, M. et al. 2014. Fate and uptake of pharmaceuticals in soil–plant systems. *J Agric Food Chem* 62(4):816–825.

Cheng, W.H., Chu, F.S. and Liou, C.Y. 2005. Simulating the emission rate of volatile organic compounds from a quiescent water surface: Model development and feasibility evaluation. *J Environ Sci Health* 40(9A):1701–1713.

Chiacchia, K.B., Houlahan, H.E. and Hostetter, R.S. 2015. Deriving effective sweep width for air-scent dog teams. *Wilderness Environ Med* 26:142–149.

Clark, R.P. 1974. Skin scales among airborne articles. *J Hygiene* 71(1):47–51.

Clark, R.P. and de Calcina-Goff, M.L. 2009. Some aspects of the airborne transmission of infection. *J R Soc Interface* 6(Supplement 6):767–782.

Conover, M.R. 2007. *Predator-prey dynamics: The role of olfaction.* Boca Raton, FL: CRC Press/Taylor & Francis.

Cousins, I.T., Angus, U., Beck, J. and Jones, K.C. 1999. A review of the processes involved in the exchange of semi-volatile organic compounds across the air–soil interface. *Sci Total Environ* 228:5–24.

Craven, B.A. 2008. A fundamental study of the anatomy, aerodynamics, and transport phenomena of canine olfaction. PhD diss., Pennsylvania State Univ.

Craven, B.A., Paterson, E.G. and Settles, G.S. 2010. The fluid dynamics of canine olfaction: Unique nasal airflow patterns as an explanation of macrosmia. *J R Soc Interface* 7:933–943.

Davies, R.R. and Noble, W.C. 1962. Dispersal of bacteria on desquamated skin. *Lancet* ii:1295–1297.

DeBose, J.L. and Nevitt, G.A. 2008. The use of odors at different spatial scales: Comparing birds with fish. *J Chem Ecol* 34(7):867–881.

DeGreef, L.E. 2010. Development of a dynamic headspace concentration technique for the non-contact sampling of human odor samples and the creation of canine training aids. PhD diss., Florida International Univ.

DeGreeff, L.E. and Furton, K.G. 2011. Collection and identification of human remains volatiles by non-contact, dynamic airflow sampling and SPME-GC/MS using various sorbent materials. *Anal Bioanal Chem* 401:1295–1307.

Dent, B.B., Forbes, S.L. and Stuart, B.H. 2004. Review of human decomposition processes in soil. *Environ Geol* 45:576–585.

Eckenrode, B.A., Ramsey, S.A., Stockham, R.A. et al. 2006. Performance evaluation of the scent transfer unit™ (STU-100) for organic compound collection and release. *J Forensic Sci* 51(4):780–789.

Edge, B.A., Paterson, E.G. and Settles, G.S. 2005. Computational study of the wake and contaminant transport of a walking human. *J Fluids Eng* 127:967–977.

Eisenhauer, P.M. 1971. *Dogs for swimmer defense*. Panama City, FL: Naval Ship and Development Laboratory Sept R&D Rept NSRDL/PCC 3469.

Ensminger, J.J. and Papet, L.E. 2011. How to prevent cueing arguments from getting canine evidence thrown out in court. *Deputy and Court Officer* 3(2):36–38.

Ewing, R.G., Waltman, M.J., Atkinson, D.A. et al. 2013. The vapor pressures of explosives. *Trends Anal Chem* 42:35–48.

Fjellanger, R. 2003. The REST concept. In *Mine detection dogs: Training, operations and odour detection*, ed. I.G. McLean, 53–105. Geneva: Geneva International Centre for Humanitarian Demining.

France, D.L., Griffin, T.J., Swanburg, J.G. et al. 1997. Necrosearch revisited: Further multidisciplinary approaches to the detection of clandestine graves. In *Forensic taphonomy: The postmortem fate of human remains*, ed. W.D. Haglund and M.H. Sorg, 497–510. Boca Raton, FL: CRC Press.

Frankel, R. 2014. *War dogs: Tales of canine heroism, history, and love*. New York: Palgrave Macmillan/St. Martin's Press.

Furton, K.G. and Harper, R.J. 2017. US Patent Number 9,706,755 B2.

Furton, K.G. and Myers, L.J. 2001. The scientific foundation and efficacy of the use of canines as chemical detectors for explosives. *Talanta* 54:487–500.

Furton, K.G., Hong, Y., Hsu, Y. et al. 2002. Identification of odor signature chemicals in cocaine using solid-phase microextraction–gas chromatography and detector-dog response to isolated compounds spiked on U.S. paper currency. *J Chromatogr Sci* 40:147–155.

Gary, H.L. 1974. Snow accumulation and snow melt as influenced by a small clearing in a Lodgepole Pine forest. *Water Resour Res* 10:348–353.

Gazit, I. and Terkel, J. 2003a. Explosives detection by sniffer dogs following strenuous physical activity. *Appl Anim Behav Sci* 81:149–161.

Gazit, I. and Terkel, J. 2003b. Domination of olfaction over vision in explosives detection by dogs. *Appl Anim Behav Sci* 82:65–73.

Gazit, I., Goldblatt, A. and Terkel, J. 2005a. Formation of an olfactory search image for explosives odours in sniffer dogs. *Ethology* 111:669–680.

Gazit, I., Goldblatt, A. and Terkel, J. 2005b. The role of context specificity in learning: The effects of training context on explosives detection in dogs. *Anim Cognit* 8:143–150.

GICHD. 2004. *Training of mine detection dogs in Bosnia and Herzegovina (NPA Global Training Centre).* Geneva: Geneva International Centre for Humanitarian Demining.

Gill-King, H. 1997. Chemical and ultrastructural aspects of decomposition. In *Forensic taphonomy: The postmortem fate of human remains*, ed. W.D. Haglund and M.H. Sorg, 93–108. Boca Raton, FL: CRC Press.

Goldblatt, A. 2017. REST. Paper presented at the International Working Dog Conference, Banff, Canada.

Goldblatt, A., Gazit, I. and Terkel, J. 2009. Olfaction and explosives detector dogs. In *Canine ergonomics: The science of working dogs*, ed. W. S. Helton, 135–174. Boca Raton, FL: CRC Press/Taylor & Francis.

Goodwin, K.M. 2010. Using canines to detect spotted knapweed: Field surveys and characterization of plant volatiles. M.S. Thesis, Montana State University.

Gosink, J.P. and Osterkamp, T.E. 1983. Measurements and analyses of velocity profiles and frazil ice crystal rise velocities during periods of frazil ice formation in rivers. *Annals of Glaciol* 4:79–84.

Graham, H. 1979. Convectional turbulence and the air scenting dog. *Search Rescue Dogs Tech Note* 2:1–4.

Graham, H. 1994. Probability of detection for search dogs or how long is your shadow? *Response Mag* Winter:1–7.

Graham, H. and Graham, J. 1985. Training for water search. *Dog Sports Mag* January:1–2.

Graham, H. and Graham, J. 1987. Taking back from the river. *Response Mag* September/October:34–37.

Grandjean, P.D. and Clero, D. 2011. Why must training and nutrition stay closely related in working dogs? Paper presented at the Penn Vet Working Dog Center Conference, Pearl River, New York.

Hall, N.J., Smith, D.W. and Wynne, C.D.L. 2013. Training domestic dogs (Canis lupus familiaris) on a novel discrete trials odor-detection task. *Learn Motiv* 44(4):218–228.

Hardy, M. 1992. Water search with dogs. Paper presented at the National Association for Search and Rescue Conference. Available at http://www.pawsoflife.org/Library/Trailing%20Water/Water%20Search%20with%20Dogs%20-%20Marion%20Hardy.pdf.

Haskel, N.H., Hall, R.D., Cervenka, V.J. et al., 1997. On the body: Insect's life stage presence and their postmortem artifacts. In *Forensic taphonomy: The postmortem fate of human remains*, ed. W.D. Haglund and M.H. Sorg, 415–448. Boca Raton, FL: CRC Press.

Hepper, P.G. and Wells, D.L. 2005. How many footsteps do dogs need to determine the direction of an odour trail? *Chem Senses* 30:291–298.

Hewitt, A.D., Jenkins, T.F. and Ranney, T.A. 2001. Field gas chromatography thermionic detector system for on-site determination of explosives in soils. *ERDC TR-01-9.* Hanover, NH: US Army Cold Regions Research and Engineering Laboratory.

Hoffman,E.M., Curran, A.M., Dulgerian, N. et al. 2009. Characterization of the volatile organic compounds present in the headspace of decomposing human remains. *Forensic Sci Int* 186:6–13.

Hood, L.V., Dames, M.E. and Barry, G.T. 1973. Headspace volatiles of marijuana. *Nature* 242:402–403.

Hudson, D.T., Curran, A.M. and Furton, K.G. 2009. The stability of collected human scent under various environmental conditions. *J Forensic Sci* 54(6):1270–1277.

Irwin, K.T. 2008. Arvada case. In *Buzzards and butterflies: Human remains detection dogs*, ed. J.C. Judah, 161–169. Morrisville, NC: Coastal Books.

Janaway, R.C. 1997. The decay of buried human remains and their associated materials. In *Studies in crime: An introduction to forensic archaeology*, ed. J. Hunter, C. Roberts and A. Martin, 58–85. London: Routledge Press.

Jenkins, T.F., Walsh, M.E., Miyares, P.H. et al. 2000. Analysis of explosives-related chemical signatures in soil samples collected near buried land mines. *ERDC TR-00-5*. Hanover, NH: US Army Cold Regions Research and Engineering Laboratory.

Jezierski, T., Adamkiewicz, E., Walczak, M. et al. 2012. Factors affecting drugs and explosives detection by dogs in experimental tests. Poster presented at the Canine Science Forum, Barcelona.

Jezeirsky, T., Adamkiewicz, E., Walczak, M. et al. 2014. Efficacy of drug detection by fully-trained police dogs varies by breed, training level, type of drug and search environment. *Forensic Sci Int* 237:112–118.

Karg, G., Suckling, D.M. and Bradley, S.J. 1994. Absorption and release of pheromone of *Epiphyas postvittana* (Lepidoptera: Tortricidae) by apple leaves. *J Chem Ecology* 20(8):1825–1841.

Koenig, M. 2000. Water searches. In *Cadaver dog handbook: Forensic training and tactics for the recovery of human remains*, ed. A. Rebmann, E. David and M.H. Sorg, Boca Raton, FL: Taylor and Francis/CRC Press.

Komar, D. 1999. The use of cadaver dogs in locating scattered, scavenged human remains: Preliminary field test results. *J Forensic Sci* 44:405–408.

Lai, L.H., Guerra, P., Joshi, M. et al. 2008. Analysis of volatile components of drugs and explosives by solid phase microextraction-ion mobility spectrometry. *J Sep Sci* 31:402–412.

Lasseter, A.E., Jacobi, K.P., Farley, F. et al. 2003. Cadaver dog and handler team capabilities in the recovery of buried human remains in the southeastern United States. *J Forensic Sci* 48(3):1–5.

Lavdas, L.G. 1976. A groundhog's approach to estimating insolation. *J Air Pollution Control Assoc* 26(8):794.

Lazarowski, L. and Dorman, D.C. 2014. Explosives detection by military working dogs: Olfactory generalization from components to mixtures. *Appl Anim Behav Sci* 151:84–93.

Lidwell, O.M., Noble, W.C. and Dolphin, G.W. 1959. The use of radiation to estimate the numbers of micro-organisms in air-borne particles. *J Hyg* 57:299–308.

Lippi, G. and Cervellin, G. 2011. Canine olfactory detection of cancer versus laboratory testing: Myth or opportunity? *Clin Chem Lab Med* 49(10):1–5.

Lotspeich, E., Kitts, K. and Goodpaster, J. 2012. Headspace concentrations of explosive vapors in containers designed for canine testing and training: Theory, experiment, and canine trials. *Forensic Sci Int* 220:130–134.

Lovitz, A.M., Sloan, A.M. and Rennaker, R.L. 2012. Complex mixture discrimination and the role of contaminants. *Chem Senses* 37:533–540.

MacDonald, I.R., Leifer, I., Sassen, R.et al. 2002. Transfer of hydrocarbons from natural seeps to the water column and atmosphere. *Geofluids* 2:95–107.

Macias, M.S. 2009. The development of an optimized system of narcotic and explosive contraband mimics for calibration and training of biological detectors. PhD diss., Florida International Univ.

Macias, M.J., Harper, R.J. and Furton, K.G. 2008. A comparison of real versus simulated contraband VOCs for reliable detector dog training utilizing SPME-GC-MS. *Am Lab* 40(1):16–19.

MacIntyre, F. 1974. The top millimeter of the ocean. *Sci Am* 230(5):62–77.

Marht, L., Vickers, D., Nakamura, R. et al. 2001. Shallow drainage flows. *Boundary-Layer Meteorol* 101:243–260.

Marples, M.J. 1969. Life on the human skin. *Sci Am* 220:108–115.

Marshall, T.J. and Holmes, J.W. 1979. *Soil physics.* Cambridge: Cambridge Univ. Press.

McLean, I.G. and Sargisson, R.G. 2005. *Detection of landmines by dogs: Environmental and behavioral determinants.* Geneva: GICHD.

McMahon, M. 2014. Using distance alerts to further the search effort. *Meridian* Fall:10–14.

Mech, L.D. 1970. *The wolf: The ecology and behavior of an endangered species.* Garden City, New York: Natural History Press.

Mesloh, C. and James-Mesloh, J. 2006. Trained dogs in the crime scene search. *J Forensic Identif* 56(4):534–539.

Noble, W.C. and Davies, R.R. 1965. Studies on the dispersal of staphylococci. *J Clin Path* 18:16–19.

Nussear, K.E., Esque, T.C., Heaton, J.S. et al. 2008. Are wildlife detector dogs or people better at finding desert tortoises (*Gopherus agassizii*)? *Herpetol Conserv Biol* 3(1):103–115.

Oesterhelweg, L., Kröber, S., Rottmann, K. et al. 2008. Cadaver dogs: A study on detection of contaminated carpet squares. *Forensic Sci Int* 174:35–39.

Oke, T.R. 1987. *Boundary layer climates*, 2nd edition. New York: Routledge/Taylor & Francis.

Osterkamp, T.E. 1977. Frazil ice nucleation by mass-exchange processes at the air–water interface. *J Glaciol* 19(81):619–625.

Osterkamp, T.E. 2001. Improving POD with the air scenting SAR dog: Training for control at a distance, range, and search pattern, Part 1. *SAR Dog Alert* 21(2): Spring. Available at http://www.k9search.net.

Osterkamp, T.E. 2002. Improving POD with the air scenting SAR dog: Training for control at a distance, range, and search pattern, Part 2. *SAR Dog Alert* 23(1): Winter. Available at http://www.k9search.net.

Osterkamp, T.E. 2003. Improving POD with the air scenting SAR dog: Training for control at a distance, range, and search pattern, Part 3. *SAR Dog Alert* 23(2): Spring. Available at http://www.k9search.net.

Osterkamp, T.E. 2020. Search dogs and scent prints. *J Forensic Sci* 65(1):345–346.

Osterkamp, T.E. 2011. K9 water searches: Scent and scent transport considerations. *J Forensic Sci* 56(4):907–912.

Osterkamp, T.E. and Burn, C.R. 2002. Permafrost. In *Encyclopedia of atmospheric sciences*, ed. J.R. Holton, J. Pyle and J.A. Curry, 1717–1729. New York: Academic Press.

Oxley, J.C., Smith, J.L., Kirschenbaum, L.J. et al. 2008. Detection of explosives in hair using ion mobility spectrometry. *J Forensic Sci* 53(3):1–4.

Oxley, J.C., Smith, J.L., Shinde, K. et al. 2005. Determination of the vapor density of triacetone triperoxide (TATP) using a gas chromatography headspace technique. *Propellants Explos Pyrotech* 30(2):127–130.

Palman, D. 2011. Distant alerts. Available at http://www.mesard.org/pdf_documents/Distant%20Alerts.pdf. (accessed November 19, 2015).

Papet, J.E. 2016. Narcotic and explosive odors: Volatile organic compounds as training aids for olfactory detection. In *Canine Olfaction Science and Law: Advances in Forensic Science, Medicine, Conservation, and Environmental Remediation*, ed. T. Jezeirski, J. Ensminger and L.E. Papet, 265–278. Boca Raton, FL: CRC Press/Taylor & Francis.

Papet, J.E. and Minhinnick, S. 2016. Training a statistically superior scent discrimination canine: Where trainer wisdom meets scientific validation. In *Canine olfaction science and law: Advances in forensic science, medicine, conservation, and environmental remediation*, ed. T. Jezeirski, J. Ensminger and L.E. Papet, 173–195. Boca Raton, FL: CRC Press/Taylor & Francis.

Pearsall, M.D. and Verbruggen, H. 1982. *Scent: Training to track, search, and rescue.* Loveland, CO: Alpine Publications.

Petersen, L.W., El-Farhan, Y.H., Moldrup, P. et al. 1996. Transient diffusion, adsorption, and emission of volatile organic vapors in soils with fluctuating low water contents. *J Environ Qual* 25(5):1054–1063.

Pfiester, M., Koehler, P.G. and Pereira, R.M. 2008. Ability of bed bug-detecting canines to locate live bed bugs and viable bed bug eggs. *J Econ Entomol* 101(4):1389–1396.

Phelan, J.M. and Webb, S.W. 2002. Chemical sensing for buried landmines: Fundamental processes influencing trace chemical detection. *Sandia Rept 2002-0909.* Albuquerque, NM: Sandia National Laboratories.

Phelan, J.M. and Webb, S.W. 2003. Chemical sensing for buried landmines: Fundamental processes influencing trace chemical detection. In *Mine detection Dogs: Training, operations and odour detection*, ed. I.G. McLean, 209–286. Geneva: GICHD.

Phelan, J.M., Webb, S.W., Gozdorb, M. et al. 2001. Effect of soil wetting and drying on DNT vapor flux: Laboratory data and T2TNT model comparisons. Available at https://spie.org/publications/spie-digital-library.

Prada, P.A., Curran, A.M. and Furton, K.G. 2015. *Human scent evidence.* Boca Raton, FL: CRC Press.

Ramotowski, R.S. 2001. Composition of latent print residue. In *Advances in fingerprint technology*, ed. H.C. Leeand and R.E. Gaensslen, 63–104. Boca Raton, FL: CRC Press.

Rebmann, A., David, E. and Sorg, M.H. 2000. *Cadaver dog handbook: Forensic training and tactics for the recovery of human remains.* Boca Raton, FL: Taylor and Francis/CRC Press.

Reed, H.E., Bidlack, A.L., Hurt, A. et al. 2010. Detection distance and environmental factors in conservation detection dog surveys. *J Wildl Manage* 75(1):243–251.

Reynolds, A.J. 2017. Ten Things that helped make my team world champions. Paper presented at the International Working Dog Conference, Banff, Canada.

Riezzo, I., Neri, M., Rendine, M. et al. 2014. Cadaver dogs: Unscientific myth or reliable biological devices? *Forensic Sci Int* 244:213–221.

Rivett, M.O., Wealthall, G.P., Dearden, R.A. et al. 2011. Review of unsaturated-zone transport and attenuation of volatile organic compound (VOC) plumes leached from shallow source zones. *J Contam Hydrol* 123:130–156.

Robe, R.Q. and Frost, J.R. 2002. A method for determining effective sweep widths for land searches. *US Coast Guard Contract Number: DTCG39-00-D-R00009, Task Order Number: DTCG32-01-F-000022*. Washington, DC: The National Search and Rescue Committee.

Rolland, R.M., Hamilton, P.K., Kraus, S.D. et al. 2006. Faecal sampling using detection dogs to study reproduction and health in North Atlantic right whales (*Eubalaena glacialis*). *J Cetacean Res Manage* 8(2):121–125.

Ruzicka, R.E. and Conover, M.R. 2011. Influence of wind and humidity on foraging behavior of olfactory mesopredators. *Canadian Field-Naturalist* 125(2):132–139.

Sargisson, R.J., McLean, I.G., Brown, J. et al. 2012. Environmental determinants of landmine detection by dogs: Findings from a large-scale study in Afghanistan. *JERW Mine Action* 6(2):74–80.

Savidge, J.A., Stanford, J.W. and Reed, R.N. 2011. Canine detection of free-ranging brown treesnakes on Guam. *N Z J Ecol* 35(2):174–181.

Schade, G.W. and Goldstein, A.H. 2001. Fluxes of oxygenated volatile organic compounds from a Poderosa Pine plantation. *J Geophys Res* 106(D3):3111–3123.

Schoenfeld, T.A. and Cleland, T.A. 2005. The anatomical logic of smell. *TRENDS Neurosci* 28(11):620–627.

Schoon, A. and Haak, R. 2002. *K9 Suspect Discrimination: Training and practicing scent identification line-ups*. Calgary: Detselig Enterprises Ltd.

Schoon, A., Fjellangerb, R. and Kjeldsenc, M. et al. 2014. Using dogs to detect hidden corrosion. *Appl Anim Behav Sci* 153:43–52.

Schroeder, M.J. and Buck, C.C. 1970. *Fire Weather*. Agriculture Handbook 360, Forest Service, Boise, Idaho: US Department of Agriculture.

Settles, G.S. 2005. Sniffers: Fluid-dynamic sampling for olfactory trace detection in nature and homeland security—The 2004 Freeman Scholar Lecture. *J Fluids Eng* 127:189–218.

Settles, G.S. 2020a. Flow Visualization Video Clips of Canine Olfaction. YouTube Video: https://youtu.be/eo2sdckSMMA.

Settles, G.S. 2020b. Flow Visualization of the Human Aerodynamic Wake. YouTube Video: https://youtu.be/jQu3hcnBIkc.

Settles, G.S. 2020c. Schlieren Visualization of the Human Thermal Plume. YouTube Video: https://youtu.be/1MA-zEUepvs.

Settles, G.S. and Kester, D.A. 2001. Aerodynamic sampling for landmine trace detection. *Proc SPIE Aerosense* 4394(paper 108) April:1–10.

Settles, G.S., Kester, D.A. and Dodson-Dreibelbis, L.J. 2002. The external aerodynamics of canine olfaction. In *Sensors and sensing in biology and engineering*, ed. F.G. Barth, J.A.C. Humphrey and T.W. Secomb, 1–13, Vienna, NY: Springer.

Simonich, S.L. and Hites, R.A. 1994. Vegetation-atmosphere partitioning of polycyclic hydrocarbons. *Environ Sci Technol* 28:939–943.

Stanley, A. 1981. Utilizing air scenting search dogs to locate drowning victims: A research report. Paper presented at the National Association for Search and Rescue Conference, Virginia.

Stockham, R.A., Slavin, D.L. and Kift, W. 2004. Survivability of human scent. *Forensic Sci Comm* 6(4): October, Washington, DC: FBI.

Syrotuck, W.G. 1972. *Scent and the scenting dog.* Rome, NY: Arner Publications.

Teather, R.G. 1994. *Encyclopedia of underwater investigations.* Flagstaff, AZ: Best Publishing Co.

Thesen, A., Steen, J.B. and Doving, K.B. 1993. Behavior of dogs during olfactory tracking. *J Exp Biol* 180:247–251.

Thurston, M.E. 1996. *The lost history of the canine race: Our 15,000-year love affair with dogs.* New York: Avon Books.

Tolhurst, W.D. 1991. *The police textbook for dog handlers.* Sanborn, NY: Sharp Printing.

Vass, A.A. 2001. Beyond the grave–understanding human decomposition. *Microbiol Today* 28(Nov.):190–192.

Vass, A.A. 2012. Odor Mortis. *Forensic Sci Int* 222:234–241.

Vass, A.A., Smith, R.R., Thompson, C.V. et al. 2004. Decompositional odor analysis database. *J Forensic Sci* 49(4):1–10.

Vass, A.A., Smith, R.R., Thompson, C.V. et al. 2008. Odor analysis of decomposing buried human remains. *J Forensic Sci* 53(2):384–391.

Vu, D. 2001. SPME/GC-MS characterization of volatiles associated with methamphetamine: Toward the development of a pseudomethamphetamine training material. *J Forensic Sci* 46(5):1014–1024.

Wilson, D.A. and Stevenson, R.J. 2003. The fundamental role of memory in olfactory perception. *TRENDS Neurosci* 26(5):243–247.

Zimmermann, T. 2006. Raising the dead. *Outside Mag* 30(8):58.

Zubedat, S., Aga-Mizrachi, S., Cymerblit-Sabba, A. et al. 2014. Human–animal interface: The effects of handler's stress on the performance of canines in an explosive detection task. *Appl Anim Behav Sci* 158(9):69–75.

Index